THE COMPLETE ART
OF PRINTING
AND ENLARGING

THE COMPLETE ART
OF PRINTING
AND ENLARGING

by

Dr. O. R. CROY

Sixth Impression

THE FOCAL PRESS
LONDON AND NEW YORK

First published : 1950
Second impression : 1951
Third impression : 1953
Fourth impression : 1954
Fifth impression: 1956
Sixth impression: 1959

French Edition:
L'ART DU TIRAGE ET DE L'AGRANDISSEMENT
Éditions Prisma, Paris

German Edition:
VERGRÖSSERN MIT ALLEN FINESSEN
Heering Verlag, Seebruck am Chiemsee

Spanish Edition:
EL ARTE DE HACER BUENAS COPIAS Y AMPLICACIONES
Ediciones Omega, Barcelona

Swedish Edition:
KONSTEN ATT FÖRSTØRA
Forum Forlag, Stockholm

Danish Edition:
FORSTÖRRELSESTEKNIK MED ALLE FINESSER
Forlaget Skrifola A/S, Copenhagen

Norwegian Edition:
FORSTORRELSESTEKNIK MED ALLE FINESSER
Dreyers Forlag, Oslo

Printed in Great Britain by W. & J. Mackay & Co. Ltd., Chatham
for the Focal Press Ltd., 31 Fitzroy Square, London, W.1

CONTENTS

I. FROM NEGATIVE TO PRINT

II. FINER POINTS OF PRINT MAKING

III. COMBINATION PRINTING

IV. OFF THE BEATEN TRACK

V. AFTERTREATMENT, RETOUCHING, AND FINISHING

LIST OF FORMULAE

INTRODUCTION

The negative is but the means to the end. It becomes a picture only when we print or enlarge it.

In this book I hope to show that print making can play as creative a part in photography as does camera technique. Our raw material is the negative. But it is no more than a sketch or a plan of the final print. We do not utilise the full scope of photographic technique until we get down to it in the darkroom. That is where our picture comes to life.

I have attempted to demonstrate the immense range of things we can do with negatives—and even without a negative—far beyond the normal processes of printing. The possibilities are, of course, endless. No book can do justice to them all. Yet this one does claim to cover a wider field than ever attempted before.

To be of any real use any such book must show very clearly "how to do it". So I have left theory to one side. This is a practical book for the practically minded reader. It is the result that matters; pictures must be pictures in their own right, not because their making illustrates certain photographic phenomena or theories.

You can take this book with you into your darkroom. You will find well-tried methods, the outcome of many years of practical experience, translated into these pages and their illustrations, which are all my own and so are the very proofs of my words.

Probably the examples shown will give you many ideas of your own. All the better. For you cannot create by imitating. I can only tell about the ideas I had, and show you the methods which you, too, can use.

The methods may be mine—the pictures you will make with them will have to be your own.

Section One

FROM NEGATIVE TO PRINT

Years ago, negatives were simply printed by daylight onto printing-out-paper, or P.O.P. No darkroom of any kind was needed, just a printing frame, and a dish of toning and fixing bath. But simple as this method was, it needed a lot of time. It could take a quarter, or even half an hour before the print was finished.

Nowadays this way of printing is almost obsolete.

One reason for this may be that the sepia or brown prints produced by printing-out-paper are no longer so universally popular. We now seem to prefer black-and-white prints, as obtained by printing on development papers with artificial light.

Probably a more important reason is that daylight printing was too lengthy. With development papers the print is finished in a few seconds.

Then, as negative sizes in common use tended to become smaller and smaller, the demand turned from contact prints to enlargements. And these can only be made on the much more sensitive enlarging papers.

WHAT PRINT MAKING CONSISTS OF

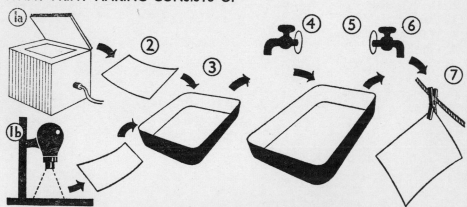

The steps in printing. **1a.** Expose the paper through the negative in a contact printer (p. 20) or **1b** in an enlarger (p. 21). Develop the exposed print **2** in the developer **3. 4.** Rinse in water or in a stop bath (p. 40). **5.** Transfer to fixing bath (p. 40). **6.** Wash in running water or by changes of water (p. 42). **7.** Hang the finished print up to dry.

In printing, then, we take the negative and turn it into a picture—into what we visualised when we pressed the button on the camera.

Most of the picture is already there on the negative. To be exact the whole image of the picture is there. Whether it is large or small does not matter, we can print or enlarge it in any size. What matters is what we make of this image.

The printing process is much the same as that of making negatives. There the light formed an image on the film. Where that image was bright, the negative is dark; where it was dark, the negative is nearly transparent.

Now we turn again to the agency of light. But we control it this time by making it pass through the negative.

Where the negative is dark, little light passes through, and the printing paper will remain nearly white. Where the negative is transparent, it will let through a lot of light and make the paper go dark.

But before we can see the picture we must develop it.

The developer acts on the silver salts in the paper where these have been affected by the light, and turns them into black silver. The more the light has acted, the more silver will be formed. Our positive image appears!

But we have not finished with the print yet. There is still plenty of light sensitive salt left in the paper. Slowly this would also turn black if exposed to light. So once the positive image is there, we must remove all the remaining silver salts. This is done in a fixing bath.

Then we must wash out of the print all the chemicals used in development and fixation, and after that dry the picture.

Finally, we finish it and prepare it for presentation. Small blemishes must be removed, the print must be cut to shape, and we shall probably mount it.

The stages in print making are therefore:

1. Exposure through the negative.
2. Development.
3. Fixing.
4. Washing and drying.
5. Finishing.

THE WORKROOM

To make prints we need a suitable workroom which we can black out.

It need not be completely blacked out, though. Any room will do if we are only going to make prints in the evening or at night. Even the street-lighting outside does not matter much. But if it is strong enough for reading a newspaper in the room, at least the curtains must be drawn.

Whether this workroom is now a completely darkened and well equipped photo-laboratory, where we can work even during the day, or whether we use an ordinary room to make do at night: the working space in either case must be laid out in much the same manner.

The best way is to work on two separate tables or benches. The one we shall call the "wet", and the other the "dry" table.

The wet table is the place for the dishes with the various solutions. As splashes are more or less unavoidable however careful we are, the table-top should be protected from the solutions. A sheet of waterproof and chemical resistant plastic or rubberised material will do well enough.

The dry table holds the printer or enlarger, the negatives, and the printing paper.

These must on no account be exposed to accidental splashes from the wet table, so the two tables should not be too close together.

DARKROOM ILLUMINATION

A darkroom lamp or safelight on or near the wet table illuminates the table and the dishes. It must be an orange or bright green light to which the printing papers are as good as insensitive.

The safelight should be near enough for watching the print comfortably while it is in the processing solutions. But it must not be too near, or it may fog the paper.

Usually the instructions with the darkroom lamp will give the minimum safe working distances. But to be quite sure, here is a simple test.

Take a strip of the most sensitive printing paper (p. 27), and fold it in the middle with the emulsion sides facing outwards. Without exposing the paper to white light, put it into the developing bath in front of the safelight. Leave it in for at least 3 minutes, with one side facing the lamp, while the other faces away from it and lies against the bottom of the developing dish. Then rinse (p. 40) and fix (p. 40).

After $\frac{1}{2}$ minute take the strip out, unfold it, and examine in white light. Both halves should be equally white. If the half which faced the lamp has the slightest trace of a grey tone, the darkroom lamp is unsafe.

16

That means it must be kept farther away from the paper, or a weaker bulb used. Then test again.

This test will always indicate the light as safe if the lamp is sufficiently far away. But that is not really the point we are after. The important thing is to find the nearest safe position for the lamp, so that it gives as much light as possible, without affecting the paper.

Furthermore, the test must be carried out under at least as stringent conditions as will be used later on. If possible, they should be even stricter to provide a safety margin. In particular, the test piece should not be pushed into the developer (p. 38) quicker than it would be normally. Development papers are considerably more sensitive dry than wet. Once they are immersed in the developer, their sensitivity goes down to as little as one-sixth.

To make quite sure, repeat this test with every type of paper in use.

THE DISHES

Lay-out of the wet table. *Left:* Developer, measure, fixer, cloth to wipe up spilt solutions. *Right:* Developing dish and forceps under safelight, rinse, fixing dish with print paddle.

Now let us get back to the three dishes on the wet table.

Reading from left to right, they contain respectively: developer; water or acid rinse; and acid fixer.

Also, from left to right, they should be progressively larger.

The developing dish must be at least as large as the biggest paper size to be used. Too large a dish, on the other hand, will need a lot of developer.

The rinsing dish is larger to make rinsing of the prints easier. And the acid rinse is so cheap, that stinginess here would be false economy.

The fixing dish is the largest of the three. The prints collect there during working, and they must have plenty of room to move about.

Finally, we also need a *washing dish* with clean water in which the prints are eventually washed. This need not stand on the wet table, but can go into the sink if there is one. The fixed prints are transferred to this dish in batches for washing later on by ordinary light. If the actual washing is to be done in this dish (it can also be a bowl), it must be larger than all the others. On the other hand, if the prints are to be washed in the sink or the bath, the dish only holds the prints until everything is ready. In that case the washing dish need be no larger than the developing dish.

There are shallow dishes and deep dishes. They can be made of various materials: porcelain, enamelled metal, stainless steel, or plastic.

For the developer a shallow porcelain dish is best. Shallow, so that the edges do not throw shadows on the print under observation; and porcelain, because the solution temperature remains more constant in it.

The rinsing dish should be deep. It has to hold a lot of liquid, so that the rinse does not become too quickly contaminated with developer. Plastic or enamelled dishes are best here; porcelain may break easily during the frequent emptying and refilling. Stainless steel dishes, though expensive, are ideal.

We also need a deep dish for the fixing bath. This again needs a lot of solution when making a whole batch of prints. With a deep dish splashes are less likely, and thus the risk of fixer getting into the other baths is reduced. Because that just must not happen.

The fixing dish, too, should be plastic (bakelite), or enamelled or stainless steel. Porcelain dishes are not really suitable for fixing. The fixing solution usually seeps through tiny cracks in the glaze. There the salts crystallise out when the dish is dried, and make the cracks still larger, until finally the glaze chips off and the dish becomes useless.

The final washing dish again may be plastic, or enamelled or stainless steel.

PRINT FORCEPS

We shall need print forceps to handle the prints in the solutions without getting our fingers wet.

It is a nuisance having to rinse and dry the fingers every time between processing one print, and exposing the next one. And wet or moist (and greasy) fingers leave visible and unpleasant marks on the fresh printing paper!

The solutions don't do the fingers any good, either. The alkalies in the developer attack, or at least soften, the skin, which then easily absorbs traces of fixer. The fixer contains quite an amount of silver which, absorbed by the skin, will stain and blacken the fingers.

These stains are not easy to remove.

Lastly, development papers can only stand the action of the solutions in this order: developing, rinsing, fixing. With the fingers dipping into any of these solutions any time, we just cannot avoid gradually contaminating the developer with traces of fixing solution and so interfering with the regular process.

Therefore: work with print forceps. It is useful to have two of them; one stays in the developer all the time, and the other in the fixer. They should preferably be different types, so that neither is immersed in the wrong solution by mistake.

PRINT PADDLE

When a print is to be immersed and moved about in a solution (particularly the fixing bath) without further attention, a print paddle is better than the print forceps. The corners of the jaws of the latter may damage the prints or at least mark them if the forceps are resting on the print.

The print paddle on the other hand consists of an ebonite, plastic, or glass ring

18

with a long handle. The whole of the ring lies on the print, not just the ends of the forcep jaws. Therefore they cannot injure the print surface.

The paddle can even be home made. Bend a glass rod in a gas flame through an angle of about 45 degrees. The bend should be about 3 in. from one end, while the rest of the rod should be longer than the dish it is going to be used with. When the paddle lies in the dish, the short end rests on the prints, while the handle projects over the edge. Thus it cannot roll away or fall in, and is always at hand.

OTHER ACCESSORIES

Other items required are a measure, a rag, and a thermometer.

With the measure we measure out the amounts of developer or other stock solutions needed to make the working baths. A 50 c.cm. one, marked in single or 2 c.cm. units, or a 2 ounce one, marked in $\frac{1}{2}$ dram (30 minim) units, is best. Larger amounts can be measured out in 4 or 8 ounce (or 100 or 200 c.cm.) bottles.

A rag should be handy to wipe up any spilt solutions. Even if the table itself is protected by a waterproof sheet, it is better to be tidy and remove all splashes immediately. There is less risk of contamination that way.

The thermometer should register temperatures between at least 50° and 160° F. (or 10° to 70° C.). Mercury thermometers are more accurate and reliable than spirit ones, but the latter are good enough for most photographic work. If a spirit thermometer is used, the spirit should be dyed blue, not red, or it will be difficult to read by the light of the darkroom lamp.

For greater convenience there are also special types of photographic dish thermometers. They are simply clipped onto the side of the dish with the bulb inside the solution, and left there for constant reference.

TEMPERATURE CONTROL

Which brings us to the question: why bother about temperature at all?

Nearly all developers work best at about 65–70° F. (18–21° C.).

There are some which almost cease to work at all much below 60° F. (15° C.). But in any case, the developer acts very slowly at low temperatures.

On the other hand, if the temperature is too high the prints easily get stained and fogged.

For consistent results, therefore, keep the developer within the above optimum range of temperatures.

Generally solutions are more likely to be too cold than too hot. In the winter especially they will have to be warmed up.

Often this is possible only by improvising, such as placing the developing dish on top of a warmed brick, or in a larger dish with warm water. But both have to be rewarmed periodically.

Here an electric dish warmer is a real help. This is nothing more than a lukewarm heating plate underneath the dish. The amount of heat given out can usually be regulated, thus keeping the developer at the right temperature. A dish thermometer in the solution all the time helps to keep a constant check on it.

19

So far we have been largely preoccupied with the wet table. Let us now turn to the dry table. There is really not much to it, except that it must be large enough to accommodate the negatives and printing papers as well as the printer or enlarger.

No direct light from the darkroom lamp should fall on this table, but it should not be so far away that we have to grope about in the dark.

As far as the apparatus itself, namely the printer or enlarger, is concerned, the number of types and models available is immense. For that reason we shall discuss principal features rather than constructional details.

Basically, we can make the print the same size as the negative, larger than the negative, or smaller than the negative.

In the first case we shall use a printer.

In the second case we shall use an enlarger.

In the third case we shall also use an enlarger which, however, must be suitably equipped for this purpose. Not every enlarger can be used for reduction (p. 21); in fact a fully automatic foolproof model is usually less suitable than a more primitive one.

PRINTERS

Whatever the type of printer, all have the same basic construction in common.

The printer is nothing more than a light-tight box with a lid that opens. In the bottom of the box a yellow-orange lamp burns all the time, and there is a white light which we can switch on and off. Immediately below the lid there is a sheet of glass across the top of the box. The negative is placed on this glass (emulsion side up), covered with printing paper (emulsion side down), and the lid closed without shifting the two. The yellow-orange light to which the paper is not sensitive helps us to see while putting the negative and paper in position.

For exposing we switch on the white light for the required time. Then we open the box and develop the paper.

There are all sorts of possible variations and refinements. For instance, some printers have four or more white lamps instead of just one, sometimes with a sheet of flashed opal glass between the lamps and the negative for more even illumination. On the other hand, we may want controlled uneven illumination to give different exposures to different parts of the negative. For this the lamps can in some cases be switched on and off singly. Similarly, we can sometimes locally control the light falling on the negative by movable masks underneath.

Printing can be made still more convenient by a timing switch. On setting this to the required exposure, the print is automatically exposed for the correct time.

Movable masking bands may be provided for giving any print a white border.

But all these gadgets do not make any difference to the fundamental principle of the light-tight box. Its great advantage is that during exposure no white light reaches the darkroom. This means that we can leave packets or boxes of printing paper open all the time.

For that reason alone the old-fashioned contact printing with a printing frame wastes a great deal of time. For every print the spring back of the frame must be opened up and closed. And before every exposure under a normal lamp we must carefully pack away all sensitive paper to protect it from the white light. All this is all right for just a few occasional contact prints, but very tedious in constant use.

ENLARGER TYPES

They, too, follow a common fundamental design.

Its important parts are: the lamphouse and lamp; the negative carrier; the bellows (or something to take their place) and focusing arrangement; the lens; and the easel.

According to the way in which these parts are assembled, there are two types of enlargers: horizontal, and vertical.

In the former all the parts are laid out, as the name implies, along a horizontal axis. The arrangement thus takes up a lot of space on the working table. Usually horizontal enlargers are rather cumbersome, and nowadays almost obsolete except for large negative sizes. On the other hand, they are the most suitable type for carbon arc point source (p. 23) illumination. Also, the maximum degree of enlargement is limited only by the size of the darkroom.

In the vertical enlarger the arrangement of the whole system is upright, with the easel lying flat on the table. The lamphouse with negative carrier and lens moves up and down a vertical column fixed to the easel or baseboard.

This is the most popular design, as it is much more convenient to handle, and does not need much working space. The range of magnifications is, however, limited by the height of the vertical column. Nevertheless, for really large prints the lamphouse of most vertical enlargers can be swivelled round, so that the apparatus is used horizontally, with the paper pinned to a vertical board.

Every enlarger is really like a camera working in reverse.

During a camera exposure the subject outside is illuminated, while the sensitive film is protected inside the dark and light-tight camera. Any light that gets to the film has to come through the lens.

With the enlarger the light is inside the apparatus, and is projected through the negative and lens onto the sensitive paper in the darkened room outside. What we photographed in the camera on a reduced scale, is now reproduced enlarged by the enlarger. The image plane here is the baseboard, while the enlarger column has a function more or less analogous to the camera stand or tripod.

REDUCTION

We can, however, also use the enlarger for making reduced prints. The difference is that the relative distances from the lens to the paper and negative are changed.

During enlarging the paper-lens distance is always greater than the negative-lens distance. When the two are the same, the negative is reproduced in the same size on the paper, as with contact printing.

If, however, the negative-lens distance is greater than the paper-lens distance, we get a reduced image. For this the enlarger must have specially long bellows.

Types of enlarger illumination. *Left:* A point source and condensers give greatest contrast and brilliance (p. 23). *Centre:* The most usual system is an opal lamp with a condenser (p. 23). *Right:* Fully diffused illumination subdues grain and small defects, but is comparatively weak and soft. It is often used in cheaper models or in enlargers for large negative sizes.

The enlarger radically differs from a camera by having a lamphouse at the back. This contains a lamp which projects its light through the negative in front of it, and then through the lens onto the easel.

To give an evenly bright image, the light must obviously be spread uniformly over the whole of the negative area.

We can achieve this necessary even light distribution by either a sheet of flashed opal glass; a double condenser; or a single condenser lens.

OPAL GLASS

A flashed opal glass sheet produces the most even illumination. Its disadvantages are that the light is both very weak, and very diffused.

Though such diffused light is eminently suitable for suppressing dirt marks, scratches, and even grain (p. 87) in the negative, it is at the same time incapable of producing the highest pin-sharp definition in the projected image. Besides, the opal glass absorbs a great deal of light. Its effect is similar to that of fog or heavy clouds, which only infra-red rays will penetrate. Similarly, comparatively more infra-red and red light of the enlarger lamp passes through the opal glass sheet. But to this the enlarging paper is least sensitive. This fact, together with the already reduced brightness of the light, leads to relatively long enlarging exposures, thus slowing down the work.

Nevertheless, enlargers with flashed opal diffusers are particularly suitable for enlarging retouched portrait negatives. On the one hand, they tone down the effect of retouching, and on the other they noticeably soften the image definition.

Opal glass by itself is usually only found in the cheaper enlargers, or in models for large negatives where a condenser of the required size would be too expensive.

22

CONDENSERS

The condenser itself is a combination of two plano-convex lenses.

Any such converging lens receives the diverging rays from a light-point over its whole area, and makes them converge again to a point some way behind it. Similarly, the rays of light are spread over the whole area of a condenser before they converge again.

Therefore if we place the condenser at the correct distance (depending on its focal length) from a point source of light, this becomes an evenly bright disc of light in the plane of the condenser. Thus a negative placed immediately underneath this disc of light is evenly illuminated.

The size of the condenser needed naturally depends on the negative size in use. The diameter of the disc of light formed must be at least as great as the diagonal of the negative, otherwise the corners of the latter will not be as bright as the centre.

While large negatives usually need a double condenser, we may with small negative sizes often get even illumination already with a single condenser, i.e. one lens only of the double condenser. The convex side of this lens faces the light, while the negative is held close to (sometimes in actual contact with) the flat side.

In practice we rarely make full use of the salient points of condenser illumination.

First of all, there is no such thing as a real point source of light.

Secondly, maximum image brightness and absolutely sharp definition—which such illumination would produce—are not necessarily ideal for enlarging.

It does not matter all that much if the image on the enlarger baseboard is not so very bright as it is not really important whether enlarging exposures are in the region of 10 seconds, or whether they are nearer 20 seconds. On the contrary, to have a sufficiently wide choice of enlarging exposures, it is better to keep the times somewhat longer rather than very short. We can cut down 20 seconds reasonably accurately even to as little as one-fifth, which is not so easy with 2 or 3 seconds.

And as far as "absolute" sharpness is concerned, we do not want every little speck of dust on the negative, as well as the grain, shown up in its full glory. This feature is particular to condenser enlargers with a point-like source of light.

In addition, this direct type of illumination also results in a very contrasty image.

The reverse is true of fully diffused illumination as produced by opal glass, where the image contrast is lower than the original negative contrast.

The best solution of this dilemma is an obvious compromise.

So the most popular system of enlarger illumination nowadays uses a condenser, but instead of a point source of light, an opal lamp is put behind it. This has a much larger light area, and thus produces a partially diffused light. With such a system a single condenser lens often serves just as well as a double condenser.

NEGATIVE CARRIER AND FOCUSING

The negative is held in its position below the condenser (or opal diffuser) by some sort of negative carrier.

This may consist of two sheets of glass or a frame to hold the edges of the negative for enlarging. Depending on its construction, it allows a more or less rapid change of negatives.

23

The focusing arrangement serves the same purpose as in the camera; it moves the negative nearer to, or farther away from, the lens to obtain a sharp image.

With most models we have to focus manually, and watch the image on the easel.

There are also semi-automatic and even fully automatic enlargers where the image is focused mechanically at every degree of enlargement as we move the lamphouse assembly up or down the enlarger column. The point of these special features is that they speed up work and to make it more or less foolproof. But if we are reasonably sure of ourselves and in no particular hurry, such refinements are not really essential.

THE ENLARGING LENS

Really essential, however, is a first-class enlarging lens. After all, to do justice to a negative, we must enlarge it with at least as good a lens as with which it was taken. But not every lens is suitable for enlarging.

Some enlarger models are supplied complete with a special enlarging lens. Often, however, we may want to use the apparatus with the camera or other lens.

The focal length of the lens should usually be the normal one for the negative size, i.e. about equal to the diagonal of the negative. Thus the focal length should be more or less the same as the ideal condenser diameter (p. 23).

A lens of shorter focal length will generally fail to cover the negative satisfactorily. This means that the corners of the negative are not fully illuminated.

Too long a focal length lens, on the other hand, will work perfectly well, but needs rather a long lens-to-paper distance. Therefore we need a long enlarger column, which is neither practical nor convenient with a small enlarger.

The lens aperture need not be particularly large for an enlarging lens. We shall do most of the work at about f 5.6–6.3. Larger apertures, particularly with a strong enlarging light, mean uncontrollably short exposure times (p. 23). Besides, the definition of the image at large apertures sometimes leaves a lot to be desired. Very small apertures like f 8 or f 11, however, unfortunately tend to emphasise the grain of the negatives.

TESTING THE LENS

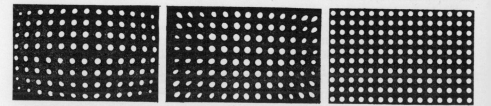

The results of lens tests. *Left:* The image shows barrel distortion. *Centre:* Near the edges the circles are no longer round. This is coma. *Right:* The perfect lens gives a uniformly bright and sharp image.

A good enlarging lens must be free from distortion, curvature of field, and coma. We can easily and quickly test the quality of a lens as follows.

24

Get a sheet of perforated paper with regular rows of small circular holes (as used sometimes for embroidery patterns). Put this into the negative carrier instead of a negative, and make an enlargement of it (p. 31).

If the rows of holes are straight and parallel, and uniformly sharp over the whole print, the lens is sufficiently corrected.

If distortion is present, the rows near the edges of the print are no longer straight, but curve inwards (pin cushion distortion) or outwards (barrel distortion). Such a lens will, for instance, never produce an accurate enlargement of an architectural subject, or of a copy of a drawing.

Generally distortion goes hand in hand with curvature of field. This means that the image of the flat perforated paper sheet is formed on a spherical surface, and consequently is not sharp all over on the flat baseboard. The edges of the print are increasingly unsharp. They will only become sharp if the lens is stopped down considerably, which, as we have seen (p. 24), is not very desirable in enlarging.

Finally, if coma is present, the images of the round holes cease to be round near the edges of the print. They become elliptical in shape, and are again unsharp.

If the lens is free from all these faults, it is good enough for enlarging.

CARE OF APPARATUS

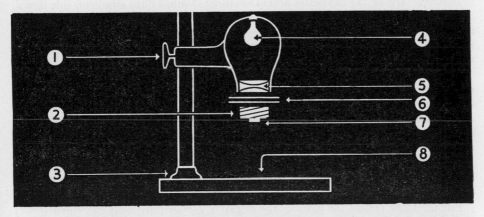

Where the enlarger needs attention. 1. Oil the lamphouse movement. 2. See that the focusing mechanism is smooth. 3. Fix the column tightly to reduce vibration to a minimum. 4. Centre the lamp correctly. Look out for dust on and between the condenser lenses 5, the negative carrier 6, the lens 7, and the baseboard 8.

Many faults in the final prints are caused by careless handling of the enlarger. First of all, the enlarger lamp must be correctly centred.

Most enlarger models have a set of spacing screws for the lampholder, by which the position of the lamp can be adjusted both horizontally and vertically. This adjustment should be carried out whenever a new lamp is put in, or when the light appears to be off-centre.

Switch on the enlarger lamp (with the room in darkness), and loosen the fixing screws gripping the lampholder. Move the lamp about inside the lamphouse until a white sheet of paper placed on the easel appears perfectly evenly lit all over. Then clamp the lamp tight in that position. To make quite sure, put a sheet of enlarging paper on the easel, and give it a short exposure. It must be completely evenly grey all over the exposed area after development. If this is not the case, the centering of the lamp is incorrect, and must be repeated.

Uneven illumination can also be caused by insufficient diffusion of the light. This is likely to happen if sprayed enlarging lamps are used instead of the opal kind. In that case recentering may not help much. The only remedy is to get a genuine opal lamp, or to shade in these "hot spots" with pencil on the bulb itself.

In time quite a lot of dust accumulates on the enlarging lens. It then acts like a soft-focus lens (p. 86) giving slightly unsharp prints of reduced contrast.

So clean the surface of the lens, and also of the condenser, periodically with a soft, clean, dry rag or a piece of chamois leather. Only a clean lens will give sharp and clear enlargements!

CARE OF THE NEGATIVES

The negatives, too, must be clean and free of dust.

Before enlarging, lay the plates and miniature (35 mm.) films emulsion side down, on a clean table. Carefully polish the back with a clean rag or chamois leather until breathing on the glass or film does not produce any irregular patterns. The surface film of condensed water vapour produced must be quite even. Do not wipe this off, but let it evaporate on its own.

Roll film and sheet film negatives should not be treated in this way, as they have a backing layer of gelatine which is easily scratched. So just polish them very carefully without breathing on them.

Alternatively, clean them with a solvent like carbon tetrachloride (p. 179). In any case, with this coating the film back is less likely to collect dirt. (The same applies to the emulsion side.)

Polish the film slowly. Violent rubbing charges the celluloid or glass with electricity, and it then attracts fine dust particles from the air. This dust, when enlarged with the negative, produces white spots and pinholes on the prints.

For the same reason the glass of the negative carrier must only be wiped slowly and gently.

A good idea is to pull the negative gently between the fingers to remove the last traces of dust, just before putting it into the negative carrier. The fingers must, of course, be absolutely clean and dry.

All this may sound a lot of bother about a little dust, but it will save a lot of time later by reducing the need for retouching (p. 178).

NEWTON'S RINGS

These are an annoying phenomenon which have nothing to do with the cleanness or otherwise of the negative, but a lot with the state of the film base.

They may occur when film negatives, particularly miniature films, show a tendency to curl. When they are sandwiched between the glass plates of the negative carrier, the film and glass are sometimes not in complete contact everywhere. The points of incomplete contact give rise to optical diffraction of the light passing through, resulting in interference fringes—shell-like shapes in all colours of the rainbow—which show up on the print.

The remedy is obvious: stop the film from curling.

We can start with precautions when we dry the film after processing. If strips of film are left hanging freely for long periods, especially in a warm dry room, they bend inward like drain-pipes. So take the film down as soon as it is dry.

Miniature films are particularly prone to curl, as they are tightly rolled up in their cassettes before exposure. After drying therefore, roll them up in the opposite way—with the emulsion facing outward—for a day or two. Then cut them up into short strips and store them in suitable negative envelopes. Films treated in this way are usually quite flat and proof against Newton's rings.

If we cannot wait the couple of days until the curl has gone out of the film, another way out is to put it in the negative carrier back to back with a piece of unexposed and fixed out sheet film—preferably matt backed. That also will prevent the formation of these rings.

PRINTING PAPERS

Finally, most important among the items we need is the light-sensitive printing paper.

PRINTING PAPERS COMPARED

Characteristics	Contact	Bromide	Chlorobromide
Main constituent	Silver chloride	Silver bromide	Silver chloride and bromide
Sensitivity	Low	High	Intermediate
Normal image colour	Blue-black	Black	Warm black to brown
Darkroom illumination	Bright yellow	Orange	Orange or light green

There are three different types, classified according to the chemical composition of the light-sensitive emulsion layer. This is either silver chloride, silver bromide, or a mixture of the two.

The sensitivity to light of silver chloride is low, that of silver bromide is comparatively high. The sensitivity of chlorobromide mixtures lies somewhere between the two.

The uses of these types also follow from their sensitivities.

Silver chloride papers are employed for making contact prints. They are therefore called contact papers (or by a confusing older name which is still popular: gaslight papers).

Silver bromide papers, or just bromide papers, on the other hand are used for enlarging. They are about 60 times as sensitive as contact papers.

Chlorobromide papers could either be regarded as slow enlarging papers, or fast contact papers, depending on the relative proportions of the two main constituents. Usually they give warm black to brown prints, as compared with the pure black to blue-black images of bromide and contact papers. They are also called portrait papers, as they are often used as the standard paper by portrait studio photographers.

While contact papers are insensitive already to bright yellow light, bromide papers must be handled only by the light of an orange darkroom lamp. In every case, test the safety of the illumination (p. 16).

CHOICE OF PAPER

To provide a wide scope for pictorial expression, photographic firms manufacture a whole range of papers of each basic type. The different kinds are distinguished by texture, and finish of the surface, as well as tint, and the thickness of the paper.

The surface texture can be smooth, velvet, fine grain, or rough grain. There are also various kinds of imitated fabric textures like silk, rayon, etc.

The surface finish may be glossy, semi-matt (or lustre), and matt.

Paper tints are white, ivory white, cream, etc.

Base thicknesses range from air mail through single weight to card (double weight).

The various makers usually designate these characteristics by a series of code letters or numbers.

The choice of a suitable paper surface and tint is largely a matter of taste. There are, however, certain more or less widely accepted ideas on how the physical characteristics of printing papers can best be matched to the subject.

For instance, a tinted paper base makes for a much warmer effect than a white one. To convey a sunny atmosphere in the print, we therefore often use an ivory or cream paper.

With high degrees of enlargement from small negatives, the negative grain may be unpleasantly obvious. So we choose a rough surface paper where the paper grain largely masks the graininess of the image.

On the other hand, for the reproduction of finest detail, glossy paper is ideal.

The table on p. 29 gives some guidance to choosing the paper to emphasise the mood and expression of the subject in the picture.

PAPER GRADES

Nearly all papers are made in several grades, ranging from soft to hard or ultra hard.

This range provides a suitable paper grade for each different negative contrast. Thus we can make prints of the same gradation from widely varying negatives. It is therefore advisable to obtain each paper required in its full range of gradations, so that any negative can be printed on it.

28

The relative sensitivity of the different grades of the same paper generally decreases as the grade gets harder. In changing from one paper grade to the next harder one with the same negative (say, if the print was not satisfactory), we must increase the exposure.

On the other hand, this decreased speed of the harder grades is compensated to some extent by the fact that among different negatives the softer ones are usually also thinner. Though such a soft negative may need a hard paper, owing to its low overall density it will not necessarily need a much longer printing exposure.

MATCHING SUBJECT AND PAPER

| Subjects | Paper Characteristics | | | |
	Surface Texture	Surface Finish	Tint	Image Colour
Against the light	Smooth	Lustre	Ivory or cream	Black
Animals	Smooth	Lustre	White or ivory	Black
Architecture	Smooth or fine grain	Glossy or lustre	White or ivory	Warm black
Broad landscapes	Rough	Lustre	Ivory or cream	Warm black
Character studies	Grained or rayon	Lustre	Ivory or cream	Brown
Children	Smooth or rayon	Lustre	Ivory	Warm black or brown
Clouds	Smooth	Lustre	White	Black
Female portraits	Smooth	Matt	Ivory	Black
Fog	Smooth	Matt	White	Black
Interiors	Smooth	Glossy or lustre	White	Black
Landscapes	Fine grain	Lustre	White or tinted	Black or warm black
Male portraits	Fine grain	Lustre	White	Black or brown
Mountains and snow	Smooth	Glossy or lustre	White	Black
Night outdoors, summer	Smooth or fine grain	Lustre	Cream	Black
Night outdoors, winter	Smooth	Glossy or lustre	White	Black
Open air	Smooth	Lustre	Ivory	Black
Plants	Smooth	Lustre	White	Black
Rain	Smooth	Glossy	White	Black
Sea	Smooth	Glossy or lustre	White	Black
Snow scenes	Smooth	Glossy or lustre	White	Black
Still life	Grained or rayon	Lustre	White or tinted	Warm tone
Sunsets	Smooth	Lustre or matt	Cream	Black
Technical and scientific	Smooth	Glossy	White	Black
Woods	Fine grain	Lustre	Ivory	Black

MAKING THE PRINT

We are now so far that we can go through the steps of making a print from beginning to end.

We will do this as if every step in the manipulation worked successfully the first time, leaving the discussion of possible mishaps and what to do about them until the end.

SORTING THE NEGATIVES

To start with, sort the negatives out for printing.

It is obviously pointless even to try to print negatives with serious technical faults such as unsharpness, severe underexposure, fog, etc. Some other faults like excessive density, grain, low contrast, and the like, can often be minimised by after treatment (p. 172) of the negative. Do this before attempting to make any prints.

Similarly, it is a waste of time to carry on with negatives which are physically damaged, for such flaws are only emphasised in the enlarged print. This includes scratches, dried-in dust, finger prints, splash marks, and footprints of flies or moths which had settled on the film during drying. As the film has plenty of opportunity to collect such injuries, the best cure is prevention. If by ill luck such troubles should appear, they must first be removed as far as possible (p. 179). It is much better to do that once—on the negative—than dozens of times, every time a print is made.

GRADING NEGATIVES

Sorting the negatives also serves a second purpose.

The individual films and plates are graded according to their density and contrast. That saves making constant test exposures every time.

The density of the negatives determines their printing exposures, and their contrast the paper grade to be used.

For a *contrasty negative* choose a *soft paper grade*.

For a *normal negative* choose a *normal paper grade*.

For a *softer negative* choose a *hard paper grade*.

For a *very soft negative* choose an *extra hard paper grade*.

Sorting the negatives and selecting the right paper grade needs a certain amount of practice which comes with experience. In the beginning we can prepare a set of negatives for comparison (p. 33) to make selection easier.

It is best to start with the hard and dense negatives, working through to the softer and thinner ones. This is because the developer also changes somewhat in use. It develops softer in the beginning than later on when it is already partly exhausted. The reason for it is the increasing bromide content formed during development. This makes the developer more contrasty, and also slower. Thus prints need longer exposures if they are developed in an exhausted developer. So it is just as well to leave those negatives to the end which need the shortest exposures.

One other symptom of the generation of bromide during development is the changing image colour, which gradually goes from black to warm black and then greenish black. This is an unmistakable sign that the developer is nearing its useful life (or that it was made up with too much potassium bromide in the beginning).

While the print contrast obtained from any negative depends mainly on the paper grade, a certain amount of variation towards soft or hard is also possible by using specially compounded developers (p. 238). For the time being, however, we shall stick to the normal formula (p. 237).

FOCUSING

Place the negative, graded from the comparison set (p. 33) as, say, a normal one, in the printer or the negative carrier of the enlarger. In the latter case adjust the enlarger for the required print size, and accurately focus the negative.

With automatic enlargers the image is focused mechanically as the print size is set, without any further manipulation.

In the semi-automatic enlarger the vertical column and the focusing movement each have a scale of numbers. Focus the image by setting the focusing knob to the same number on the focusing scale as the lamphouse on the vertical scale.

With a normal enlarger focus the negative by turning the focusing knob to and fro. At the same time watch the sharpness of the image on a white paper on the enlarger baseboard.

Sometimes, particularly when the negative is fairly dense, this is not too easy. In that case a focusing negative helps. It is easily obtainable, but can also be home made.

Cover an old film diagonally from corner to corner with scratches made by a pointed pen-knife. This removes the gelatine where the scratches are, and gives very sharply defined lines which we can focus accurately and without trouble.

A suitable focusing negative is contained in the *Focal Enlarging Chart*. It also includes marked centimetre and inch lengths. We only have to measure the length of these in the image to obtain a direct reading for the degree of enlargement.

With a very dense negative it is often easier to watch the image on a ground glass screen. There are various devices of this type on the market. They reflect the light from the enlarger onto a suitably placed screen, for examination with a magnifier.

Once the image is really sharp, the negative to be enlarged replaces the focusing negative.

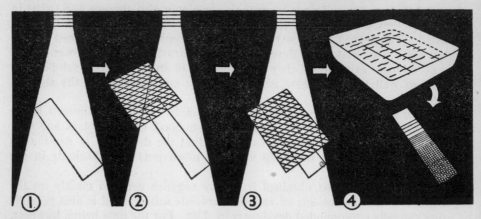

Making a test strip. **1.** Expose a strip of printing paper for 5 seconds, with the negative in the enlarger. **2.** Cover up one-fifth of the strip and expose for another 5 seconds. **3.** Carry on in this way covering up one-fifth at a time, exposing for further 5-second periods for every step until the strip is covered. **4.** Develop the test strip in the normal way (p. 38).

Before exposing the whole print, we must make a test exposure on a small strip of the printing paper to be used.

For a first test exposure we shall try 25 seconds. This, however, is not allowed to act on the whole strip at once, but divided into five periods of 5 seconds each.

Cover the strip on the baseboard or on the masking board of the enlarger over one-fifth of its length with an opaque card. Allow the light to act for the first 5 seconds. For the next 5-second exposure push the card over a further one-fifth of the strip (without moving the strip itself!) so that it now covers two-fifths. For the third 5-second period push it along another fifth, and so on.

After the complete 25 seconds we shall have exposed the strip in five steps, beginning with 5 seconds at one end, and finishing with 25 seconds at the other.

After development we can easily see which step was correctly exposed.

If necessary, make a second test strip, covering the interval between the best two neighbouring steps; for instance, the first step might receive 15 seconds, and the other four 16, 17, 18, and 19 seconds respectively. This will pin-point down the right exposure really accurately.

If all the steps appear to be too black, repeat the test with five periods of 1 or 2 seconds each.

If on the other hand all the steps are too light, make the repeated test with five 15-second steps, again pin-pointing the exact time between adjacent steps with a further strip.

The procedure is very much the same for contact printing.

In a printer, however, we may not be able to move a card behind the negative without also shifting the negative itself. In that case five small pieces of contact paper must be used instead of the one test strip, and exposed for 5, 10, 15, 20, and 25 seconds respectively. The same applies to a printing frame.

32

NEGATIVE TYPES. *Above:* The normal negative shows a full tone range with some density in the lightest parts, and not too much in the darkest. *Top left:* Dense negative. *Centre left:* Thin negative. *Bottom left:* Soft negative. *Bottom right:* Hard negative (p. 30).

CHOOSING PAPER, exposure and
development time. *Top left:* Too soft
paper. *Top right:* Too hard paper
(p. 30). *Centre left:* Overexposed
and underdeveloped print; shows
poor image tone (p. 39). *Centre
right:* Overexposed and correctly
developed print. This is too dark.
Bottom left: Underexposed and
correctly developed print. This is too
light. *Bottom right:* Forcing an underexposed print by overdevelopment
gives too much contrast with still
insufficient highlight detail (p. 41).
Opposite : Correctly exposed and
developed print on the right paper
grade.

On page 36. MAKING TEST STRIPS.
Exposing the negative in steps shows
which exposure time gives the best
result (p. 32). *Left:* The negative.
Centre: Test strip. The third step
looks about correct. *Right:* The whole
print exposed for the same time as
the third step.

34

WITH A STEP WEDGE

Another way of making test exposures is to use a step wedge.

This consists of a film which has a number of steps of increasing neutral density. Instead of exposing each step for a different time, place the whole test paper under this wedge and give it all the same exposure. The density of the steps reduces the intensity of the light, and thus the effective exposure which each part of the test paper gets. To obtain the exposure for the correct step, divide the exposure time for the whole test piece by a factor corresponding to that step on the step wedge.

One such step wedge is the Exposure Negative of the *Focal Enlarging Chart*. This has 10 steps. To use it, focus the negative to be enlarged in the enlarger onto a white sheet of paper on the baseboard in the usual way (p. 31). Instead of a test strip lay a piece of the enlarging paper, about 3 in. square, on the easel or in the paper holder, and cover it with the Exposure Negative. Expose this for 1 minute.

After development examine the paper, and choose the correctly exposed portion. Then multiply the 1-minute exposure by a factor ranging from 1/30 to 4/5, depending on which step was correct. A calculator disc on the Focal Enlarging Chart automatically indicates the correct printing exposure.

If all the steps are too light or too dark, repeat the test with a longer or shorter overall exposure, respectively.

This method can also be used with a contact printer or printing frame.

EXPOSURE

Exposing in the enlarger. 1. With the negative focused, swing the orange filter in front of the lens and switch on the enlarger. 2. Place the paper in position on the baseboard, moving it about to get the best picture area. 3. Switch off the enlarger. 4. Swing the orange filter out of the way. 5. Wait 10 seconds for vibration to die down before switching on. 6. Expose.

Let us assume we found the correct exposure for the whole print to be 20 seconds.

Now put a whole sheet of the printing paper of the required size for the print on the enlarger baseboard, placing it in the right position with the help of an orange filter over the enlarger lens.

AP—C*

With a printer, simply sandwich the paper together with the negative.

Expose for 20 seconds. This time, of course, there are no 5-second steps (nor do we use a step wedge), but give a continuous 20-second exposure.

During enlarging one point needs special attention, namely enlarger vibration. Like camera shake when taking the picture, enlarger vibration during enlarging produces unsharp pictures.

There are many things that can cause the enlarger to vibrate, and thus spoil the print. The most obvious is touching the enlarger during exposure. This includes the practice of exposing by removing and replacing the orange filter over the lens, also leaning or knocking against the table on which the enlarger is standing. Enlargers vary in their stability; frequently even walking about in the room during exposure can cause them to vibrate.

Not so obvious causes of vibration are heavy traffic outside in the street (particularly if the enlarger is not very solidly built), railway trains passing nearby, or other people tramping about in the house. In that case it is best to wait until the disturbance has subsided.

This, then, is the procedure for vibration-free exposure:

Switch on the enlarger with the orange filter over the lens.

Place the paper in position.

Switch off the enlarger.

Remove the orange filter.

Stand or sit still and wait for at least 10 seconds.

Switch on the enlarger for the exposure. Do not move about unnecessarily, and do not touch the apparatus.

Switch off when the time is up.

DEVELOPING

Immersing the print in the developer. I. Lift up the left edge of the dish. 2. Let go. When the developer has reached the left edge again, push in the print. 3. The liquid will flood back, and 4 cover the print.

The next step after exposure is to immerse the print in the dish with the developer solution.

Hold the edge of the print in the right hand, emulsion side facing upwards, with the paper slanting downwards above the dish.

Then with the left hand raise the left edge of the developer dish for a moment and let go. This causes most of the developer solution to flow towards the right-hand side of the dish, and then flood back in a wave against the left-hand side.

At this moment push the paper into the dish, and let go. The wave of developer flooding back again from the left of the dish will now spread over the paper in one even sweep.

That is the important point: the developer must wet the whole print area at the same time. Otherwise patches of uneven density may appear.

All this sounds much more complicated than it really is. But it is important to acquire the knack of immersing the paper properly. Therefore try it with a few sheets of plain paper in a dish of water. A little practice will soon show how it works best.

As soon as the paper is completely flooded with the solution, seize it by the extreme edge with the print forceps.

Move it about, keeping it fully immersed all the time.

In addition, rock the dish gently, so that the developer constantly flows over the print in all directions.

Meanwhile the image begins to appear, and becomes more and more distinct until it is fully developed. And the development time is one of the most important factors of good print quality.

At the optimum developing temperature of 65-68° F. (18-20° C.) the time must be not less than 2 minutes, and it should not be much more, either.

This is often easier said than done. But full development is the acid test which will show up whether all the other conditions for a successful print have been ful-filled. And comparison of test prints has some value only if development is standardised.

Apart from losing all basis for comparing results, haphazard development times also affect print quality. A print that is taken out of the developer too soon will look grey and flat, without any real blacks. Prolonged or "forced" development on the other hand leads to fog and stains.

When a print goes black quicker than it should, make another with a shorter exposure time. If it has not reached its full density at the end of 2, or at the most 2½ minutes, give the next one more exposure.

Standardisation applies to development temperature as well as development time. Therefore always keep the developer at 65-68° F. (18-20° C.).

For the best results, then, development time and temperature must always be correct, and exposure adjusted accordingly until the print is right. There is no substitute for correct exposure and correct development. Any compensation in the developer can only be achieved at the expense of print quality.

RINSING

When the 2 minutes for development are up, grip the paper near the middle of the right-hand edge, and slowly pull it out of the solution over the right-hand side of the developer dish.

This way most of the developer solution is wiped off the back of the print, and flows back into the dish. This not only saves developer, but also reduces contamination of the rinse and fixing bath later on.

Now drop the print into the rinse bath. The forceps must, however, not be immersed, particularly if it is an acid rinse, because this would contaminate the developer when the next print is handled. The print forceps therefore go back to the developer dish straightaway.

At this point the second pair of forceps comes into use (p. 18). Its normal place is in the fixing bath. Once development is finished and the print is in the rinse, handle it with these fixer forceps.

It does not matter much if a few drops of fixer get into the rinse, but neither rinse nor fixer must get into the developer.

The purpose of the rinse is to remove as much developer as possible within a few seconds. It can be plain water (change it frequently!), but an acid rinse (Nos. 14 or 15, p. 240) is better. There the alkaline developer left in the emulsion is neutralised and its action stopped, as it only works in alkaline solution. Hence the rinse is also called the stop bath.

Move the print about in the rinse with the help of the fixing bath forceps for about 10 seconds. During this time most of the developer carried over with the print becomes more or less ineffective.

Then lift the print out to drain. As soon as the liquid is only dripping off in single drops, push the paper, emulsion side down, under the surface of the fixing solution (Nos. 16 and 18, pp. 240, 241).

FIXING

Transferring the print to the fixer. 1. Pull the print over the edge of the developer dish. 2. Drop it into the rinse. 3. Lift out and drain. 4. Put it in the fixer and keep submerged with the print paddle.

Move the print about in the fixer for the first $\frac{1}{4}$ minute or so to let the solution get at the paper everywhere. During this time the last traces of developer absorbed in the gelatine layer and the paper base are rendered harmless by being neutralised and removed.

If the print is left to its own devices the moment it is in the fixing bath (or even allowed to stick to other prints) these traces of developer, which are not always completely neutralised in the rinse, may still give rise to yellow or brown stains on the print.

Particularly with a plain water rinse, the acid fixing bath after it has the whole task of neutralising the developer. If the solution has no chance to get at the whole print immediately, parts of the picture may go on developing, giving uneven areas of density.

So keep the prints on the move when they first get into the fixing bath. This is best done with the print paddle (p. 18).

The main purpose of the fixing bath is to render the undeveloped parts of the image insensitive to light. This it does by dissolving the light-sensitive silver chloride or bromide out of the emulsion layer.

Already after about $\frac{1}{4}$ minute the print will not be harmed by white light, provided that the acid fixing bath was really acid, and not exhausted, and that the print was moved about with the print paddle during the first few moments of immersion.

WHAT THE PRINT SHOULD LOOK LIKE

We can therefore turn on the white light at this stage. Have an ordinary lamp at hand, placed so that it shines on the fixing dish. But before switching on make sure there is no sensitive paper lying about exposed on the printing table. Put it away into its box or into a light-tight drawer.

Now turn the print over, face up, in the fixing dish for inspection.

If all has gone well, the deepest shadows, and the deepest shadows only, should be pure black. The shadow detail must, however, not be buried. The gradation should carry through right into the very darkest grey, with the tones clearly separated everywhere.

On holding the print up against the light no additional detail should become visible which we cannot see on the print when it is lying in the dish.

At the same time, the highlights must not be burned out. They should also show full detail and gradation. Only the extreme highlights may be white paper, in fact even they should have a very slight tone.

Check this by turning over one corner of the print with the print forceps, so that the back of the paper is next to the lightest image part. As the paper base is pure white (or the pure paper tint in the case of tinted papers), the slightest grey tone is immediately apparent.

Between the faintest highlight and the deepest shadow all the delicate half tones should be there in full.

If the print does not come up to standard, remake it under modified conditions of exposure, paper grade, etc. (p. 39).

If the print passes muster as good enough, turn it over again in the fixing bath, and weigh down with the print paddle so that it remains under the surface of the solution. Then switch off the white light while making the next picture. Leave the print in the fixing bath for about another 10 minutes.

Longer fixing will do no harm, except that it may prolong the subsequent washing time (p. 42). However, if the print is left in the fixing bath for hours (especially if the fixer is strongly acid), it may lose some density in the highlight, destroying the gradation there.

WASHING

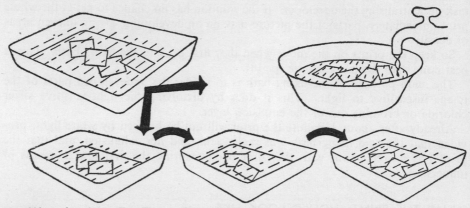

Ways of washing. *Top:* The simplest way is by running water. The prints are put into a large bowl and water is allowed to run in at one side and overflow at the other. In this way clean water reaches the prints all the time. *Bottom:* For washing by changes of water the prints are placed in a small dish, and the water renewed every 3–5 minutes. About 6–8 changes are needed.

When a few prints have collected in the fixing bath, lift them all out (except for the last two or three) with the fixer forceps. Drain off most of the liquid from one corner, and put the batch of prints into the washing dish or into an intermediate dish of water (p. 17), ready to be put into the sink for washing.

Once they are in the washing water, the prints can be handled with the fingers.

Washing is the last stage of processing. Its task is completely to remove and wash away all the chemicals absorbed in the print from the time it was immersed in the first solution.

The sensitive paper which before processing contained only insoluble silver salts in its emulsion, now carries the metallic silver grains and a swollen gelatine layer in which the soluble silver and other salts are hidden. And hidden is the right word; for the salts which are to be washed away are actually inside this watery jelly.

Washing is thus by no means a simple process of sweeping them away with a spray or jet of water. The salts must rather be enticed out of the swollen gelatine. And they will diffuse out quickest if there is plenty of clean water outside to carry them away immediately.

So the print surface must be in contact all the time with fresh water into which the chemicals can diffuse, while the chemical laden water is continually replaced.

Experience has shown that washing should take at least 30 minutes in running water, with the prints kept moving all the time.

Alternatively, wash the prints for about 45 minutes in several changes of water, leaving them in the same change of water for about 5 minutes each time.

The chemicals must also be washed out of the paper base. The thicker the paper, the longer this will take.

The above washing times are just about right for single weight papers; for double weight prints allow one and a half times to twice as long.

42

DRYING

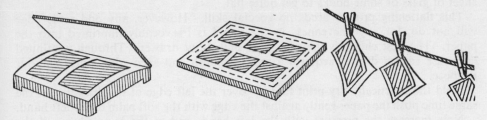

Methods of drying prints. *Left:* Glazing on a heated glazing press (p. 44). *Centre:* Laying the prints face down on a sheet of muslin stretched over a frame. *Right:* Hanging up by one corner.

Finally, we must dry the print.

There are several ways of getting the sheet of paper back into its original flat and dry form. To some extent these depend on the paper itself.

Papers with a glossy surface are dried and glazed on a heated glazing drum, or on cold glazing plates or sheets of glass.

Papers with other surfaces are allowed to dry naturally.

The second way is the simpler one. The best method is to hang the prints from a line with wooden spring clothes pegs. Each grips a print by one extreme corner.

The picture side with the gelatine layer curls inwards during drying. If we hang two prints back to back from the same peg, they will not curl so violently.

Some people prefer to dry prints flat and face down on muslin stretched over frames, or blotting paper laid over wire netting. The disadvantage of this method is that any drops remaining on the back of the print may leave their marks in the paper. Such drying marks are often difficult to remove, even if the print is re-soaked. Prints to be dried in this way must therefore be drained well beforehand.

If the prints dry too rapidly, the surface may be uneven and wavy. This is particularly liable to happen on a hot and dry day or in central heated rooms. So make sure the air is not too dry, by having a wet towel hanging up in the same room.

FLATTENING THE PRINT

Taking out the curl. **I.** Hold the print face down over the edge of a drawer. **2.** Press down with one hand. **3.** At the same time pull the print across the edge with the other hand.

Prints that have curled greatly during drying are better not allowed to become quite bone dry. When they have still a trace of moisture left in them, we can pull

43

them over an edge to straighten them out, and leave them lying under a heavy sheet of glass or some books to get quite flat.

This flattening process needs no special skill. However, any odd table edge will not do, for any unevenness in the wood is irrevocably imprinted into the paper. The best choice is the edge of a pulled-out drawer. Through continued daily use such a drawer acquires a really smooth and even edge—ideal for our purpose.

Hold the practically dry print face up over the left edge of the drawer. At the same time push the paper gently against the edge with the soft palm of the left hand.

Now increase the pressure with the left hand, and at the same time pull the paper upwards with the right. Both pressure and pulling must become stronger at the same time. If the left hand presses too strongly before the right has started pulling, a kink forms in the paper which is almost impossible to straighten out later on.

Pull through in this way from one corner to the diagonally opposite one altogether four times, once from each corner.

The print which was originally curled, is now curved outwards. It then only has to lie under pressure for a few hours to become really flat.

HOT GLAZING

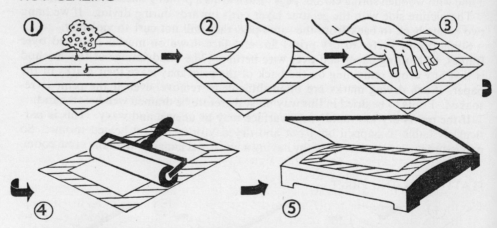

How to glaze a print. **1.** Pour a few drops of water over the heated glazing plate. **2.** Carefully lower the print onto the glazing plate. **3.** Tap the back of the print with the fingers to expel any air. **4.** Squeegee down, first in one direction, then in the other. **5.** Place the glazing plate into the hot glazer and fasten down the cloth apron. Leave until dry.

We can obtain a high glaze on glossy papers in a heated glazing press.

Such a press can also be used to dry prints with other than glossy surfaces. In that case we place the prints with the back onto the glazing plate, squeegee off surplus moisture, and put the whole into the hot glazer. This may, however, lead to some unpleasant surprises as large prints on double-weight paper in particular may come out of the press with a wavy surface which will defy all straightening. The point is, ordinary papers just have to be dried slowly.

With glossy prints there is no danger of the paper surface going into waves during drying. The reason lies in the principle of hot glazing itself. In this process the emulsion surface of the print is pressed into close contact with the glazing plate. During drying, therefore, the print clings to the glazing plate and takes on its mirror-smooth surface. After drying the paper falls off the plate as soon as the press is opened.

All this sounds very simple and promising. But we can only get a satisfactory high glaze by handling the process in the right way. The main secret of success lies in an absolutely clean glazing plate. So clean it thoroughly first as described on page 46. We can then start glazing.

First heat up the glazing press.

As soon as it has reached its working temperature, open it, take out the glazing plate, and lay it on a flat surface (a sheet of glass is best).

Then carefully wipe over the chromium surface with a clean wet sponge; partly to cool it down somewhat, and partly to leave a few drops of water on the surface.

Also wipe the surface of the prints (soaking in water after the wash) with the same sponge to remove any possible grit or dirt.

Next, pull the first print out of the water, and lay it with the emulsion side downwards onto the glazing plate. There is a special way of doing this, and a lot depends on it.

The point is that no air bubble must find its way between the glazing surface and the print. There must therefore be enough water clinging to both to push out all the air trapped between the two. Moreover, the air must also be allowed to get out.

The paper is best transferred from the water to the glazing plate as quickly as possible. Hold the paper with both hands at its opposite edges above the glazing plate. With the left hand place the left paper edge onto the surface. Then, slowly lower the other edge with the right hand, until this too lies on the glazing surface. While the arched paper is gradually lowered in this way, the water flows out underneath from left to right. At the same time it pushes the air out in front of it before the paper and plate come into contact.

As soon as the paper is in position, test for the absence of air underneath. Gently tap and push the paper back from every side with the tips of all five fingers. At first it will feel as if the paper were sticking to the surface. But after a few taps it becomes slippery and starts to slide in the direction in which it is tapped. That is a sure sign that there is as good as no more air trapped underneath.

Then press down the print by squeegeeing with a roller squeegee. This removes the surplus water, and also drives out any small air bubbles still remaining between the two surfaces.

Single large prints can be squeegeed directly.

Where several small prints have been placed on the glazing plate, cover the whole surface with a large rubber sheet, or at least a large blotting paper, before going over it with the roller squeegee. The sheet prevents small prints from sticking to the roller and leaving the surface.

45

The direction of squeegeeing is important, too. The pressure must start from the end at which the prints were lowered onto the plate first, and where most of the water has thus remained. As we had first lowered the left-hand edge of the print, the roller must also start from the left edge, so pull it gently, with slight pressure, to the right over the print.

This first squeegeeing, then, gets rid of any air that may still be present. Then pull the roller squeegee over the prints a second time. This time the direction does not matter, and the pressure can be greater, for now the water itself has to be squeegeed out.

Finally put the plate with the prints on it into the glazing press and fasten the pressure frame with the apron over it. Make sure that the cloth apron is properly tensioned, for the prints have to be pressed down all the time during drying, and must not move.

For this reason don't open the press too soon. We can find out whether the prints are dry just as well with the press closed by simply feeling the apron with the fingers. Besides, just before drying is complete, a crackling noise can be heard, indicating that the print surface is leaving the glazing plate.

The dry prints are at first violently curled inwards. The gelatine layer has been strongly dried out by the heat and has become quite horny. Just let the prints lie about for a while; the gelatine soon absorbs some moisture from the air, and the prints uncurl again. It would be wrong to flatten them under pressure straightaway after glazing, as then no air could get to them.

COLD GLAZING

A heated glazing press is, however, not absolutely essential. While cold glazing methods are laborious and take up a lot of time, they are good enough for glazing an occasional print when it is not worth buying an expensive glazing machine.

All we need is a flawless flat sheet of glass. First clean it thoroughly.

After superficial washing with soap and warm water, wipe it over with a mixture of 3 parts each of French chalk, water, and methylated spirit, with 1 part concentrated ammonia added.

When dry, rub off the white coating with a soft cloth, polishing the glass surface at the same time. Then rub the glass over again with a fresh cloth with a little talcum powder on it.

Press the glossy print onto the glass in the same way as for hot glazing (p. 44). Any airbells are easily detected from the other side of the glass.

Then wipe over the back of the prints with a cloth, and put the glass plate in a cool place to dry.

With an absolutely clean plate the prints should fall off of their own accord as soon as they are dry. Should they still stick to the plate, they can usually be lifted off by carefully going underneath the edges with a knife.

If, however, the plate was not clean, there is no remedy: the prints will cling as if they were glued on. The only thing to do is to put the whole glazing plate with the print into water and hope for the best; it may soak off without tearing.

46

Section II

FINER POINTS OF PRINT MAKING

CONTROLLING PROPORTIONS

Now that we have gone over the basic principles and general technique of the printing process, let us turn to its more special methods.

The scope for perfecting the picture is wide. We should be sadly neglecting this range of possibilities if we were satisfied with the type of average product which at the best reproduces only what was in the negative, or even less than that. We must be concerned with getting as much out of a negative as it will possibly yield. The higher the standard, the better.

For that reason we shall now take a look at gradually more advanced and subtle methods that will help us to obtain prints which are not just copies of our negatives but pictures in their own right.

But a word of warning first.

Clever and out-of-the-way working methods must never become an end in themselves. This book, which mainly deals with the refinements of positive technique, would entirely miss its point if it were interpreted as a guide merely to photographic dabbling.

Even though this dabbling as such may at times contribute to the particular character of a picture, in the large majority of cases it cannot add anything to either expression or content, nor enhance the pictorial value.

All the many dodges and techniques explained in the following sections are therefore not meant to be imitated on any odd negative just for their own sake, except perhaps for gaining practice. Rather, they are examples to suggest possibilities when a negative or an idea for a special picture really shouts for treatment outside normally accepted limits.

The emphasis is always on achieving a certain result, not on working a certain technique.

SELECTION

Photographically we only can depict the world around us more or less the way it really is.

If four people stand chatting at a street corner, we cannot easily make a picture in which there are only three. And when we find a dreamy secluded spot which time would seem to have passed by were it not for the intrusion of a misplaced telegraph pole, then a painter can leave that out. But as a rule we must photograph the pole with the rest of the scene, whether we like it or not.

The point of photography is to select that part of the subject which contains just the essence of the whole. This part is the view in the finder. That is why every beginner is told: "Get your picture in the viewfinder!"

48

Though this rule is a good one to start with, we shall often disregard it later on; sometimes by design, and sometimes through force of circumstances.

However that may be, we can often make good in enlarging what we failed to achieve for one reason or another in exposing the negative. Some people definitely prefer to settle the final picture boundaries when the negative is enlarged. In hundreds of cases there is just no time for long deliberation before taking the picture. But we have plenty of time for quiet consideration in the darkroom.

So when enlarging we must pay attention not only to the choice of paper, to exposure, and development, but also to selection of the best part of the negative.

LEAVING OUT

Leave out as much as possible until only the really essential part of the subject is left.

The masking frames which hold the paper during enlarging are often fitted with movable framing strips.

To arrive at the most favourable picture area, first set these strips for the full paper size to be used. Project and focus the negative on this frame, and then push the enlarger head further and further up the column until nothing more can be left off the two opposite edges without interfering with what is essential to the picture.

Next, move in the other two framing strips to cut off everything else that is not important.

PICTURE SHAPE

The overall shape of the picture is often fixed in advance (as it is the case with prints designed for publication in books or magazines). However, when the effect only matters, do not be afraid to finish up with whatever picture shape comes naturally; whether this is a square, or even a long rectangular print.

A slim upright picture shape emphasises the majestic in a subject. A cathedral, for instance, gains in dignity. That is not an arbitrary idea, but is present in the subconscious human imagination. It is like wearing a top hat; the increased effect of slimness makes the wearer look more distinguished.

In the same way a low horizontal format has the opposite effect. It gives an impression of peace, even of the timeless. Something lying stretched out is resting, if not dead, and in either case it will be still. Thus an expanse of sea and sky appears particularly impressive when it is trimmed to a long horizontal shape.

The square shape, however, has a special role. Its popularity is not due to pictorial design, but to necessity, or at least convenience.

The square picture appeared more or less at the same time as the square negative format of the twin-lens reflex camera. The original idea was to take upright and horizontal pictures on the same negative format without having to turn the camera through 90 degrees half the time. In practice the vague intention to "cut off something" has led to the modern square picture shape.

Owing to its uniform dimensions it has something impersonal about it. It presents the subject as it is, without any emphasis. The square shape is suitable for any subject of more or less even proportions. Such subjects stand centrally in the picture without any dead space around them.

A more indirect merit of the square shape is that it represents the happy medium between upright and horizontal pictures. This is useful if we want to collect a large number of pictures in an album—or even in a book—because it permits a uniform lay-out.

SUGGESTIVE CROPPING

We can emphasise movement by turning the masking frame so that the direction of movement slopes slightly downwards. This gives the impression that, for example, a car is coming out of the picture.

With crowd pictures, the left- and right-hand print borders should cut into the persons standing near the edge. Even half a dozen people can be made to seem like part of a large crowd in this way. If they are entirely left in the picture without cutting into them, the result will look like a group smaller than the picture area.

In portraits heads should be kept near to the top edge, and have more space in front of the face than behind it.

ORDER OF IMPORTANCE

It is not out of place to compare a picture with the page of a book. From habit we often "read" a picture subconsciously like a printed text. And in reading, at any rate with European languages, the eye always moves from left to right, and from top to bottom, line by line. This is perhaps why a picture often seems to appeal more, if its parts are arranged, according to their importance, from top left to bottom right.

To give a simple example, to many people it will look more natural if a flower is placed in the top left third of the picture area, with the stem going towards the bottom right. The same print reversed left to right would not seem as pleasing.

BORDERS

Making a black border. 1. Expose the print in the normal way. 2. Switch off, and place an opaque mask over the picture area, leaving the border clear. 3. Expose again, but without a negative in the enlarger.

It makes some difference whether the picture has a white margin, a black one, or none at all.

50

A border round the picture isolates it from its surroundings. It makes the print stand out, as if we were seeing the subject through a window. On the other hand, pictures without a border often merge into the world around them.

Prints with white margins come more or less of their own accord. A white margin is formed during exposure under the framing strips of the masking frame.

The width of such a margin is largely a matter of taste. Very wide margins with their brilliant whiteness, however, tend to make the pictures appear darker. Therefore such prints sometimes seem heavy.

A black border makes the picture look correspondingly lighter. The eye can compare the tones with the pure black of the margins.

Making a black border needs a little more preparation.

With plate negatives we can cut the emulsion layer with a sharp knife along a straight ruler, and scrape the margins clear of emulsion. With film negatives this procedure would damage the film base itself, so we make the margin during printing.

Cut a piece of opaque card to the size of the final picture shape. After enlarging, leave the paper in position on the baseboard and place the card over it, leaving just the margins free. The card is best weighed down. Remove the negative from the carrier, and give the print margins an additional exposure to the clear and unobstructed enlarging light. On development the margin will go intensely black.

CORRECTION OF CONVERGING VERTICALS

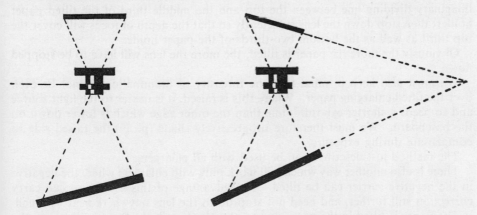

Straightening converging verticals. *Left:* The straightforward method is to tilt the baseboard up at the end where the verticals diverge. *Right:* A greater degree of correction is possible by also tilting the negative carrier in the opposite direction. To get the image sharp all over, the planes of the baseboard and negative carrier should intersect in the plane of the lens board (p. 52).

If we do not hold the camera level, but tilt it upward or downward while taking the picture, the picture will come out distorted. This will be all the more obvious the greater the angle of tilt.

In many cases the distortion is not apparent or does not matter. But wherever there are vertical lines which must be rendered parallel, they will seem to converge and so give away that the camera was tilted. Houses become narrower at the top if the camera is looking up at them from a worm's eye view, or they taper towards the bottom when we are looking down from above.

This does not necessarily conflict with our ideas of photography. In fact, distortion of this type is often produced intentionally for the sake of pictorial effect, putting dramatic exaggeration before realism.

In photographing architecture or technical subjects—and with many other pictures when the distortion is obviously accidental—it is, however, irritating and so some correction is desirable.

Once unwanted distortion is present in the negative, we can remove it by reversing the process from which it arose. In other words, we tilt the enlarging paper by raising that side of the paper holder or masking frame where the lines diverge. So the distance between this part of the paper and the enlarger lens is reduced and the degree of enlargement becomes progressively less towards the edge. In this way the diverging lines move closer together, and with an adequate tilt they will be as close as they are further down on the paper resting on the baseboard. The masking frame is then fixed in that position by pushing a box or some other object of suitable height underneath the raised side. Two darkroom pins stuck into the easel on the opposite side will stop the frame from slipping.

This would rectify the converging lines, but the image is no longer sharp. Raising the paper moved the image out of focus and we must now refocus it. Focus on an imaginary dividing line between the top and the middle third of the tilted paper holder; then stop down the lens sufficiently so that the depth of focus will cover the top third as well as the bottom two-thirds of the paper holder.

Obviously the more the paper is tilted, the more the lens will have to be stopped down.

We must also keep in mind that the intensity of illumination cannot be even over the tilted enlarging paper. Where this is raised, it is nearer to the light source and so needs a shorter exposure time than the other edge which is lower down on the baseboard. We must therefore progressively shade (p. 59) the raised side to compensate during exposure.

The method just described can be used with all enlargers.

There is also another way which will work only with enlargers where the negative in the negative carrier can be tilted. The advantage of this is that we can carry correction still further, and need not stop down the lens anywhere near as much.

The paper is tilted in the same way as already described. But we also raise the negative, again at the side towards which the lines diverge. This is the side opposite to the raised side of the paper holder (p. 51). The raised edge having been moved away from the lens is enlarged less than the other, and so the converging lines move apart. At the same time they are pulled still further apart by the already existing tilt of the paper.

The extent of correction possible is thus doubled. Also, as the negative and paper are both tilted towards each other, less stopping down or depth of focus will be needed to get a sharp image throughout.

PICTORIAL SELECTION. One negative may provide a number of different prints, each a picture itself. The best portion is easily selected during enlarging (p. 48). *Top left:* Print from the complete negative.

53

PICTURE SHAPE. *Above:* A sub
like this is best trimmed to a ver
shape. *Right:* The subject looks
in a horizontal format, half the p
area is empty (p. 49).

CONVERGING VERTICALS. If the camera was tilted upwards while taking the picture, vertical lines will converge towards the top. We can rectify this by tilting the paper holder (and perhaps the negative carrier as well) during enlarging (p. 51). *Above:* Straight print. *Left:* Corrected during enlarging.

55

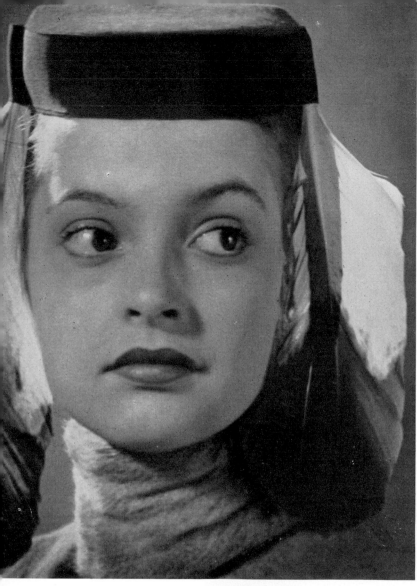

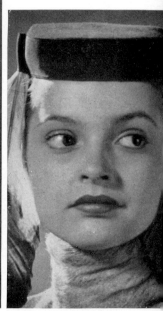

INTENTIONAL DISTORTION. Tilting the paper holder during enlarging also distorts the image proportions. In this way we might improve the shape of a face (p. 57) in a portrait. *Above right:* Straight print. *Above left:* Enlarged with the bottom edge of the paper raised up. *Right:* By carrying the process further and actually bending the paper on the enlarging easel (p. 57) the results can be quite ludicrous.

PICTORIAL DISTORTION

These methods of correction are not only useful for making the best of a bad job. We can also employ them for intentional distortion as a means to pictorial ends.

In portraiture, for instance, broad faces can be made narrower.

When we only tilt the paper holder, the whole image is, as we have seen, elongated. It is now the hypotenuse of a triangle of which it was one side when lying flat, and the hypotenuse is always the longest side of any triangle. Moreover, tilting compresses that part of the image which is nearest to the lens because it is enlarged less.

In practice therefore when tilting a face for slimming, the top of the head should be lower down (nearer the baseboard) than the chin. In this way the forehead will remain broad, while the rest of the face will be elongated towards the chin. At the same time the width of the cheek portion, which needs slimming most, is reduced (p. 56).

STRETCHING A POINT

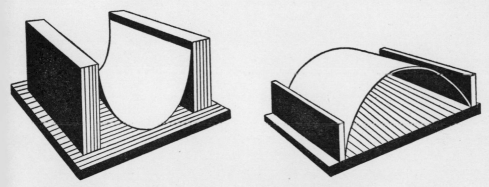

Bending the paper under the enlarger to produce intentional distortion. *Left:* To bend the paper inwards, it is best supported hanging between two small filing boxes or plate boxes. *Right:* To bend the paper outwards, two books or heavy strips are laid down and the paper pushed up between them. In the first case the centre, and in the second the edges, require extra exposure.

In addition to beautifying people with fat faces we can go still further, and bend the enlarging paper to get specially bizarre effects.

There are two possibilities: we can bend the paper either outwards or inwards. In the first case the parts of the image near the centre become smaller, and in the second case larger, than the parts near the edges. In addition, the whole image is stretched.

To bend the bromide paper outwards, place two thin books on the enlarger baseboard and weigh them down. Lay the paper between the books, and bend upwards in the centre by pushing the books together (p. 56).

If the paper is to be bent inwards, put two fairly heavy boxes of suitable height (small filing or plate boxes) near the left- and right-hand edges of the baseboard. Place the paper between them so that its edges bend up, with the middle hanging down between the boxes. Here, again, the degree of bending depends on the distance between the boxes (p. 57).

In either case the edges will have to be strongly overprinted, as the light falls on them only very obliquely.

Naturally, the more the paper is bent, the more the enlarger lens must be stopped down.

CONTROLLING THE TONES

TONE CONTROL DURING EXPOSURE

One of the rules of making good prints is to use the softest paper grade which, while still preserving the shadow detail, will give properly graded highlights and well separated medium tones. Though a harder paper may separate the medium tones better, shadow tones are submerged in black and highlight tones are lost.

To follow this useful rule, we sometimes have to help the negative a little by locally brightening up or toning down certain parts of the projected image.

Between the illuminated negative in the enlarger and the bromide paper on the baseboard there is plenty of room to interpose various paper masks, or even the hands. This produces shadows on the paper; these will affect the result, since they reduce the light projected through some part of the negative.

The longer the shadow remains in one place, the stronger its effect. If it is produced only during a small part of the total exposure time, the shaded part of the print will merely have slightly less exposure than the areas next to it.

Let us take as an example a landscape with sky and clouds. Inevitably the sky part of the negative is much denser than the rest. If we expose the print so that the foreground has just the right depth of tone, the sky will still appear very light and chalky by comparison; the clouds may be hardly visible. If the exposure is long enough for the sky to print through, the foreground will be a mere silhouette.

The best way out is to expose correctly for the foreground, and then shade this portion until the sky has had enough time to print through as well.

For instance, the landscape alone may need 10 seconds, while the sky is sufficiently dark only after 16 seconds exposure. So we expose the whole print for 16 seconds, but during 6 seconds of this time we hold back the landscape by shading.

SHADING TECHNIQUE

Tools for shading and spot printing. *Left:* Various shaped masks fixed to a wire holder will hold back portions within the picture area (p. 60). *Right:* Openings cut into a large card will serve in a similar way for local overprinting (p. 61).

This "holding back" of certain parts of the picture sounds more complicated than it really is. Admittedly it needs a little practice, but that is soon acquired.

59

Hardly any equipment is necessary. All sorts of shapes can be formed by contorting and turning the hands and fingers in every way—not unlike a game of shadow figures on the wall.

To start with it may be better though to cut a few masks out of cardboard. Some shapes crop up again and again in shading, like circles, squares, and triangles, and a few of these in two or three sizes should fill all needs.

For shading areas near the edges of the print, simply hold the masks with the fingers. For spots inside the print, fix them to thin wire. The shadow of the latter has no effect.

By tilting the mask we can vary the shape of the shadow. For example, a circle becomes an ellipse, a square can be made to produce a rectangular shadow, and triangles become slimmer or fatter. The more the mask is tilted, the narrower the shadow will be.

The size of the shadow and the sharpness of its outline depend on how high we hold the mask above the paper.

The lower to the paper we hold a mask, the smaller and sharper the shadow will be. So we must keep it slightly moving all the time to avoid registering tell-tale contours on the print. The brightness of the rest of the image will not appreciably be affected by all this.

If we hold the mask high up near the lens, the shadow becomes large and less well defined. Also the brightness of the image is reduced, for the nearer the mask is to the lens, the more it acts like a lens stop, decreasing the overall light. We must therefore increase the exposure time.

To compensate for varying brightness of the image (for instance when the paper holder is tilted to correct distortion; p. 51), use a fairly large sheet of cardboard for shading. Slowly move it from the brighter edge to the darker and back, remaining above the bright parts for a longer time. The required exposure adjustment is thus obtained by progressive shading.

SPOT PRINTING

There is no really sharp distinction between shading and spot printing. We could say that with shading, parts of the image are held back during exposure so that the corresponding print areas do not become too dark. In the case of spot printing, parts of the print are overexposed in order to gain sufficient detail in the highlights.

But this is really saying the same thing the other way round. For while one part of the print is shaded, the rest is relatively overprinted, and vice versa.

When we are faced with a subject like our landscape (p. 59), where the dark foreground and light sky can be assumed to be of equal size, shading and spot printing become identical. It does not matter whether we regard the exposure time as 16 seconds and shade half the print for 6 seconds, or fix the exposure at 10 seconds and overprint the other half for 6 seconds. The result is exactly the same.

60

In practice the difference between the two techniques is in fact mainly a matter of comparative sizes. If the shadows to be controlled form the smaller part of the image, they are shaded. If on the other hand the highlights are smaller and fewer, they are spot printed.

Small areas are best printed up in this manner with the help of a card with a hole cut in it. After exposing the whole print normally, hold this card in the path of the light so that the whole image is covered except for the highlights to be spot printed. Naturally, the card must again be kept moving all the time to diffuse the outlines of the overprinted portion.

EXPOSURE CONTROL IN CONTACT PRINTING

Modern contact printers also allow suitable masks to be inserted between the negative and the light source during exposure.

In some cases the lamps, if there are several, can be manipulated individually (p. 20).

For example, with our landscape we can switch off the lamps under the foreground part of the negative and expose the print only by the light of the lamps behind the sky portion. In this way the sky receives more light.

Fine control of small picture areas is very limited with contact printers, because it is almost impossible to observe the image during exposure.

With a printing frame the possibilities for shading and spot printing are also restricted, particularly in the smaller sizes.

FLASHING

Tools for flashing. An ordinary pocket torch with a cardboard sleeve round the bulb will make a useful miniature spotlight. This can be used for darkening corners or other parts of the print by "painting" over them with light (p. 62).

We can improve prints by additional exposure—independently of the enlarging exposure itself. This technique is known as flashing.

For instance, we can make a print softer by exposing the bromide paper for a short time to a yellow safelight as used for contact papers. This slightly fogs the print, but its highlights can be cleared later (p. 200).

To obliterate the marginal detail in a picture (e.g. portraits) remove the negative from the enlarger and give the print an additional exposure—shading the main picture area (e.g. the head) with an oval mask. The light is now very strong, so we need some means of reducing it to keep the flashing exposure at a controllable level.

It is not advisable to stop down the enlarger lens because the outline of the shadow becomes sharper. The best way is to develop a film or plate by daylight just long enough to produce an even medium grey tone. The resulting neutral density plate then takes the place of the negative during the flashing operation and reduces the excessively strong enlarger illumination.

Where uneven flashing is more suitable, we can use an ordinary pocket electric torch. This is fitted with a funnel-shaped paper hood so that it produces a narrow cone of light. We can now "paint" over with the thin beam of light those parts of the print which should be darkened during enlarging. In this way we may produce all sorts of shadows and abstract designs to add to the image proper.

The light itself should not be so strong as to blacken the image completely straightaway. Where required, a full black is produced instead by repeated "overpainting".

VIGNETTING

Making a Vignette. 1. Trace the outline of the area for vignetting on a card. 2. Cut out the mask. 3. Expose the print with the mask in position, to obtain a softly diffused outline fading into white (p. 68).

We can, as we have seen, make a portrait with a light background stand out of the picture by darkening its corners and edges. In the same way, with pictures against a dark background—or any other background for that matter—the eye is drawn more strongly towards the centre if the edges are faded out by vignetting.

To make a vignette, fix an opaque card some distance above the paper on the baseboard by laying it across two piles of books, or using a masking stage (p. 123).

The card should completely shade the paper underneath. Its height above the baseboard is best found by experiment.

Switch on the enlarger with the negative in the carrier, and sketch the outline of the required vignette on the opaque card.

Cut away the portion inside this outline with a pair of scissors and put the card back in the same place as before.

Expose the print through this hole. The light can of course only act in the middle of the print, while the contours of the vignetting mask gradually fade into white towards the outside.

The nearer the mask to the paper, the more abrupt the fade—the farther away the softer its effect. If the vignetting mask is placed directly on the photographic paper, it will be reproduced completely sharp.

However, sharp vignetting rarely looks good. The same effect could be produced anyway by cutting the required part out of the finished print with scissors, and pasting it on a piece of white paper.

For an unusual effect and discriminating use here is one idea for vignetting with sharp contours (p. 69).

Put down a large dry developing dish on the enlarger baseboard and place the paper holder or masking frame inside it. After focusing and exposure tests, swing the orange filter in front of the lens and insert the bromide paper—preferably glossy surfaced—in the paper holder. Now sprinkle granulated animal charcoal (medicinal grade) over the whole paper surface. Switch on the enlarger with the orange filter in position. This prevents exposure, but allows the details of the image to be observed.

Next, with a fine brush sweep away the charcoal from those parts of the paper where the image is to print through, leaving untouched the portions to be vignetted.

When that is done, switch off the enlarger light, remove the orange filter, and expose in the normal way.

Finally take the paper out of the holder, let the charcoal slide off (the dish is there to catch it), and process as usual.

Variations are possible by using different sprinkling media, e.g. pins, rice, granulated sugar, fine wood or cork shavings, etc.

Also, instead of leaving the grains in one place during the whole of the exposure period, they can be shifted about two or three times. In this way we produce grey particle shapes as well as pure white ones on the print.

TONE CONTROL DURING PROCESSING

We can selectively modify parts of the picture during development, too. The limits are narrower though, than during exposure.

The methods available are based on two facts.

Firstly, the density of the print increases slightly during prolonged development.

Secondly, the speed of development and the energy of the developer increase if the solutions are warmed up. According to the position and size of the picture areas to be treated, some correction is thus possible by local overdevelopment: either through forcing, or through warming up the developer.

To bring up our landscape and sky yet again, the procedure there would be to develop until the foreground is just dense enough. Then the paper is partly pulled out of the developing dish with the forceps, so that only the sky portion remains in the solution, and is developed for a little longer.

Obviously any extra density obtainable in this way is severely limited. This method is therefore only a help in borderline cases where just that little bit of additional density puts the final touch to the picture. But at the best this extra bit is not much more than we could expect from the exposure given. Beyond a certain length of time, forcing becomes pointless and only produces yellow stains (p. 39).

The developer on the print can be warmed up locally in two ways.

We can rub with the finger tips over parts of the print needing extra density to bring out detail, while the print is immersed in the developer. This continually brings fresh solution to those spots, and also by the warmth of the hand increases the speed of development there. As, however, the fingers often get cold faster than they can influence the developer by their warmth, the effect is very slight in practice.

A better method is to lift the print out of the developer, drain it, and breathe onto the areas in question, bringing the mouth very near to the paper. The risk of yellow stained prints, as well as of aerial fog is considerable, though.

These methods are therefore only suggested as a last resort for improving a print when other methods of compensation such as shading and spot printing were impracticable or when we just did not think of them when we made the print.

STRENGTHENING THE HIGHLIGHTS

When the print is on the whole good except for too light and bare highlights, some improvement is possible after development. One condition for this treatment is that the print should have been fully developed so that the shadows cannot subsequently gain more density.

Transfer the print straight from the developer to a dishful of water at about 90–105° F. (30–40° C.). Owing to the sudden increase in temperature the developer absorbed in the emulsion layer is spurred on to increased activity. The shadows may become just a shade darker, but in the highlights where there is hardly any developable silver the developer will remain effective for much longer, and can now with its increased energy bring out as much detail as will come out.

As the warm water treatment greatly softens the emulsion, it must not be carried on for too long. But we can enhance its effect by using a warm 5 per cent solution of sodium carbonate instead of plain water.

VARIABLE CONTRAST DEVELOPMENT

We can control the print quality during development by adjusting the composition of the developer. Thus we can increase contrast by using a contrast developer (No. 3, p. 238) or decrease it by using a soft-working formula (No. 4, p. 238).

This method of contrast control is considerably more limited than the range of contrasts obtainable by changing from one paper grade to another.

The amount of compensation possible by varying the developer is, in fact, at the most equivalent to about half a paper grade each way. It is therefore useful when we need a print gradation intermediate between two paper contrast grades. For instance, a print on normal paper may be just a trifle too soft, but it would be still much better than on the next harder grade.

But developer compensation cannot, and is not meant to, take the place of the various paper grades. So always try to get the best possible print on a suitable paper grade by normal development first.

SOFTER PRINTS BY PRE-TREATMENT

We shall sometimes come across negatives which are so contrasty with the high-lights completely blocked up, that even the softest paper with all forms of process-

64

SHADING. When parts of the picture print too dark we can shade them (p. 59) during part of the exposure time. *Left:* Straight print. *Above :* Left-hand portion shaded during enlarging.

LOCAL OVERPRINTING. When parts of the picture print too light they are given extra exposure (p. 60). If the areas in question are small, we can do that by means of a card with a suitably shaped hole in it. For larger areas, as in this case, the rest of the print is simply shaded. *Right*: Straight print. *Above*: Enlargement with part of the picture overprinted.

FLASHING. To darken the edges or corners of the print the main part is shaded while the areas to be darkened are exposed without a negative in the enlarger (p. 61). A specially adapted pocket torch can also be used (p. 61, 62). *Centre left and bottom left:* Straight prints. *Top left:* Foreground and sky darkened. *Above right:* Corners flashed in.

67

VIGNETTING. Unwanted details are
held back by means of a cut-out mask
supported some way above the printing paper during the exposure
(p. 62). *Right:* Straight print. *Above:*
Vignetted enlargement.

CONTACT VIGNETTE. A variation of the normal vignetting method is to cover the print surface with some granular material leaving only the subject itself free (p. 63). *Left:* Straight print. *Above:* Enlargement printed with granulated charcoal covering the paper during exposure.

69

HIGH KEY. To make a high key print the negative is printed on soft paper with increased exposure and developed in a dilute developer (p. 77). *Bottom:* Normal print. *Top:* High key print. *Right:* Subjects consisting mainly of light tones with very few blacks are specially suitable for this treatment.

70

LOW KEY. For a low key picture the normal tone range is restricted mainly to the dark or near-dark tones. *Left:* Normal print. *Above:* Low-key enlargement.

71

Opposite: POSTERIZATION.
print consists only of three to
Again two negatives are needed
the highlights and for the shad
All tone gradation is destroyed
making another set of contr
duplicates until the negatives
just opaque masks. These are t
printed on one sheet of bron
paper, again in exact register (p.

Page 74, top left: First stage high
negative as for normal tone sep
tion. *Top centre:* Contrasty high
negative without tone gradation
posterizing. *Bottom left:* First s
shadow negative. *Bottom centre:* H
contrast shadow negative. Ce
row: If we use a third negative
print will have altogether four tc
Right hand column: Each posteri
negative by itself would print
as a silhouette.

TONE SEPARATION. The tone
range of the print is compressed at
the expense of the middle tones only,
leaving the highlight and shadow
gradation unchanged. This is achieved
by making two duplicate negatives,
one with full highlight detail but no
shadows, and the other with good
shadow gradation and almost opaque
highlights. The two are then printed,
one after the other, in exact register on one sheet of bromide paper
(p. 78). *Right:* Straight print. *Above:*
Tone separation with two negatives.

72

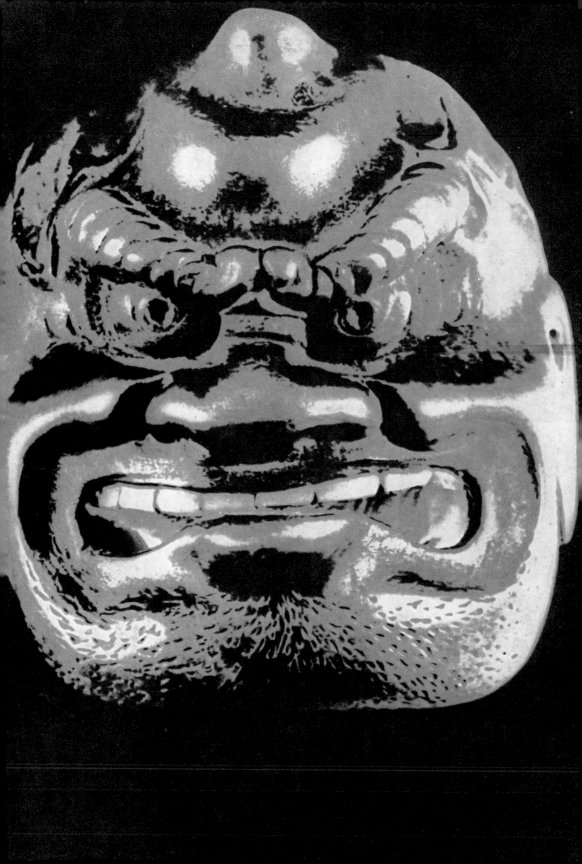

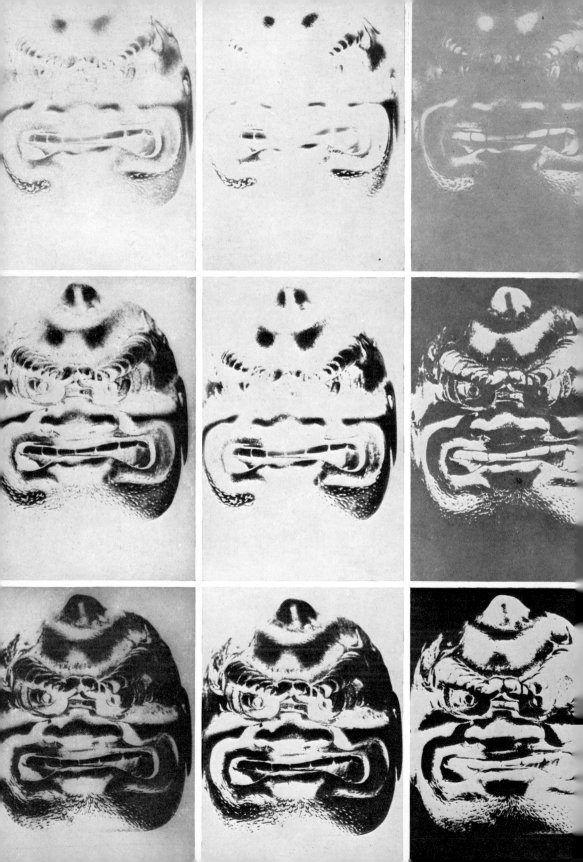

CHEMICAL TONE SEPARATION.
Partial bleaching and redevelopment of a very contrasty negative can reduce the tone range in a manner somewhat similar to tone separation (p. 82). *Left:* Straight print. *Above:* Enlargement from bleached and redeveloped negative.

75

CLEARING THE HIGHLIGHTS (p. 200). *Above left:* Original print. *Above right:* Highlights cleared in Farmer's reducer.

OPTICAL INTENSIFICATION. Very thin underexposed negatives can be made printable by copying the negative by dark-ground illumination (p. 175). *Left:* Flat and detailless print from original negative. *Right:* Print from copy negative.

ing compensation will not help. In that case the *Sterry* forebath of potassium bichromate may come in useful.

Bathe the normally exposed (or if necessary slightly overexposed) print before development in a 1 per cent potassium bichromate solution for 1 minute. Then drain and without rinsing transfer to the developer.

The rest of the processing (acid rinse, fixing, washing) follows in the usual way. The developer must, however, be renewed repeatedly.

Through this forebath the gradation of the picture becomes much softer, in a way which can never be achieved with ultra-soft paper and soft developers. Only the image colour falls off slightly; instead of blue-black or deep black, the print has a greenish brown tone.

We can avoid this change of tone by using a 10 per cent thorium nitrate solution. The difference between this and the Sterry effect is that the print does not become softer or more grey all over. Only the deep shadows gain in transparency and show increased detail. Moreover, the image colour is not affected at all.

The exposure time must be increased with the thorium nitrate forebath.

For instance, an enlargement which needed 20 seconds exposure on soft paper may be found too hard. So expose the next print for three times as long, i.e. 60 seconds. Then immerse it for 3 minutes in a 10 per cent thorium nitrate solution, rinse briefly, and develop as usual.

If the thorium nitrate solution is turbid, add a few drops of nitric acid until it is clear.

HIGH KEY

There are subjects without any blacks to them, even without shadows.

A branch thickly covered with blossom set against the sky, or a platinum blonde in a white silk dress with a white background belong to this category—provided they are both photographed in diffuse front light.

It would be wrong to handle such pictures in the normal way, so that they show the usual full range of tones. It is far more important to preserve and emphasise the delicacy of the light tones. That is done by high-key technique.

Strictly speaking, it is not a special process; it is simply variation of the usual technique for a special purpose, namely for obtaining a pale, ethereal picture.

We definitely cannot achieve that by shortening the development time. Taking the print out of the developer prematurely leads to unpleasant image tones (p. 39). On the other hand, the enlarging exposure must not be cut short, either, because the highlight gradation would be lost, or with forced development the whole print may show chemical fog (p. 39).

The correct way to go about it is as follows:

Only the softest paper grade is of any use here. Conduct the enlarging process so that the tone range of the print runs from pure white to light medium grey, and abruptly stops there.

After finding the correct exposure by means of usual test strips, expose the print for double that time. Develop it in a diluted developer instead of the normal solution. According to the tone range of the negative, this dilution should be between 5 and 10 times. The more contrasty the negative, the greater the dilution. The development time is, of course, also increased. A warm tone formula (e.g. No. 6, p. 239) is particularly suitable.

With black tone developers there is some danger of yellow fog, particularly in hot weather. This can be prevented by adding extra potassium bromide, but that would again increase the contrast. For our purposes a developer improver does the trick. (The formula No. 1 on p. 237 contains such a developer improver, and needs no further additions.)

A high-key print is rarely successful on the first attempt. We must adjust the working details exactly to each individual negative. Often we may have to bring in one or the other subsidiary control method. These may include the *Sterry* effect (p. 77), forcing the highlights in a warm water bath (p. 64), diffusion during enlargement (p. 86), and finally reducing or clearing solutions.

LOW KEY

A heavy dark picture, with a full weight of black in it, needs low-key technique. It is suitable for dramatic subjects.

Use a relatively contrasty paper which ensures full black tones, without however drowning the shadow detail. Exposure must be full, though not excessive. Develop the print to completion.

Development can be followed by an afterbath in warm water (p. 64), provided the shadows still show enough detail.

TONE SEPARATION

The steps of tone separation. 1. Make a positive transparency from the original negative and scratch two registration marks on it. 2. From the transparency make two negatives; a thin highlight one, and a dense shadow negative. 3. Print the shadow negative. 4. Print the highlight negative in exact register (p. 72).

Tone separation technique will increase the scale of tones in the print.

While the tone range of a negative from the brightest white to the deepest black

78

may in extreme cases cover as much as 1 : 1000, the paper positive can reproduce a tone range of only about 1 : 30. The full gradation in the various grey tones is therefore considerably compressed.

The whole tone range can only be shown in a transparency, because we look through it by transmitted light. With a print, however, we look at it by reflected light. While the black tones will still reflect a little light, the whitest tone cannot reflect more light than falls on the white paper base. And at the best, reflection is not complete. The diffused white of a print can never reach the real brilliance of the light falling on it.

In printing, therefore, we must choose between two alternatives. We either aim at the best reproduction of the half tones, together with part of the highlights, with the shadows blocked up. Or we work for a good reproduction of the half tones and most of the shadows, but with no detail in the highlights.

We could attempt to bring most of the negative tones into the very restricted positive range by using a soft printing paper. But then all the medium tones will merely merge and so make the print look flat, even if it contains a pure white and a full black somewhere. We must try to separate those medium tones and yet retain both highlights and shadows.

Tone separation methods therefore aim at increasing the reproducible range of tones in a print. They do this in a fairly roundabout way.

To make things easier for the paper, we suitably change the negative. We break it down into two (or even more) separation negatives of which one shows up the highlight gradation, and the other the shadows. Both negatives are then printed successively onto the same sheet of printing paper in exact register. They are thus combined again to give a single positive print. The tones on the print are now more separated, giving full shadow gradation and detailed highlights.

What has really happened, is that the tone scales of the highlights and shadows in the negative have to some extent become superimposed. Thus, to give an arbitrary example, the shadow brightnesses originally may have ranged from 1 to 50; and the highlights from 100 to 200. In the print they are now from 1 to 25, and from 20 to 30 respectively. That means that we have cut out or falsified some of the intermediate tone gradation but the result is nevertheless better than if the ranges had been 1 to 8 and 25 to 30, respectively.

For all tone separation methods a contrasty original negative is essential. The highlights should be so heavy that they are difficult to print successfully without completely blocking the shadows. For the invention of the tone separation process arose from the search for a way to print such hard negatives at all.

The steps of making a print by tone separation are:

1. Make two separation negatives from the original negative.
2. Print the shadow negative, giving it a normal exposure.
3. Print the highlight negative on the same sheet of paper in exact register, giving it a greatly reduced exposure.

Before preparing the separation negatives, make two registration marks on opposite edges of the original negative. Whether these are crosses scratched in with a needle, or just two fine pin pricks, is immaterial. Important is that the marks should be easily recognisable.

Now make two duplicate negatives from this original. One of them must show its fullest gradation in the highlights, while the shadow detail can be completely absent. The other must have full shadow detail, while the highlights need not show through at all. The registration marks must be distinctly visible on both negatives.

The original negative can even serve as the shadow negative, provided the highlights are dense enough.

Put this into a printing frame in contact with a sheet of direct reversal film and expose as for contact printing. Develop, bleach to reverse, and redevelop in the solutions recommended for the particular reversal film used. This will give the highlight negative.

A few tests will be necessary to arrive at the right exposure. This will be longer than usual, for the final highlight negative must be very thin and soft. One way of making sure of that is to reduce the time of the second development, or to use the second developer at only one-quarter the recommended strength. We can then watch the reversal negative as it develops up, and stop development when it looks right.

Another method is to use an intermediate positive transparency.

Prepare this by printing the original negative by contact or with the enlarger onto a lantern plate or a slow sheet film. Develop this positive in the normal way (p. 38), and scratch the two registration marks on it.

Now make two negatives from the intermediate positive.

Print it first onto a slow contrasty negative emulsion or on a hard grade of lantern plate. Expose fairly heavily to get the highlights almost blocked up. Then develop in a contrast developer (p. 238). This will be the shadow negative.

Then print the transparency again, but this time on a soft working negative material or a soft grade of lantern plate. Develop in a low contrast developer (p. 238) until the highlights appear just sufficiently dense, then fix and wash. This will be the highlight negative.

With the intermediate transparency the separation negatives can be any size, as long as both are exactly the same; we can make them either by contact or by enlargement.

When combining the two separation negatives into a final print, first print the shadow negative.

Focus it accurately and mark the registration points on the baseboard with pin pricks. With an orange filter in front of the enlarger lens, we may even make the marks on the bromide paper itself. When we subsequently put the highlight negative in the negative carrier, we can register the corresponding marks accurately on the paper, again with the orange filter in front of the lens.

Find the exposure times by separate test strips for each negative. The strips must, of course, be developed for the same time. While the shadow negative usually requires a normal exposure, only a very short time is needed for the highlight one.

The final result will depend on the relative exposure times, the number of separation negatives used, and on their differences in gradation and density. The effect can range from purely photographic to a completely graphic posterised impression (p. 73).

80

TONE SEPARATION WITH MINIATURE NEGATIVES

Make first an enlarged positive transparency—about quarter-plate size ($3\frac{1}{4} \times 4\frac{1}{4}$ in.) or 9×12 cm.—from the original negative.

After scratching two registration marks in suitable corners, make the separation negatives by copying the transparency on miniature film with the camera. The best film material is document film or a positive film with a very contrasty emulsion.

Place the transparency about 1–2 in. in front of a sheet of ground glass. Illuminate this from behind with one or two ordinary pearl lamps, making sure that the whole transparency is evenly bright. To avoid stray light shining into the camera lens, mount the transparency in a frame, made by cutting a hole of the right size in a large sheet of cardboard. This should shield all light except that actually passing through the transparency itself. This arrangement is similar to the one used for copying negatives by dark ground illumination (p. 175), except that here we have a ground glass screen interposed between the transparency and the lamps, providing a bright background.

Set up the miniature camera in front of the illuminated transparency, so that the image more or less fills the whole negative area. With a 2 in. (5 cm.) lens on the camera, the distance between the lens and the transparency will have to be about 10 in. (25 cm.). To focus the camera at this close range, use a $\frac{1}{2}$ in. (1.3 cm.) extension tube if available, or alternatively put a 4 or 4.25 dioptre supplementary lens in front of the camera lens.

The exposure times of the two separation negatives should be in the ratio of 1 : 20. In other words, if one needs 2 seconds, the other would need 40 seconds.

The actual exposures depend of course on the density of the transparency and on the illumination. As the miniature film is cheap enough, make a whole series of exposures after calculating the approximate time needed for the lamps used, etc. For instance, at f 11, this series might be 1/5, $\frac{1}{2}$, 1, and 2 seconds. Then make the second series with the exposures increased 20 times, thus: 4, 10, 20, and 40 seconds. It is very important that neither the camera nor the rest of the set-up should move between exposures.

Develop the film in a fine grain developer, and after processing select a pair of negatives. Look for the most suitable thin negative in the first series, and then choose the corresponding dense negative of the second set.

By shifting the complete filmstrip to and fro in the negative carrier, the dense and thin negative chosen are quickly and easily interchanged during enlarging.

The enlarging exposures are also in the ratio of 1 : 20. Use hard paper.

POSTERISATION

We can go further with the tone separation process, and carry it to extremes in order to produce effects like that of an advertising poster.

A negative can, for instance, be split up into four separation negatives, each of which should contain only one tone. The composite print will then contain (besides white) only four tones—light grey, medium grey, dark grey, and black—in detailless masses without any tone transition.

First of all, we must prepare the necessary separation negatives. For the sake of clarity we shall assume here that we are going to use three of them; the procedure with a larger number follows the same principle.

We therefore need a highlight negative showing density in only the extreme highlights, with clear film or glass everywhere else.

Further, we need a medium tone negative which shows a single image tone in all highlight and half tone areas.

The third will be a shadow negative with density in all parts of the image except the deepest shadows which are to print black.

We can prepare these negatives either by contact printing from a positive transparency, or by enlarging. The important point is that each negative must have one black image tone only, with extreme contrast between areas of image and of no image. In other words, there must be no tone gradation. So a high contrast process film or plate, or (with miniature negatives) contrasty positive film, is essential for all three separation negatives. In addition they should be developed in a contrast developer of the caustic hydroquinone type (No. 3, p. 238).

The relative exposure times to produce the three negatives are usually in the ratio 1 : 2 : 5. Find the best exposure for the highlight negative by means of test pieces or a test strip, and then increase this time accordingly for the other two.

Each separation negative must be fully developed to produce sufficient density. The highlight negative will need at least 4 minutes, the other two as much as 6, or even 8 minutes of development.

After development, parts of the image which should be absolutely clear may still show some faint detail. This must completely disappear.

Treat the negatives therefore as far as possible in *Farmer's* reducer (p. 243), and if necessary make a further set of duplicates. By preparing these via another set of transparencies, again using high contrast film and high contrast development, we shall achieve the absolute black-and-white silhouette effect we require.

Finally, print the three separation negatives on one sheet of printing paper, using the registration marks to superimpose the images accurately (p. 80).

The highlight negative will produce a light grey tone over the whole of the picture, except for the extreme highlights which remain white.

The medium tone negative protects the highlights and medium tone areas from further exposure, but allows a dark tone to print through in the shadows.

The shadow negative then protects all but the deepest shadows which are allowed to print completely black.

The relative depth and separation of the tones in the print will depend on the printing exposure of each negative, and on the gradation of the printing paper.

These exposures are best found by test strips (p. 32); as a rough guide, provided the black is equally dense on all three negatives, a ratio of exposure times of 1 : 3 : 8 should work fairly well on a hard paper grade.

CHEMICAL TONE SEPARATION

While for the normal tone separation methods we have to make additional negatives and combine them in printing, we can also extend the tone range, under certain conditions, by bleaching and redeveloping the negative. The effect of this chemical tone separation strongly resembles that of ordinary tone separation, though the process does of course not allow the same scope of control. On the other hand, it is much simpler.

Again we start with a hard dense negative. Thin-layer films are not suitable.

Either the original negative can be used, or a duplicate.

Develop this duplicate in a contrasty developer (e.g. No. 3, p. 238) until the highlights are blackened right through the emulsion and are clearly visible from the back of the film or plate. Fix and wash in the usual way.

First bleach the negative—original or duplicate—in the same bleaching bath as used for sulphide toning (No. 41, p. 245), but at half the working strength.

Bleaching takes 4–8 minutes, depending on the thickness of the emulsion layer. The black silver image disappears more and more and turns into creamy white silver bromide. The shadows go first, followed by the halftones and later the highlights. The process can be watched (by subdued daylight or artificial light) from the back of the negative as it eats its way deeper and deeper into the emulsion.

Continue bleaching until only the extreme highlights are left black. Then rinse the negative and wash for 30 minutes in running water.

Finally redevelop in a surface developer (No. 5, p. 238).

In this developer the image near the surface of the emulsion develops rapidly long before the solution affects the deeper emulsion layers. Stop development at the right moment by immersing the negative in a 2 per cent solution of acetic acid. This stage is reached when the surface image is completely black, while the halftones as seen from the back of the negative are still covered with the yellowish white silver bromide. Apart from the shadows, only the previously unbleached black highlights should really show through the back.

Dissolve away the undeveloped silver bromide in an acid fixing bath (No. 16, p. 240), and wash and dry the negative in the usual way.

The resulting negative will show a rich detail with completely unblocked highlights. Depending on how far we carry the bleaching process, we can keep the highlight areas larger or smaller and thus denser or more delicate.

MASKING

Printing with a positive mask. 1. Make a thin low contrast positive transparency. 2. Bind up negative and transparency in register, with a clear spacer in between. 3. Enlarge like a single negative.

There is yet another way of decreasing the tone range of a negative: we can print it bound up in accurate register with a low contrast positive made from it.

This is the last resort for very hard negatives, especially when the shadows are comparatively thin.

This positive mask reduces the overall contrast of the negative, particularly in the shadows. The latter may in fact lose almost all detail. We can avoid that by making the positive an unsharp mask. The low contrast unsharp shadow detail in the positive will not then greatly affect the image detail in the negative.

The effect of the unsharp mask goes even further. The sharp image of the original negative is usually surrounded by a very weak unsharp image due to light scatter, halation, etc. The unsharp positive image tends to cancel this lack of sharpness in the negative, and may actually increase the negative definition.

To prepare the mask, make a contact positive transparency from the negative. During this printing operation insert a spacer (i.e. a clear sheet of cut film) between the negative and the positive material to produce the slight diffusion intended.

Adjust the printing exposure for the mask to obtain a very thin transparency, and reduce the development time to keep down contrast. Usually it will be sufficient if the mask shows just a fairly weak image in the shadows.

Bind up the negative and positive in accurate register. If necessary, the spacer can again be inserted to increase the unsharpness of the mask when the sharp negative is focused in the enlarger. Enlarge the combination as one negative.

To decrease the effect of the mask, reduce it in *Farmer's* reducer (No. 35, p. 243) before binding up with the negative. Conversely, to increase the effect, reduce the density of the negative in the same way.

CONTROLLING THE IMAGE COLOUR

With bromide papers we are usually limited to black images. Any attempt to modify these by special development generally give images of an unpleasant greenish-brown appearance.

Chlorobromide papers on the other hand lend themselves well to controlled development methods to produce a whole range of tones from warm black to reddish brown. The exact colour produced under any given conditions depends on the make and grade of paper, and the developer (No. 6, p. 239).

In principle, the method consists of overexposing the print and developing it in a diluted developer with extra potassium bromide added. The greater the degree of overexposure, the more diluted the developer, and the higher the potassium bromide content, the warmer will be the final tone.

One point to bear in mind with warm tone development is that with increasing warmth of tone the print becomes softer. For very warm tones, therefore, choose a more contrasty paper grade.

DIRECT COLOUR DEVELOPMENT

This method of producing coloured images is similar to that used in colour photography.

Here a colour coupling developer with certain additions—the couplers—produces dyes together with the silver image. The amount of dye formed is propor-

84

tional to the density of the silver developed. We can then dissolve away the silver, leaving a pure dye image in any colour depending on the coupler used.

The variety of colours obtainable is almost unlimited. We can mix the couplers in any proportions, and we may remove the silver wholly or only partly, leaving the colours in any brilliance we desire.

The process is very simple, but needs clean working. Nearly all types of paper except contact (chloride) emulsions are suitable. Slightly increased exposure times may sometimes be necessary.

Develop the print in the coupling developer made by mixing the main developer (No. 7, p. 239) with the chosen coupler or couplers (Nos. 8-13, p. 239). Then rinse and fix in a fixing bath of 25 per cent hypo with about 4 per cent of sodium sulphite crystals added. Finally wash for not more than 30 minutes. Longer washing may reduce the brilliance of the colours.

At this stage the dye image is still largely masked by the silver. To bring out the colours more prominently we may remove the black silver image.

A suitable formula is *Farmer's* reducer (No. 35, p. 243) with about 1 part of 10 per cent sodium carbonate solution added to every 200 parts of reducer. As the silver image becomes weaker in the reducer, the colours become progressively purer and more brilliant. Stop the process when the desired effect is reached, and wash again for 15 minutes.

To reduce the strength of the dye image which may at times appear too intense, immerse the print in a 1 per cent hydrochloric acid solution followed by a 15 minute wash.

SOFT FOCUS

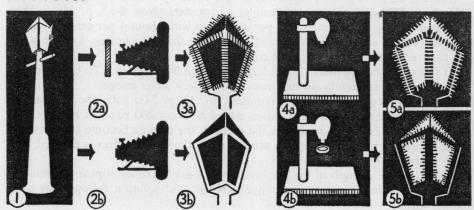

Soft focus in camera and enlarger. Subject I is photographed with a soft focus disc 2a in front of camera. The negative 3a on enlarging 4a gives diffused print 5a with highlights spreading into shadows, giving a soft halo-like glow (p. 93). Diffusion of straight negative 3b during enlarging 4b gives soft print 5b with shadows spreading into highlights (p. 94).

Working with soft-focus lenses is really part of camera technique. We can only obtain the genuine soft-focus effect when exposing the negative in the camera. All the same, soft-focus diffusion finds its application in enlarging as well, though the effect obtained is somewhat different.

A soft-focus lens is not completely corrected for spherical aberration. While the centre of the lens forms a sharp image on the film, the rays from the edge produce a slightly out-of-focus image superimposed on the sharp one. The sharp image is therefore surrounded by a soft halo. The dark parts of the negative image overflow into the light ones; in terms of the positive image light parts will spread into their dark surrounds. This spreading of light from the highlights into the shadows is a characteristic feature of soft-focus lenses.

Logically, the effect is reversed by introducing the same technique during enlarging. Again, the dark parts of the image spread out, at the expense of the light ones. But this time it happens to the positive and the dark parts are now the shadows; it is these that spread. This tones down the brightness of the image. What we gain is not radiance but something like soft gloom. While we obtain the genuine soft-focus effect with the halo round the highlights when we take the picture, we produce a mellowing veil during enlarging.

Yet soft-focus or diffusion through enlarging is popular. It softens pin-sharp definition, and tones down fine and often irrelevant detail. In portraits it plays down disturbing facial lines and wrinkles, thus reducing the need for subsequent retouching.

To imitate the true soft-focus effect of a camera exposure during enlarging, we must go a round-about way. First, we must make a straight positive transparency from the negative, and make a second negative from that by same-size reproduction in the enlarger. The diffusion is introduced during this stage in making the duplicate negative. In this way we recreate the conditions of diffusion in the camera and obtain the same result.

There is no need to use a special soft-focus lens for enlarging. Diffusion discs or soft-focus attachments placed in front of the lens are equally suitable.

These are glass discs with an irregular surface. The irregularities partially impede the otherwise unobstructed passage of the light, and refract some of the rays, thus producing the halo result. Most diffusion discs on the market have concentric rings ground or moulded in. There are, however, also types with sets of black lines.

A print made with a soft-focus attachment in front of the enlarger lens will appear softer in gradation than a straight enlargement. The difference amounts to about half a paper grade. If, for instance, an ordinary enlargement looks just right on normal paper, the same enlargement diffused will look as if it had been made on an intermediate grade between normal and soft. This must be kept in mind when choosing the paper grade.

CONTROLLED DIFFUSION

We can control the soft-focus effect.

The harder the paper grade, the more apparent it will be.

On the other hand, we can decrease it by stopping down the enlarger lens.

There is also another way of varying the diffusion, namely by splitting the exposure into two periods. First expose the print through the soft-focus disc, and complete the exposure without it. The advantage of this method is that the basic image inside the halo becomes sharper. The halo itself can still be increased or decreased by adjusting the relative length of the two exposures.

We can even produce a soft-focus image of sorts without any accessories at all, though it will not suppress blemishes needing retouching. Focus the negative at full aperture so that the image is not quite pin-sharp, but reaches absolute sharpness when the lens is stopped down. Give a short exposure at full aperture, and then complete the full exposure at a small stop. Naturally, allowance must be made for the reduced aperture with the second exposure. The sharp image in the print is then surrounded by a woolly soft outline.

SUBDUING GRAIN

At high degrees of enlargement the negative grain can at times be disturbingly apparent. Apart from various round-about methods of minimising grain by aftertreatment (p. 176), choice of enlarger illumination (p. 22), or use of rough surfaced papers (p. 22), diffusion during enlarging can do much to alleviate the nuisance.

We shall of course have to plan our working procedure with a view to subduing the grain rather than to producing a particular soft-focus effect. Therefore the methods mainly of importance are those where diffusion takes place during only part of the exposure time. There the individual grains are superimposed by their diffused images.

The relative exposure times with and without diffusion must be found by test strips. The grain should just disappear before the image softness becomes too apparent.

For keeping down the grain we can also use a grease-plate as diffusing disc. This is a clear glass plate such as a negative with its emulsion layer removed. Rub a minute amount of vaseline over it in a circular motion with the finger tips. Hold this plate underneath the enlarging lens, and move it about during part of the exposure.

HOME-MADE DIFFUSION DISCS

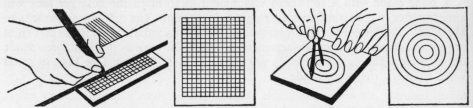

Two ways of making a diffusion disc. *Left:* Ruling sets of straight lines on the gelatine surface of an unexposed, fixed out plate with a pointed tool. *Right:* Scratching concentric circles with a pair of compasses.

There are two ways of making them.

For the first, take a sheet film or plate, and without exposing, completely fix and wash it. Then engrave a pattern of lines on it with a needle.

The pattern can be two sets of parallel lines at right angles to each other. Use a ruler to get the lines really straight.

Alternatively, cut a set of concentric circles with a pair of compasses, using one point for centring, and the other to engrave the circles. As the centre of the gelatine layer should not be pierced, it is best protected by a piece of indiarubber on which the compass point (or the pencil lead of the compass), rests. This rubber also stops the point from slipping.

The degree of diffusion depends on the distances between the lines or circles. If they are far apart, the soft-focus effect will be slight; lines closer together produce greater diffusion.

The difference between straight and circular line patterns is that straight line patterns tend to produce an uneven effect near the edges of the print. This becomes particularly apparent if the picture contains round shapes.

The other method of making diffusion discs is more ingenious, but also a little more involved.

Draw a series of concentric circles in Indian ink on white drawing paper, and copy the drawing on a contrasty process plate or film. Adjust the scale of reproduction to the diameter of the enlarging lens with which the diffusion disc will be used. If, for instance, the diameter of the lens is 1 in., the diameter of the outermost circle in the negative should also be 1 in.

From this negative—which shows the circles as clear glass or film against the dead black background—make a positive transparency. The image will now consist of black lines on clear glass.

That, in itself, is really the soft-focus disc. The effect is, however, not very strong, as the lines are black, and do not produce much refraction. They also reduce the brightness of the projected image.

The disc can be improved by treating the transparency in *Farmer's* reducer (p. 243), until the image has all gone. After drying, the circles will be seen as a deepened relief in the gelatine when the plate is held obliquely to the light. This relief is quite enough to produce some diffusion.

Incidentally, if the negative instead of the transparency is bleached, a high relief will be left, which also has a similar effect.

TEXTURE SCREENS

One of the questions that crops up most frequently in the search for particular pictorial effects is that of the most suitable paper texture. Though the choice of paper surfaces is very great, it is, in view of the endless pictorial possibilities, still rather limited. However, any paper surface can be given a special texture effect with the help of a screen.

Such a screen should have a more or less irregular pattern. It inevitably will have a density of its own and so the exposure times are increased.

Naturally not every subject can be printed with a texture screen. Negatives rich in fine detail are definitely unsuitable. On the other hand, broad areas without detail can well be broken up by printing-in a screen.

For contact printing we can only put the screen between the negative and the paper.

In enlarging we may use the screen in contact with either the negative or the bromide paper. Both methods have their peculiarities.

If the structure of the screen is to be reproduced really sharp and a suitable material like tissue, crepe georgette, or muslin is available, it should be printed in contact with the paper.

But simply covering the paper with the material will not do; the two must be pressed into intimate contact. The best way is to put both into a printing frame of the right size, when the spring back will press them together during exposure. Only a screen of hard and stiff material, such as perforated card, can simply be laid on top of the paper.

Stiff screens of this type have the advantage that we can use them for a limited effect—either to cover only parts of the print, or to cover it only during part of the exposure time. The latter procedure is particularly important when coarse textures are to be printed in.

Such large patterns are only successful if the photographic image underneath is still easily recognisable. It must be a continuous image, even if with reduced density, right under the covered portions, and show through them. Otherwise the picture will just appear chopped into little pieces like a jig-saw puzzle and become almost undecipherable.

For coarse texture screen effects, therefore, expose the enlargements with the screen for only one-fifth of the total exposure time. Expose them straight, without any screen at all during the remaining four-fifths.

The other possibility is to enlarge a normal negative together with a special texture negative. We can make the latter by copying a material like sacking, a coarse plaster wall, grained wood, etc. Place the two negatives in contact with their emulsion sides facing, and enlarge as one negative.

In addition, the image can be slightly diffused, which gives a special effect. With a screen consisting of fine lines, such as a reproduction of open gauze, the white lines almost completely disappear in the shadows owing to the spread of light through diffusion. The pattern remains really noticeable only in the highlights.

HOME-MADE SCREENS

Though a whole range of different printing screens is available on the market, it is worth while trying to make them to one's own liking. Home made texture screens possess an individual personal note not found in the bought article nor in anybody else's pictures either.

Almost any texture can be used for making a texture screen. It can be an area of sand, a frying pan full of rice, a piece of hand made paper, or a lampshade parchment, the fine cracks in the glaze of a tile, the fur of an animal, and so on.

Often the texture has to be emphasised before photographing it. Rough paper, for instance, is best rubbed over first with graphite or powdered charcoal. This sticks mainly to the raised portions of the paper surface and brings out the paper grain.

Similarly, the texture of woven materials, grained leather, and the like can be made more distinct by moistening it with oil paint.

Spread some black oil paint over a glass surface and work it to and fro with a roller squeegee until the paint is evenly distributed over the roller surface. Then roll the squeegee more or less lightly over the surface to be photographed, so that the raised parts of the texture are blackened. Finally clean the squeegee with turpentine.

When photographing a texture surface, a normal negative is not necessarily the best. The most suitable type of negative for this purpose will be thin and delicate, but it should still clearly show the texture image.

PHOTOMOSAICS

There are certain kinds of glass used in the building trade which carry an embossed pattern on one side—the bathroom window type. They let light through, but we cannot see anything through them.

90

We may use this glass as an extreme type of texture screen to obtain an unusual effect. The irregular surface structure of the glass usually consists of little more or less semi-spherical hills and valleys. The individual hills can be compared to minute lenses. Each one acts separately, collecting the light into bundles of rays.

If we place such a sheet of glass in the path of the light from the enlarger lens, the uniform beam of light is dispersed into a large number of small beams. And if the beam of light is the projected image of a negative, this is similarly broken up into many small part images corresponding to the miniature lenses.

During this splitting up process of the negative image a kind of tone separation occurs. Those parts of the glass which receive the light from the thinner parts of the negative naturally produce brighter beams than those under the dense portions. At the same time the density of each light circle corresponds to the overall density of the negative area by which it is formed. The result is a relative concentration of the tone values with sharply separated individual light points (p. 98).

To work this idea we must first find the approximate focal length of the lenticular units by experiment. Every sheet of this type of glass behaves differently, depending on the depth and shape of the surface structure. The distance between the paper and the glass sheet must be great enough for the individual light beams to be formed, but not so great that the image is completely diffused. Usually the distances are so small (about $\frac{1}{8}$–$\frac{1}{2}$ in.) that the effect cannot be observed by looking underneath the glass. The only thing to do, therefore, is to experiment with test strips until the desired result is obtained.

Once the distance is found, it will be the same for all negatives as long as the degree of enlargement remains the same. But this distance is changed when we push the lamphouse up or down the enlarger column.

In practice the following is the quickest way for finding the right distance for the glass sheet.

Put four similar wedge-shaped pieces of wood side by side. Draw a set of straight lines across the inclined planes of each with a ruler, so that the lines are about $\frac{1}{8}$ in. apart. Number these lines consecutively, starting from the thin edge of the wedge. Now place the sheet of glass over the paper holder so that its corners each rest on one of these wedges.

Vary the distance of the glass above the paper by moving the wedges closer together or further apart, with each corner on a line of the same number on each wedge. The actual distance of the glass plate need not even be known, it can be defined in terms of the scale on the wedges. This then gives a means of easily reproducing the same distance every time—just go by the scale numbers.

Finally, not all embossed types of "bathroom window" glass are suitable for this technique. They must in fact show indications of such lens elements, though these need not necessarily be round.

RETICULATION

Carrying on with our quest for special texture results, we can even turn to the usually dreaded effect of reticulation.

This occurs in the negative when the temperature of the developer (or of the fixing bath) is too high. The gelatine swells excessively and its surface forms tiny wrinkles. They have different shapes, but are always of uniform size, so that the whole surface looks a bit like something akin to a miniature jig-saw puzzle.

To produce reticulation on purpose from the outset we merely have to develop the negative in a developer at about 105–115° F. (40–45° C.). The reticulation will then appear of its own accord.

To bring about reticulation by aftertreatment, bathe the negative in a 10 per cent solution of sodium carbonate at about 120–125° F. (50° C.). When the negative surface feels grainy (carefully run the finger tips over it to feel for the reticulation), wash in cold water. Use negatives that have been fixed in an acid hardening fixer (p. 240), otherwise the gelatine may melt.

Whichever of the above methods is used, the reticulation is inevitably there for good, and cannot be removed again. If we only want the effect for one or two occasions without spoiling the negative, we must produce it by a more round-about way. For this a clean glass plate of the same size as the final print is sprayed with a special lacquer by means of an atomiser or fixatif spray.

To prepare the lacquer, boil a few old rollfilm negatives in water to remove all the gelatine layer. After drying, cut the films into small shreds and dissolve them in a mixture of equal parts of acetone and amyl acetate. After a little while the solution will be quite clear. The idea is to dissolve enough film to obtain a slightly thick syrupy solution. The thicker the lacquer, the better; though it must still be thin enough for spraying. If it will no longer spray in the atomiser, add a little more solvent.

Spray this lacquer several times over a glass plate. Leave to dry each time before going over the surface again. As the mixture is very inflammable, spraying is best carried out in the open air. After six or seven applications a distinctly rough texture will be noticed—and felt—on the surface. The plate is then ready.

During enlarging hold this prepared plate about $\frac{1}{16}$ to $\frac{1}{8}$ in. (2–3 mm.) above the bromide paper. The irregular lacquered layer will break up the image into small particles strongly resembling reticulation.

SOFT FOCUS. *Left:* If a diffusing disc or soft focus lens (p. 86) is used during enlarging, the shadow areas of the image spread into the lighter parts. Note particularly the background shadows. *Above:* In a true soft focus picture (p. 86) the light print areas spread into the dark ones, e.g., the outline of the face, and the highlights on the hair.

DIFFUSION DURING ENLARGE-
MENT often improves certain subjects like low key portraits which lose
much of their harshness. *Right:*
Straight print. *Above:* Enlargement
with diffusion.

94

CONTROLLING DIFFUSION. The softness of the outlines can be controlled by exposing through the diffusing disc for part of the time only (p. 87). *Above:* Best degree of softness. *Left:* Too much diffusion obliterates all image details. *Right:* Too little does not produce any noticeable effect at all.

95

SUBDUING GRAIN. Partial diffusion will help in reducing graininess in the enlarged print. The degree of softness must be adjusted so that the grain just disappears before the loss of definition becomes disturbing (p. 87). *Above left:* Grainy enlargement. *Above right:* Grain subdued by diffusion. *Right:* Magnified sections of the prints above.

96

TEXTURE SCREENS. The appearance of certain types of print can be enhanced by using a texture screen (in this case a sheet of muslin) in contact with either the negative or the paper during exposure. *Left:* Original print. *Right:* Texture screen in contact with paper. *Above:* Texture screen in contact with negative, diffused with a soft focus attachment (p. 89).

97

PHOTOMOSAICS. Certain kinds of glass—the type used in bathroom windows—held just above the paper during exposure will break up the image to produce a mosaic-like effect (p. 90). *Right:* Straight print. *Above:* Printed with glass screen.

98

RETICULATION. Produced either directly on the negative, or by means of a specially sprayed glass plate, reticulation will also give the print a special texture effect (p. 91). *Left:* Straight print. *Above:* Printed with sprayed glass plate $\frac{1}{16}$ inch above the bromide paper.

MELTING OF THE EMUL
Partial melting of the emulsio
of the negative can produce gre
effects (p. 105).

Section III

COMBINATION PRINTING

We have already used combination printing in tone separation (p. 78) to alter the picture itself, without adding foreign picture elements. But we can go further and combine different picture elements to form one new composite unit. That is photomontage.

The methods of photomontage are varied. According to the particular technique employed we could distinguish photomontage by simple combination printing from photomontage by combination printing in several stages often involving the use of masks, and lastly cut and paste montage. Some cases may call for a combination of all three.

ADDING A MOON

A moon by combination printing. **1.** Take a picture of the moon with a long focus lens. **2.** Put the moon negative face to face with a suitable landscape negative. **3.** Enlarge the two together as one negative (p. 109).

At first sight we might ask: why do in such a round-about way what we can also achieve directly? But this objection is not really valid.

Firstly, true moonlight pictures still need considerable camera exposure times. During the many minutes that are required, the moon moves on quite a bit in the sky; it will come out not as a round disc, but as a sausage-like elongated shape.

Secondly, if we should really take the picture at, say, dusk when it is not yet really dark, and include the moon in it, the result is usually not very convincing. The trouble is that the moon is much too small in proportion as compared with our mental picture of a moonlit landscape.

We cannot therefore achieve a truly suggestive impression of a moonlit night by straight photography. So the use of photomontage is certainly justified here.

On a suitable occasion—a clear moonlit night—take a picture of the moon. Just the moon, nothing else. In other words, point the camera at the sky, and bring the moon into the viewfinder in the best position for subsequent combination.

With an average speed film an exposure of $\frac{1}{2}$ second at f 6.3 will be just about right. In this time the moon would not move noticeably.

If the usual negative size for the landscape is $2\frac{1}{4} \times 2\frac{1}{4}$ in. (6×6 cm.) or $2\frac{1}{4} \times 3\frac{1}{4}$ in. (6×9 cm.), the moon is best photographed on a quarter-plate ($3\frac{1}{4} \times 4\frac{1}{4}$ in. or 9×12 cm.) negative. We can easily move the smaller negative about within the area of the larger one, and so get the moon in the most suitable part of the picture area. Also, the larger camera produces a larger image of the moon.

That is the main point. We must photograph the moon with a longer focal length lens than the landscape to go with it. Otherwise it will be too small, and no longer convincing. The moon should in fact be almost twice as large as it would appear normally. So if we use the same camera for both the landscape picture and the moon, the latter should still be photographed with a longer focal length lens.

Where the camera lens is not interchangeable, the only way out is to make an enlarged copy negative of the moon picture.

For combination place together the two negatives of landscape and moon, emulsion sides facing, and shift them about until the moon is in the right place. Then put them in that position in the negative carrier like a single negative.

With infra-red materials it is possible to make landscape pictures in sunshine which are indistinguishable from moonlight photographs if the sky is cloudless. Such pictures become even more realistic by printing in a moon as just described. But watch out for the shadows: they must tally with the position of the moon!

Any normal landscape taken by daylight can also be turned into a moonlight picture by printing it dark. The negative should be fairly thin. Usually the image of the moon is, however, so dense that it will still be pure white even if the landscape is overprinted to a silhouette. A contrasty enlarging paper helps.

FALLING SNOW

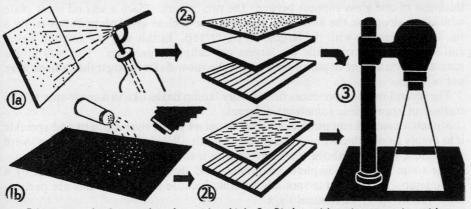

Faking snow. **1a.** Spray a glass plate with red ink. **2a.** Bind up with a winter negative, with a spacer in between. **3.** Enlarge the two together. Alternatively, **1b** sprinkle salt onto a sheet of black velvet and photograph it, moving the velvet during the exposure. **2b.** Combine this negative with a winter landscape. **3.** Enlarge the two together like one negative (p. 110).

Taking pictures while it is snowing is easy enough. But making sure the falling snow will really be visible is more difficult.

Apart from the fact that this type of outdoor work may not do the camera much good, the snow-flakes falling closest to the lens often prevent a clear view. We would have to work from a deep doorway, or through the open window in order to keep the falling snow-flakes at least a couple of yards away from the camera.

Another difficulty is that while it snows the weather is usually very dull. In the diffused uniform light the white flakes hardly show up against the white background.

So we are justified in reproducing falling snow by other means. There are two alternative methods of doing this. They will each show a different type of falling snow.

The first produces large slowly falling flakes on a calm day.

To start with, fix and wash a few unexposed sheet films or plates. Even spoilt plates can be used if they are first bleached out in *Farmer's* reducer (p. 243). In any case, they must be absolutely clear. Once they are, spray some red ink over the emulsion side with a spray or an atomiser. Spray some of the plates from a near distance, others from farther away so as to get different drop sizes. Do all that at an angle so that the drop shape will be slightly oblong, and not quite circular.

When dry, enlarge one of these "snow" negatives together with a normal winter negative.

To avoid too sharp and therefore unnatural snow-flakes, keep the two negatives separated by two or three clear glass plates. If both negatives are themselves glass ones, it may be enough to put them in the enlarger with the emulsion sides facing away from each other. When the picture negative is focused at a large aperture, the snow-flakes will be just sufficiently blurred.

To make the falling snow still more realistic and denser, place a snow negative with very fine "flakes" directly on the subject negative so that there is just the thickness of one glass support between the two images. Place a second snow plate with larger drops on the first snow negative, and a clear glass plate, followed by a third snow negative with the largest drops, on top. In this way the smallest flakes still seem fairly sharp, while the largest are definitely unsharp. This will give a natural impression of depth of field—as if the snow-flakes nearest the camera were out of focus.

The second method produces fine rapidly falling flakes like in a snow-storm. The method of approach is somewhat different.

Stretch a piece of smooth black velvet or velvet paper over a board and sprinkle it as evenly as possible with ordinary cooking salt. We shall copy this "scene" with the camera vertically above the board, but in a somewhat unusual way.

The room must be completely darkened, and the velvet lit from one side by a single lamp. A spotlight is specially suitable because the salt crystals are particularly well lit up by directional light.

During exposure, slowly move the board in an oblique direction. This produces fine, not quite sharply defined small traces which correspond to the patterns produced by fast falling snow when driven by the wind and photographed at a slow shutter speed.

The resulting negative, made on a contrasty film or plate, should show some gradation in the tracks of the salt crystals. The heaviest desinty must not be quite black. Too heavy a snow negative must be reduced, for the effective density will still be increased by the density of the subject negative.

Finally, combine the two negatives face to face and again enlarge as before.

But do not print a snow-storm into a picture obviously taken in strong sunshine. The sun shadows will show through even the thickest "blizzard", and are apt to look incongruous.

RAIN

Artificial rain can also be produced by combination printing. The method is similar to the one just described.

Here again we sprinkle salt over velvet and copy it. But the area of the velvet must be twice as large and the salt very finely distributed over it.

During copying pull the velvet board through its whole length so that each salt grain leaves a track obliquely across the whole negative. This forms streaks corresponding to falling rain drops.

To make sure of getting really straight streaks (for rain drops do not as a rule fall crooked), lay the board on the floor against a wall. Set up camera above it with its side at a slight angle to the wall. The board can then be pulled along it evenly and absolutely straight.

The negative should be somewhat underdeveloped. It must be thin and soft, for rain is transparent.

Such a rain negative can obviously only be combined with a picture taken during or just after the rain. The print must show the whole wetness produced by the rain.

We can also convey the impression of rainy weather in a different way, namely by showing a picture as if it had been taken through a rain splashed window. Photographing a glass really wet with rain and combining the negative with another does not, however, produce very good results.

A more useful rain negative is obtained by placing a mirror or a chromium glazing plate on the floor, and spraying water over it. Slowly raise up one edge until the droplets begin to flow. Then photograph them in this condition.

To avoid showing a reflected picture of the camera, take the surface obliquely, and prop up a neutral light grey card more or less opposite. From the camera position the card should be seen mirrored covering the whole of the shiny surface. Against the grey background the drops will show both highlights and shadows, and a three dimensional quality which cannot be obtained on a normal wet window.

Among the trick negatives we have mentioned so far this is the first one which would not have a completely clear background. This density, though not very great, inevitably increases the enlarging exposure time when we enlarge the rain negative in contact with the normal view. In addition the whole print becomes softer, as all the light halftones of the subject negative will now be covered by a uniform grey. But this is not necessarily a drawback—when it rains, the weather is dull, anyway. And if a hard printing paper is used, the details are still sufficiently resolved, and so the contrast can be brightened up.

Under normal conditions we can hardly ever photograph a whole rainbow. The

105

Making a rainbow. **1.** Draw sets of concentric semi-circles in red ink on a clear fixed-out plate. **2.** Combine this plate with a suitable negative, with a spacer in between. **3.** Enlarge the combination like a single negative.

angle of view required is so great that even a wide angle lens cannot easily get all of it into the negative.

We can make a rainbow negative artificially for combination printing as follows.

Fix out an unexposed plate and wash and dry. Place a piece of indiarubber on the gelatine side near the middle of one of the longer edges of the plate. This takes the point of a pair of compasses, and protects the gelatine layer from damage.

Fill the drawing pen of the compass with dilute red ink or red water colour, and draw arc after arc side by side until the rainbow is wide enough. Even a double rainbow is feasible, but as in Nature, it should be much fainter.

After every arc the ink must be allowed to dry before drawing the next. The liquid swells the gelantine and makes it extremely sensitive to mechanical damage. So if it is still wet when the next arc is drawn over it, the drawing pen would just plough through the gelatine layer like butter.

The final density should only be reached after drawing over the same place about six or seven times. In this way we can smoothly grade it off across its width like a real rainbow, with a suggestion of lighter or darker colour bands.

Finally, print the rainbow negative together with a landscape in much the same way as a sprayed snow negative (p. 103).

COMBINATION PRINTING BY STAGES

Generally two negatives can be combined simultaneously in one printing stage only if one of them shows the subject against a clear background. If on the other hand the subject is a thin image within a dense one, the negatives must be combined by successive printing in two or more part exposures.

In such cases one negative is enlarged first and the undeveloped bromide paper exposed again to the second negative.

All manipulation must of course be very exact so that the individually exposed parts will accurately fit together.

PRODUCING FOREGROUND MOTIFS

Printing in a foreground. **1.** Make a lay-out sketch of the main picture on a piece of paper. **2.** Print the main negative. **3.** Position the foreground image with the help of the layout sketch. **4.** Print the foreground negative (p. 111).

Let us choose the following example: an expanse of sky is to be broken up by printing in a few branches or twigs.

To start with, prepare a full-sized lay-out sketch for the landscape.

Expose the bromide paper to the landscape negative.

Next focus the branch negative on the lay-out sketch in the paper holder and adjust it until the size and position of the image fits in with the landscape.

Finally, replace the lay-out sketch by the exposed bromide paper, and expose again, this time to the branch negative.

Now let us look at these steps in more detail.

First of all, a negative with suitable branches on it must be available.

If necessary and considered worth the trouble, we can make it when convenient at a suitable opportunity by simply photographing a few branches or twigs against the brilliant sky. Develop the plate or film to as high a contrast as possible to obtain a very dense sky with the branches against it in almost transparent silhouette. Such a negative can then be used in combination with other negatives of any gradation.

Once the need arises to liven up a large expanse of sky area and so improve the picture, we select a branch negative which will match the picture both for shape and the season of the year.

For the first stage of printing, focus the negative of the landscape on a sheet of plain white paper of the same size as the final print. Take a pencil and, with the enlarger light switched on, trace the main outlines of the landscape on this paper. At the same time decide where the branches are to go.

Find the necessary time by test strips for the first exposure (p. 32), i.e. for printing the landscape negative.

After the first exposure remove the bromide paper and put the plain paper with the lay-out sketch again in its place.

Special care is needed in positioning the bromide paper, as this position will have to be found again exactly when it comes to the second exposure. Only an accurate masking frame or paper holder is really good enough for this job, and double weight paper is preferable.

Single weight papers are not easily positioned with sufficient accuracy. If there is no other choice insert them in a cut film sheath or frame of the right size and leave them there until development. Such a frame will also do if no good paper holder is available.

Put the plain paper with the sketched lay-out into a second cut film holder. To allow accurate interchange of the two, push four darkroom pins into the baseboard, two each touching two adjacent edges of the holder. By placing one holder against these locating pins so that it touches all four at the same time, we can guarantee identical positioning also for the other holder.

When working with a masking frame, mark the top edge of the paper on the back; otherwise we may easily replace it upside down. With cut film holders the position of the feeding slit usually shows which edge is which.

With the lay-out sketch under the enlarger, replace the landscape negative by the branch negative. Readjust the focus and degree of enlargement until the branches fit best into the sky area. The paper holder can be moved about at will, but when the right position is found it must be fixed again by the locating pins.

Determine the second exposure with test strips. Choose this exposure so that while the branches are sufficiently dense, the sky around them should not show any tone.

Again replace the sketch by the already exposed bromide paper, positioning it with the help of the locating pins, and expose for the second time.

Where the sky of the landscape was empty and almost white, the required exposure for the branch negative is simply that found by the test strip. If, however, the sky of the first negative already produced some tone, the time which would give the same tone without a negative in the carrier must be deducted from the second exposure. Otherwise the grey of the sky and the dark grey of the branches would together produce a black detailless silhouette which is not always desirable. There is no need to be particularly exacting about this, though. Usually shortening the second exposure time by something like 10 per cent will just about do the trick.

Finally develop, fix, etc., in the usual way. If, after fixing, the two exposure times

108

SIMPLE COMBINATION PRINTING.
To fake a moonlit view, a normal negative is enlarged in contact with a specially prepared moon negative (p. 102). *Left:* Print from original negative. *Right:* Print from moon negative. *Above:* Combination of moon and view overprinted to give night effect.

AP—I

ARTIFICIAL SNOW. The technique is the same as for printing-in a moon (p. 109). *Left:* Print from snow negative made by photographing salt sprinkled on to velvet (p. 103). *Right:* Print of original snow landscape. *Above left:* Snowscape in blizzard. *Above right:* To produce the effect of slowly falling snow, a glass plate sprayed with red ink is used as snow negative (p. 104).

ADDING A FOREGROUND. A normal landscape negative is printed in the usual way and then the foreground introduced by a second exposure from another negative (p. 107). *Left:* Original view. *Right:* Combination print with branches added. *Above:* How an ant sees the world. In this case the foreground can only be faked as it would be impossible to obtain both the foreground and the background sharp in a single straight exposure.

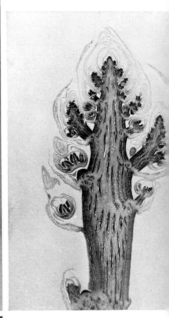

SUCCESSIVE COMBINATION
PRINTING from two similar negatives
(p. 117). *Left:* Print of asparagus bud.
Right: Lay-out sketch for registering
the two exposures. *Above right:*
Print of section of shoot. *Above left:*
"X-ray view" of an asparagus shoot.

112

SUPERIMPOSITION IN SERIES (p. 117). *Left*: Prints from the individual negatives of grandmother, mother, and daughter. *Above*: Family likeness pictured in a combination print by enlarging the three negatives successively on the same sheet of printing paper. In each case the eyes were taken as registration points to superimpose the images accurately (p. 118).

113

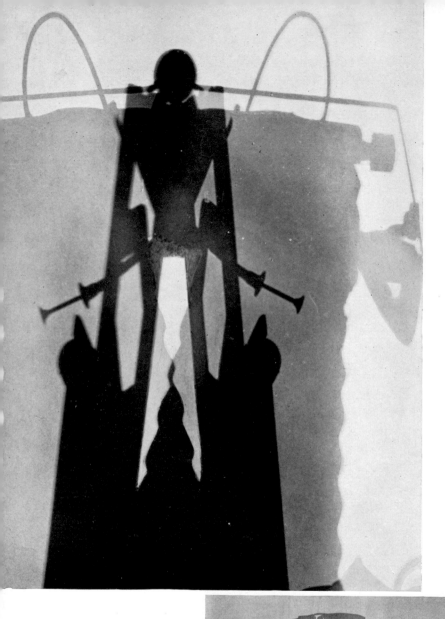

DUPLICATION. We can print the same negative twice, once normally and once reversed left to right, to obtain fantastic shapes by the over-lapping of the image (p. 118). *Right:* Straight print. *Above:* Enlargement by double printing.

114

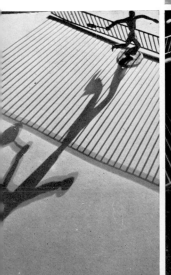

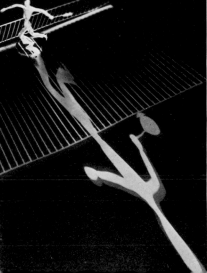

NEGATIVE - POSITIVE COMBINATION. Duplication effects are not confined to the negative only. We can also double print it with a transparency made from it (p. 119). *Left:* Positive print from negative. *Right:* Negative print from positive transparency. *Above:* Negative and transparency printed one after the other on the same sheet of bromide paper.

115

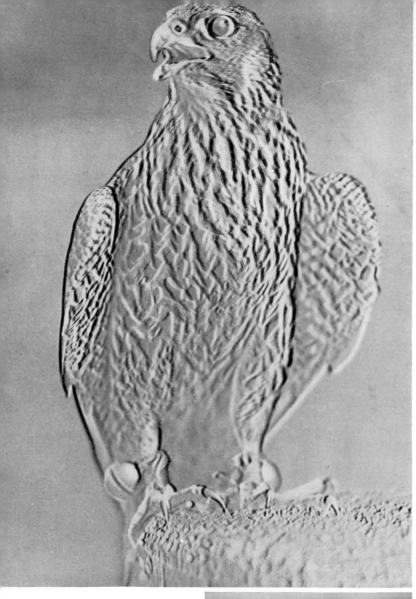

BAS RELIEF. If the negative is printed in contact but slightly out of register with a positive transparency made from it, the effect resembles that of an embossed relief (p. 119). *Left:* Negative. *Right:* Positive. *Above:* Combination bas-relief.

116

do not seem to match sufficiently, the combination print can be repeated with appropriate adjustments.

To make the decision easier, make three enlargements straightaway from the landscape negative, and pack them away in a light-tight box. If we have to repeat the print, we simply place one of these pre-exposed sheets of paper in position under the second negative which is already in the enlarger, anyway. As required, we then exposed longer or shorter than for the first combination print, until the two exposure times give a well balanced picture.

MULTIPLE IMAGES

Sometimes it is impossible to photograph every important part of a subject in one shot. We may be forced to take two or more separate shots so that we can record the different aspects of the matter in several individual pictures. Eventually we combine these multiple images by printing them on one piece of paper in two or more stages.

Let us take as an example an asparagus tip. The outwardly closed bud hides an exceptionally detailed and delicately developed shoot. A section of this shoot already shows all the beginnings of the fully grown plant. The relationship of the inside of the asparagus shoot to the outside can, however, only be shown by a multiple picture—a combination of photographs of the closed tip and of the shoot in section.

The procedure is the same as already described (p. 107), with the difference that we are here dealing with two negatives of similar gradation. The image of each covers more or less the whole picture area, so that the one must be well and truly superimposed on the other. We must therefore decide beforehand which of the two is to dominate in the final picture.

In our case this is the sectional view, with just an indication of the outline of the closed bud. So we print the negative of the section for two-thirds of the total exposure time, leaving one-third for the whole tip itself. A fifty-fifty division of exposure is not suitable here, because it would only lead to an indistinct result with grey blending into grey.

Focus the negatives and adjust them as before, with the help of a pencilled lay-out.

When making test strips, develop the strips from both negatives for the same time, making sure that the highlights remain clear and almost pure white.

In the combination print reduce the exposure for the section of the shoot to two-thirds, and the second exposure for the outline of the whole bud to one-third.

Multiple photographs of this type are suitable for presenting not only subjects in natural science, biology, botany, etc., but also for advertising and technical pictures. In fact, they are successful whenever internal detail of a subject as well as external shape has to be shown, as if the outer cover of the object were transparent.

SUPERIMPOSITION IN SERIES

The greater the number of negatives to be combined, the more accurately and carefully must the individual steps be carried out. When things become more complicated, a pencilled lay-out sketch is no longer adequate, as it only shows the relationship of the general shapes, but does not indicate detail. Besides, it is impossible to trace outlines accurately to the nearest one-hundredth of an inch. A more exact guide is necessary to fit the separate images together.

For this purpose we must determine at least two registration points. These should be two clearly visible points of fine detail in the negative, preferably some distance apart. They may be present as parts of the image, or they can be produced by pricking small crosses with a fine needle into the gelatine on opposite edges of the negative.

Let us take a case where parts of the image are already suitable registration points. An example would be the superimposition of several portraits (p. 113).

Such an experiment might perhaps show what features are common to a number of persons. For instance within a family the sisters and brothers, or several generations, would show a degree of family likeness. Thus by printing together pictures of grandfather, father, and son, the resulting face would correspond to some extent to each of the individual ones.

It does not really matter if the outlines of the different faces are not identical. Faces are, after all, differently proportioned in every case. The centres of the faces must, however, coincide; particularly the eyes.

For this reason we print the three portraits (which must of course have been taken showing the same expression, full-face, with the same lighting and exposure) on top of each other so that the eyes are exactly superimposed. The eyes are, in fact, our registration points.

First focus the largest image carefully on a piece of plain paper, and mark the centre of the pupils with small crosses with a sharply pointed pencil. Every following negative is subsequently focused so that the centres of the pupils come to lie exactly on these two little crosses.

For each negative again find the full exposure time by test strips at a standard development time. For printing, reduce the correct exposure time in each case to one-third—as there are three negatives; with four negatives each would be reduced to one-quarter. In addition cut each of these part exposures by about one-tenth of the time just found. The resulting combination print will receive the correct total exposure to produce the necessary density.

The extra one-tenth reduction is advisable to obtain really clear highlights. These easily become grey through the partial superimposition of individual large areas; so it is better to keep them a little lighter by slight underexposure. This underexposure also gives the picture extra contrast, for the methods of successive combination printing tend to soften the print gradation.

DUPLICATION

Duplication technique serves to show the most important parts of the negative image double. The effect is similar to that obtained by photographing a subject together with its mirror image. Duplication methods during enlarging also permit mutual overlapping of the subject and its mirror image.

According to the result desired, we may work the process in one stage by simple combination, or in two stages by successive exposure.

For the first case two identical (or nearly identical) negatives must be available. They should be thin and soft, for they will be printed together simultaneously, and their densities are thereby added.

Place the two negatives face to face in the negative carrier so that one is the right way round, and the other reversed left to right. Expose and process the same as for direct combination prints.

When successive combination serves the purpose in view better, print the same negative in two exposures; once the right way round, and once either reversed left to right or turned upside down. By suitable adjustment of the successive exposures, half of the picture can be emphasised or suppressed at will.

This superimposition of the most transparent shadows usually creates unexpectedly grotesque and ludicrous shapes. The method is therefore useful for certain out-of-the-way pictorial effects in commercial photography.

NEGATIVE-POSITIVE DUPLICATION

An extension of the above method lies in printing a negative together with a transparency printed from it. This again can be done by either simultaneous or successive combination.

The picture obtained is composed of both negative and positive images. Placed crosswise on top of each other and enlarged together, they produce effects similar to duplication. In addition the tone values of one half are the reverse of those of the other.

Another application of negative-positive duplication is masking of negatives to reduce their tone range (p. 83).

BAS RELIEF

Combining a negative and its positive transparency during enlarging in a different way again, will produce an effect similar to that of an embossed flat-relief.

Make a soft transparency from a soft negative. Neither the former nor the latter must show really opaque areas. If the two are exactly superimposed and held up to the light, the negative and positive images cancel each other out. All that will be visible will be a more or less even grey area.

If, however, the two images are slightly displaced, transparent contours appear round the main outlines, and the details begin to show some gradation. The resulting impression of a relief is increased the more the negative and positive are displaced, until at a certain stage it altogether disappears again. The most effective displacement is found by trial and error, and the two put into the negative carrier in that position.

Once the best position is found, fix the negative and transparency relative to each other—if films are used—by pushing a needle through opposite corners and threading a thin thread through the holes. With plates, tape two edges together with thin gummed paper strips before putting the combination in the enlarger.

The final result after enlarging shows the main subject with undiminished clarity, and with white illuminated contours on one side and corresponding shadows on the other. The tone range of the halftones is at the same time reduced to an almost uniform grey. Consequently this technique is suitable only for subjects with large shapes and bold outlines. Masses of detail just will not show up; at the best they merely give an impression of a blurred picture.

THREE-DIMENSIONAL TRANSPARENCIES

Making it look plastic. **1.** Make a transparency with the negative focused on the lantern plate on top of a 1 inch thick board. **2.** Remove the board and make a second transparency. **3.** Combine the two transparencies with a frame as spacer.

As a special application of duplication we can combine two positive transparencies—one sharp and one unsharp—to produce a picture which appears to stand in space.

Lay a $\frac{1}{2}$ in. thick board on the enlarger baseboard, and focus the image on a sheet of white paper on top of it. Replace the white sheet by a piece of black paper, and lay a lantern plate or positive film on it. Expose and process in the usual way (p. 37). The result should be a thin transparency.

Remove the board and place the black paper with another lantern plate directly on the baseboard. Make a second transparency from the same negative under the same conditions, without, however, refocusing the enlarger. This then gives an unsharp and slightly larger image.

We now have two transparencies which only together should make up the required density.

Fix them in a frame so that the sharp image is in front of the unsharp one. The distance between the two must again be $\frac{1}{2}$ in. This is easily done by cutting $\frac{1}{2}$ in. strips of thick cardboard and using them as spacers between the edges of the transparencies. The picture elements should be in register when the combination is viewed straight from the front. Finally back the frame by a sheet of opal glass.

On looking through the frame at eye level against the light, a special three-dimensional effect is visible. The explanation is that we look through the sharp front transparency into depth, as it were, which loses itself in unsharpness.

120

With the methods of combination printing discussed so far the whole of every single negative had a share in the complete print.

On the other hand, we may sometimes have to leave out individual picture elements altogether in combination printing, so that sections of different negatives are united without overlapping.

PRINTING IN CLOUDS

How to add clouds. **1.** Make a lay-out sketch of the landscape. **2.** Print the cloud negative, shading the foreground up to the outline of the lay-out. **3.** Print the landscape, and hold back the sky by shading (p. 134).

This is the simplest of the masked combination printing methods. We turn to it when we have a landscape with an empty sky and wish to put a few clouds into it.

To start with we need a suitable cloud negative. A good idea is to record different types of clouds in different types of light whenever an occasion arises, so as to have a selection for future use. Spring clouds, summer clouds, and autumn clouds are not the same, just as a morning sky is different from an evening one, and delicate white clouds look different from those heralding a thunderstorm.

Suitable cloud negatives are made with a yellow filter and preferably shortened exposure times. The best place to take them is in the open country or from the roof of a house, with the camera pointing at just above the skyline. Tilting the camera directly upwards produces distorted cloud shapes which will not combine successfully with a picture taken with the camera held level. Such shapes would only look natural when combined with a negative also taken looking up from below.

It is best to choose a grouping which shows a wide bank of clouds stretching upwards from the horizon, with the open sky and smaller cloud masses above.

If now clouds are to be printed into a landscape, select a cloud negative from the range available. Apart from considerations of season, the clouds must also correspond to the landscape negative in their distribution of light and shade. Where the landscape shadows point to the right, the shadow sides of the clouds must also

121

be on the right, with the light rims on the left. If they are the other way round, reverse the sky negative left to right when enlarging.

First focus the landscape negative in the enlarger, and trace the skyline on a plain sheet of paper.

Then put the cloud negative in and find its position with the help of the lay-out sketch. All the details sticking up above the horizon should come to lie within the broad lower cloud bank. If they reach into the blue part of the sky, the densities of the two would overlap and would give the trick away.

With the cloud negative correctly in position, shade the paper with the hands and fingers so as to produce a shadow of the same shape as the landscape skyline. During exposure this shadow will have to cover the landscape up to the indicated horizon while the clouds are printed in.

It is by no means necessary to be dead accurate, nor is a cut-out mask essential. But the shadow should more or less fit. Some guide is perhaps useful to help in remembering its shape and height in the picture area later on. The shape will probably be reproduced by referring to the lay-out, while we can make a faint mark on the paper holder or even on the extreme edge of the paper itself, to indicate the height of the horizon.

Print the sky negative first, shading the landscape portion which will be printed in later. Move the hands a little during exposure, to avoid a hard edge to the shadow. Moreover, a slightly shortened exposure is preferable to an excessive one, so that the sky remains sufficiently delicate and the clouds come out really white. Under these conditions the shadow outline will blend invisibly into the large white basic cloud bank. This is why such cloud banks are so useful and well worth while looking out for when collecting sky pictures.

The second exposure then follows with the negative of the landscape in the enlarger. No further precautions are needed where the sky is really dense, but if it is thin enough to print through as grey, the sky area must be shaded for the second exposure. This is not too difficult, as the outline to be shaded is clearly visible in the form of the projected image.

After development the finished print will show whether the exposure times were correctly suited to each other. If not, repeat with suitably altered exposures.

MASKING TECHNIQUE

Conditions are not always as favourable as where we had a cloud bank to play about with. More frequently there are different shapes of definite tone value side by side. There approximate shading with the hands is no longer good enough. Instead, we must create accurately positioned boundaries, which is only possible with masks suitably cut for each occasion.

We must provide some means to hold the masks so that they cannot move between successive exposures. Place a sufficiently large flawless sheet of plate glass across two supports of equal height (such as piles of books). It will then be like a bridge above the paper holder. This glass plate carries the masks.

While such a makeshift arrangement is quite adequate for odd occasions, for more frequent work of this kind a masking stage is very useful.

THE MASKING STAGE

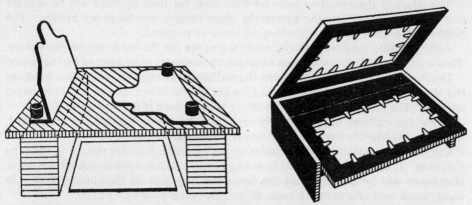

Aids for masked combination printing. *Left:* A simple masking stage may consist of a sheet of glass supported on two blocks above the enlarger baseboard. The masks are weighed down on the glass. *Right:* A specially constructed masking table provides wider scope. The masks are held in place by the spring clips while the paper holder goes underneath.

A masking stage is a sort of box with a frame top which carries a sheet of plate glass. The front of the box is open to allow the paper holder or masking frame to be pushed underneath and to be withdrawn, as well as to insert the paper itself. Special guides in the base position the paper holder.

The sides should be made of double slotted movable boards which can be raised or lowered, and fastened with wing nuts at any height from the baseboard.

The top frame with the plate glass has pressure springs all round, and the various masks are clamped underneath these springs.

The top is fastened to the back of the box with two hinges so that it always closes down in the same position.

As a further refinement we can fit a second frame and glass plate. This would be pushed underneath the first one and supported by two battens. We can do with a second stage as it is sometimes useful to have two independently movable masks.

MASK AND COUNTERMASK

Making the masks. 1. Trace the outline of the masked portions on an opaque card on the masking stage. 2. Cut out the mask. 3. Fit the mask and countermask together on the masking stage, and weigh down ready for the exposure.

123

Masks are made of white opaque paper.

The effect of their shadow must be tried first, for their outlines will be sharper and their shape smaller, the nearer the glass plate is to the paper holder. The height of the glass plate is therefore adjusted as required.

After focusing the first negative, place the paper for the mask on the glass plate. Then trace in pencil the outline up to which the image is to be printed on the paper.

Don't refocus the enlarger to show the outline more clearly. That would change the size of the mask and it would no longer fit the image on the bromide paper later on. The image can be traced without trouble even if it is not quite sharp.

Draw the outlines always slightly smaller than the image on the baseboard, since the shadow always spreads beyond the mask.

Cut out the mask either with scissors or with a knife. See that the cut is right the first time. It cannot be corrected later on, for any additional bits cut off the mask afterwards will be missing from the corresponding part of the countermask. In short, mask and countermask must fit exactly—like a jig-saw puzzle.

After cutting out, place the first mask again in its original position, so that the shadow thrown can be checked against the actual outline of the projected image. If the effect is in order, weigh down the paper with a few small weights, and stick the outer edge of the mask to the glass plate with a gummed paper strip. This allows it to be folded away out of the path of the enlarger light, and to be replaced again exactly when required without any trouble.

Then fit the countermask exactly to the basic mask, weigh it down, and tape down to the opposite edge of the glass plate. As soon as this is done, remove the weights from the basic mask and fold it out of the way. This completes the preparations for the first exposure.

EXPOSING THROUGH THE MASKS

Exposing. **1.** Fold away the first mask, place the paper in position and make the first exposure. **2.** Change the negatives in the negative carrier. **3.** Fold down the mask and fold away the countermask. Make the second exposure (p. 133).

After finding the exposure time by test strips, print the first negative onto the final bromide paper. In doing this make sure that the paper can be replaced in exactly the same position relative to the masking box and cut-out masks (p. 108).

Now exchange the first negative for the second one, and fold down the basic mask (and keep it down with a few weights) against the countermask. Then fold away the countermask. Adjust the position of the negative image relative to the

124

masking box until the part of the second negative to be printed in exactly fits the unmasked portion left by folding back the countermask.

As long as the adjustment is small it is immaterial whether we do this by moving the negative in the carrier or by moving the mask box and paper holder assembly as a whole. When greater movement is necessary adjust only the negative in the negative carrier. Otherwise the light rays from the enlarger lens might fall on the masks at a changed angle. This would alter both the exact position and the exact shape of the mask shadows on the paper.

For the same reason the degree of enlargement of the two negatives must be the same. If, for instance, we reduce it for the second negative, we would alter the width of the diffused shadow contour. It would in this case become greater and overlap the shaded area of the first enlargement. The result is a white line along the border of the shaded portions, and it becomes increasingly wider going outwards from the centre of the print.

Finally, carry on with the second exposure in the same way.

After development the result can at last be checked to see whether the work was accurate enough, and whether the shapes of the masks were correct.

If that is not the case, there is nothing for it but to start all over again.

CHEMICAL MASKING

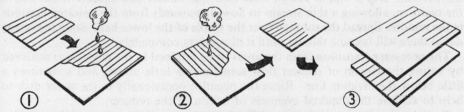

Combining chemically masked negatives. 1. Partially reduce the first negative to dissolve away the area not wanted. 2. Remove the corresponding portions of the second negative. 3. Put the two negatives together, adjust the relative image positions, and print.

We sometimes have to modify one of the negatives before we can print it in combination with the other. This may be the case when we only want to print isolated details into an existing picture without printing in other elements of the second negative.

The most useful method here is one involving partial reduction (for combination printing in one stage) or partial blocking out (for printing in several stages).

In practice the first method is much more frequent. For example, let us imagine the following case.

A picture is to show a large perfume flask filling the foreground in the lower part of the print, while the background in the upper part depicts a scene such as a dancing couple. Such a shot is impossible by pure camera technique. The best way of tackling it is combination printing with partial reduction.

First take a picture of the perfume flask. Already during exposure plan its position for the final effect, and arrange it so that it will take up the right amount of picture space at the bottom of the negative. It is better not to plan for the whole negative area, but to arrange the subject to fit a smaller imaginary negative size. This will allow more room for adjustment later on.

Make the second exposure of the dancing couple on a negative of the same size as the first, again utilising only part of the full picture area. Remember in this case the subject will have to come in the top half of the negative.

When the two negatives are exposed and developed, we have to prepare them to fit each other. All trouble, however, would be wasted if we allow the gradation of the two to be so widely different that we cannot enlarge them onto a paper of the same grade. Uniform contrast of the two negatives is absolutely essential; remember that when exposing and developing them.

The next step is the partial reduction. The idea is completely to remove the image in the upper half of the perfume flask negative, and the lower half of the one of the dancing couple.

Use *Farmer's* reducer. Make this up according to the formula No. 35 on p. 243, and pour it into a white dish. Place a large dish with plain water next to it. There should be plenty of light on the working place.

While plate negatives can be handled just as they are, films are best taped to old plates to have a better hold on them.

Hold the negative sloping slightly downwards with the portion to be reduced at the bottom. Dip a wad of cotton wool into the reducer and squeeze it out above the negative, allowing a thin stream to flow downwards from the required contour in the middle. Spread the solution over the whole of the lower half. Soon the image detail there will become thinner until it disappears completely.

The necessary transition from the areas to be retained in the negative is achieved by letting the stream of reducer flow sometimes a little above, and sometimes a little below the dividing line. Rinse the negative occasionally in the water dish to help to achieve the required evenness of action of the reducer.

Partial reduction is a little more difficult when part of the centre of the negative is to be removed without affecting the marginal portions. The areas in question are then best dabbed with a soft camel hair brush, rinsing the negative in the water dish each time to remove surplus reducer.

Both these methods give gradually diffused outlines.

Where sharp outlines are required, all the work must be done on the dry negative, which is not rinsed at all until the very end.

Paint in the contours with a fine pointed brush filled with reducer. As the reducer is quickly used up, dip the brush frequently in the solution. It is, however, quite sufficient to reduce just a band along the outline. Remove the rest with a wad of cotton wool soaked in the reducer.

It is also possible to save time by using just the 10 per cent potassium ferricyanide solution for painting over instead of the mixed reducer. Allow the solution to act until the silver image to be reduced has all gone a yellowish white. These portions will be completely dissolved away as soon as the negative is transferred to an ordinary plain hypo fixing bath.

This method is suitable for all cases where image parts in the middle of the negative are retained, removing only the surrounding detail. If on the other hand

126

the edges are to be retained and part of the image to be removed from the centre, leaving sharp outlines, a different procedure is necessary.

This time paint the areas of the negative which are not to be reduced with an asphalt varnish (e.g. 1 part india rubber and 50 parts asphalt to 150 parts petrol). No air bubbles must be allowed to form. When dry, simply put the negative into the reducer until all unprotected areas are completely reduced. Then wash and dry the negative normally, and finally remove the asphalt varnish with a wad of cotton wool soaked in benzene or petrol.

The point of all these methods is that the treated negatives should fit together. The outlines must neither overlap, nor leave clear parts in between. When they coincide on the whole (except perhaps for minor inconsistencies which can be removed later by retouching), put them together in the negative carrier and enlarge.

Here is another example of the technique and the story behind it (p. 135). It was a story published in newspapers all over the world.

A photographer who had taken a picture of a wedding group outside the church door said that he found after developing his plates the bride appeared without her clothes on. Her dress had simply vanished in the photograph!

The report which went with this hoax explained that the bride had been wearing a nylon wedding dress, and that nylon became transparent when photographed.

The problem was to provide a suitable illustration to this tall transatlantic tale. It was done by combination printing with partially reduced negatives.

A girl was first photographed in a nylon dress. The photographer then took a second picture of the same girl in the same pose, but minus the dress.

All of the first negative was removed by reducer applied with a brush, except for the dress. Even the dress was to some extent reduced until only a thin image of it remained visible. The last stage was combining the two negatives and enlarging them together. The final print showed an ethereal indication of the dress over the undressed girl.

MULTIFACED PORTRAITS

There are people whose profile is surprisingly different from what we would expect after seeing full-face view. By combining both in the same picture we come nearer to a complete likeness.

A good and reliable method of creating such multifaced portraits is to combine partially reduced negatives.

Take a portrait of the profile against a light background, and a second one full-face against a black background.

Gradually reduce the profile negative towards the back of the head, until all detail has disappeared in the places to be occupied by the full-face view in the finished print.

The second negative needs no further treatment as owing to the black background the negative image is already clear glass all round the head.

Then enlarge the two negatives together as if they were one.

Such multifaced portraits can, of course, also be made by successive combination printing with the help of a mask and countermask (p. 123).

CUT AND PASTE MONTAGE

Combination printing as a rule aims at diffused or unsharp outlines where the picture elements blend into each other. When sharp and exact outlines are wanted, the best process is cut and paste montage.

Cut and paste montage consists of cutting some part out of one picture and putting it into another.

Therefore as a first condition, both pictures must be on the same type of paper. They must have the same image colour, and identical density and gradation.

Secondly, lighting, perspective, and proportions must match.

Finally, the cut-out edges must completely merge into the composite picture. Hence the need for really accurate cutting technique. Moreover, the picture to be pasted in must be on thin paper. Cutting edges become the more disturbingly obvious the thicker the paper.

As to suitable tools—we shall need scissors or a knife, or both. But not every knife or scissors will do!

The scissors must be really sharp. The usual household ones, used and misused on cloth, string, paper, cardboard, or thin wire, are just no good. Suitable instruments are new manicuring and surgical scissors. Two pairs are preferable: a straight-bladed one and a curved pair, for straight and curved outlines.

TECHNIQUE WITH SCISSORS

Cutting with scissors. 1. Roughly cut away the bulk of the unwanted area. 2. Cut accurately along the outline. 3. To cut out pointed details jutting into an outline cut into the corner from *both* directions.

In cutting out go roughly round the outlines first to get rid of most of the bits of surplus paper. This makes the print easier to handle for accurate cutting, as now only small pieces have to be cut off.

Always cut pointed bits inwards from the outside, where they jut into the main outline. In other words, make two cuts towards the converging point. But do not cut right into the corner; continue the cut only until the pointed piece in between

128

is just about ready to fall off. Get hold of this piece with the fingers, and tear it off from the back of the print.

Tear inwards, not away from the cut. In this way the face of the print is not damaged, only the paper fibre underneath frays out a little near the edge.

If the scissors cut into the corner, and then turn round to cut out of it, the extreme point is unavoidably broadened. Quite frequently it tears as well.

CUTTING WITH A KNIFE

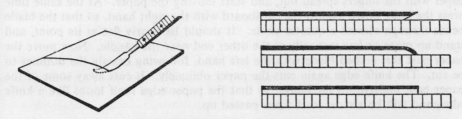

How to use a knife. *Left:* Cut by moving the print past the bent knife. *Right:* This will give an oblique cut *(top)* where the edge can be stuck down flat *(centre)*. A scissor cut *(bottom)* can never be stuck down really flat.

A knife, which is preferable anyway, is at times essential when cutting small portions from inside the picture. The blade must be the thinnest possible with a very keen edge. A surgical scalpel is best.

The knife must naturally be kept sharp all the time. For that reason a whetstone is just as essential as of the knife itself. Resharpen the blade (p.188) as soon as cutting requires the slightest extra effort.

We also need an absolutely smooth support underneath the print to be cut.

Glass, though often recommended, is definitely unsuitable. As soon as the cutting edge has cut through the last strands of the paper, it comes up against the glass, and is immediately blunted, as glass is harder than steel. And a blunt knife is no good for further cutting.

Therefore the support must be softer than the knife. It must also be homogeneous, and not have parts of different hardness. This disposes of wood with its uneven grain. A suitable support, on the other hand, is hard cardboard, the so-called pasteboard. Still better are sheets of zinc.

If the knife has a thick wedge-shaped cutting edge the broad shoulder pushes the paper edges apart like a plough, however sharp the edge may be. As a result, the cut edges curl upwards and are very difficult to smooth down again—hence the need for a really thin blade. In addition a thick blade loses its keenness much quicker than a thin one.

There are two ways of cutting with the knife: either vertically through the paper, or obliquely.

Oblique cutting has a special advantage in that the edge can be bevelled off underneath. In other words, the paper support gets thinner towards the edge. At the edge itself there is hardly any paper left at all, and on pasting up, the image layer there comes into more or less direct contact with the other surface. In this

129

way the pasted on edge is really level, and will not give the show away by causing shadows. The whole technique of cut and paste montage depends on avoiding these edge shadows.

From the point of view of the result, it does not matter whether the knife cuts along the stationary paper, or whether the paper moves past a stationary knife. Let us use the latter alternative.

Put the print down on the pasteboard support, and pierce the paper outside the cutting line with the knife held in the right hand. Press down the left hand on the paper with the fingers spread out, and start moving the paper. At the same time press the knife down against the cardboard with the right hand, so that the blade bends through almost a quarter circle. It should lie nearly flat at its point, and stand up more or less vertically at the other end near the handle. Now move the paper past this arched blade with the left hand, following exactly the outlines to be cut. The knife edge again cuts the paper obliquely. It cuts away some of the paper base underneath the image, so that the paper edge itself looks like a knife edge, and will be almost level when pasted up.

WHERE TO CUT

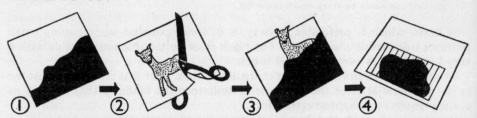

Montage behind the foreground. 1. Cut a slit along the foreground line. 2. Cut out the shape to be inserted. 3. Push into the slit between the foreground and background. 4. Stick down at the back with adhesive tape (p. 138).

When we come to pasting up, anything that belongs to the foreground must really be kept in the foreground. Thus if a man is supposed to be standing behind a bush in a wood, the order of objects from foreground to background is: bush—man—trees. When we therefore want to paste the man into the picture behind the bush but in front of the trees, we must obviously cut him out where he borders onto the background. Where, however, he borders onto the foreground, it is better to do the cutting on the bush.

This means that we cut a slit into the background print along the contour of the bush. The slit should be just wide enough to push through the cut-out of the man. So he automatically comes between the bush and the trees, as intended. All we have to do now is to stick some gummed paper over the slit on the back of the print to fix the figure in position, and to stick down the figure to the front (p. 138).

It is not always necessary to cut certain shapes out completely. We can leave parts of the background with the cut-out, if these parts will match the background of the second print. We thus disguise the presence of a cutting line and make cutting easier.

130

It is worth while to sit down and plan where to cut before picking up the knife. For instance, the picture to be cut out may show the subject against a leafy background. Pasted up on the second print, the subject would also border on a leafy background. So we leave some of the first background on the cut-out and merely cut along a wavy line which subsequently will blend well into the foliage of the second background.

FINISHING THE EDGES

Making the cutting edge invisible. *Left:* Jagged cuts are evened out with emery paper. *Centre:* Smoothing down the edges with sand paper will make them really thin. *Right:* Alternatively, the edges can be painted with water colour.

As the cutting edges of the pasted up composite print easily show shadows during copying, we must make them as invisible as possible.

Oblique cutting (p. 129) is one way. It is, however, not always easy. Besides, many people prefer cutting with scissors, which only allow a vertical cut. So the edges will often have to be finished off afterwards.

We can do this in two ways: by smoothing down, and by painting.

For smoothing down we need fine sandpaper. Lay the cut-out picture face down on a flat piece of cardboard, and rub down the edges, stroking them outwards from the centre. The sandpaper must not be so coarse as to fray the paper. For the same reason, pressure should not be too great. Continue smoothing until the edges are as thin as possible.

Irregularities in cutting can also be smoothed down with sandpaper. It is, for instance, almost impossible even with the greatest care to cut out a round shape without leaving any jaggedness at all. Therefore use sandpaper or pumice stone to even out the slightly uneven edge due to applying the scissors repeatedly. Put down the paper or stone on the table and rotate the round shape with its edge in contact with the rubbing surface.

The other method of finishing the edges is to paint them. This is recommended particularly with very complicated and detailed cutting edges which are not easily reached with sandpaper or might be damaged by it.

Fill a fine brush with spotting medium, and paint over the white paper edges with the side of the brush. Hold the cut-out face up horizontally in the left hand, while holding the brush vertically in the right hand with the point up and pulling it sideways along the outlines.

The depth of colour should of course match the neighbouring tone. Thus adjoining a black area paint the edge also black, near a grey area paint it grey, while edges near white areas are left as they are.

131

ASSEMBLING THE COMPOSITE

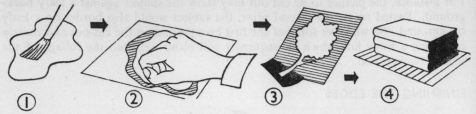

Sticking down the montage. **1.** Cover back of cut-out with adhesive. **2.** Stick down on background print. **3.** Apply adhesive to thin details from underneath with a small strip of paper and stick down. **4.** Put under pressure until the adhesive is dry.

The final step of pasting together needs a great deal of care.

We can use either ordinary photo mounting paste or rubber solution.

The latter has the advantage that, if mounting was not satisfactory, the two prints can again be separated without leaving any trace of the rubber solution. It is also much cleaner to work with.

Paste on the other hand makes a really permanent job of it. But once the prints are stuck together, their position cannot be changed any more.

Lay the cut-out print face down on a sheet of newspaper and apply the mountant. Press the print against the paper with two fingers. It must not move while the sticky solution is being applied. If it does move, the picture edges are immediately soiled by the mountant.

Then carefully lift the print off the newspaper, lay it in the right position on the second print, and press down. Wipe the face of the cut-out with gentle pressure from the centre out with a clean soft cloth. Press down edges with special care.

At this stage careless manipulation can spoil the whole work, for the edges have become moist through the paste. The gelatine is therefore swollen and extremely sensitive to injury. So press down the edges carefully with just the finger tips. Immediately wipe away any traces of mountant oozing out.

Herein lies the greatest drawback of paste mountants as compared with rubber solution. The latter does not soften the gelatine layer, while traces of solution on the print do not matter much. They are easily rubbed off afterwards.

During working the fingers must remain clean and dry to avoid soiling the print surface with finger prints. A shallow box or dish within reach with talcum powder or French chalk in it helps a lot. Whenever the fingers become sticky with mountant, dip them into the talcum powder. This takes away all stickiness, and we can continue work immediately.

Very fine details or thin strips are best not stuck down straight away, but are left dry while dealing with the main areas. Afterwards cut a plain paper tongue and half smear one side with mountant. Use this tongue to apply the mountant to the last fine corners and strips by going under them and spreading the mountant on the underside. Then stick down these parts on the background, too.

Finally, leave the composite print for a few hours under moderate pressure underneath a glass plate, so that it dries really flat. Minor flaws will then need retouching (p. 142) before we rephotograph the print.

COMBINATION PRINTING WITH MASKS (p. 122). *Top left:* Straight print of statuette. *Centre left:* Straight print of background. *Bottom left:* Masked print of statuette. *Bottom right:* Countermasked print of background. *Above right:* Statuette negative printed through mask, followed by background negative printed through countermask onto the same sheet of bromide paper (p. 123).

AP—L 133

PRINTING IN CLOUDS. Clouds introduced into a landscape will often add a touch of sunniness even if the view itself is fairly dull, mainly because we rarely see well defined cloud shapes against the blue sky in dull weather. The technique is similar to that of masked combination printing, but simpler (p. 121). *Left:* Print from cloud negative. *Right:* Print from landscape negative. *Above:* Landscape and clouds combined.

134

COMBINATION OF PARTIALLY
REDUCED NEGATIVES. Sometimes
chemical reduction of the negative
has to take the place of masking (pp.
125-127). *Above left:* Print from first
negative. *Left:* Print from first
negative after reducing away unwanted detail. *Right:* Print from
second negative. *Above right:* "The
transparent nylon dress." Second
negative printed in contact with
reduced first negative.

SIMULTANEOUS PORTRAITS. A single photograph of a person can never convey more than a small fraction of personality. So why not combine two views? *Left:* Full face view taken against black background. *Right:* Print from partially reduced profile view. *Above:* Full face and profile combined and printed as one negative (p. 127).

136

CUT AND PASTE MONTAGE (p. 128). *Left*: The fly was cut out of one enlargement and stuck in the middle of the print of the man's face. Fine detail like the feet could not be cut out accurately; they were later painted in. *Above*: It was impossible to cut the head with its fussy outline. Therefore the foreground which has straight and easy contours was cut out and stuck to the print of the ostrich.

BLENDING IN WITH THE BACK-
GROUND. *Left:* Background print.
A slit was cut where the foreground
joins the background (p. 130). *Right:*
From the Zoo. The pattern of the
wire netting was carefully retouched
away before cutting out the animal.
Above: The leopard was finally pushed
into the slit and stuck down.

138

PHOTOMONTAGE AND PAINT-ING. The globe was suitably re-touched and then cut out and stuck down on to the background. *Above left:* Original print of globe. *Left:* Halo background. *Above right:* Finished montage. The rockets were painted in, and their tracks added with the airbrush (p. 207).

139

UNIVERSAL CARBONS
Above All

VARIOUS TYPES OF LETTERING. *Above:* Black lettering by successive printing of the lettering negative onto the same sheet of paper as the foreground (p. 145). *Left:* Cut-out lettering by printing the negative in contact with a suitable panel with the letters cut out. The panel could also be placed in contact with the paper during part or the whole of the exposure (p. 148). *Right:* White letters by printing the negative in contact with a specially prepared positive lettering transparency (p. 146).

140

HARRIS

CRICHTON'
EXPERTS IN OLD ENGLISH SI

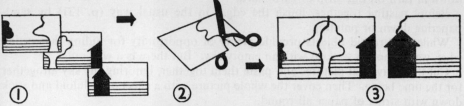

Mounting a panoram. **1.** Make sure the edges of neighbouring prints contain overlapping details. **2.** Cut along a suitable easily camouflaged outline. **3.** Mount the component prints with the overlapping parts of the image in exact register.

Panorams are a special application of cut-and-paste montage.

A panoram is a series of pictures—usually of a landscape—each showing a section of the whole view as wide as the camera lens can cover. These sections are then joined together side by side to form one continuous picture which in this way can include an angle of view of as much as 360 degrees.

Planning a panoram begins with making the individual exposures.

To allow a certain amount of latitude later on when pasting together, it is best not to utilise the full field of view of the camera for each exposure. So leave some overlap (at least $\frac{1}{4}-\frac{1}{2}$ in., or about 1 cm.) between each picture and its neighbour.

If possible, avoid having the open sky near the margins of the single views. It is much better to have an object (e.g. a tree or a house) projecting well above the skyline near the picture edge. Such an object should appear near the common edge of each of two neighbouring exposures, if possible.

From this set of individual negatives first prepare a series of exactly similar enlargements. They must be identical in both gradation and density. Accuracy at this stage is essential if we want to make a really invisible join later on.

Moreover, each enlargement must include the full area of its negative.

After drying, the prints have to be joined together side by side on a strip of stiff cardboard. Here cutting techique is important.

Avoid making the cutting edge coincide with the edge of one of the prints. For instance, a tree may (because we have purposely placed it there) jut into both the left-hand edge of one print and the right-hand edge of the next one. So cut through the foliage on one print, following if possible some irregular outline common to both prints. Naturally nothing must be cut away from one print that is not present in the other. Any generosity of overlap comes in very useful here.

After making sure the cut parts of the tree fit satisfactorily over the corresponding parts of the other print, carry on cutting along the tree trunk. Follow this outline accurately until the foreground. There again cut along stones, grass, etc.

The point of it all, whatever the marginal object may be, is to have as irregular a join as possible between the one picture and parts of the next. It should blend in with the image detail and so camouflage the cutting line itself.

Naturally only one of the prints need be cut for each join. The cut edge is then superimposed on the image portions of the other print. We can do this either by cutting both sides of every other print, or cutting one side of every print. The latter method is more practical, as we can then progress print by print, pasting each down in turn on our strip of cardboard.

Before pasting together, finish the edges in the usual way (p. 131) by sand-papering down or painting.

While foreground objects provide plenty of opportunity for hiding the cutting edge, we are not so well off with an empty sky. But there is a way out.

Cut the individual pictures and paste them together, ignoring the sky altogether for the time being. Then cover the whole picture with a sheet of celluloid and stick down with strips of paper all round.

Now mix some black and some white air brush paint (p. 208) until the tone is exactly the same as that of the sky. Judge the colour by a dry sample of the mixed paint; it is usually darker when wet.

Wipe the celluloid with a rag moistened with petrol to remove all grease. Then spray the paint with an air brush (p. 207) onto the celluloid over the boundary between the two prints until the join is completely hidden underneath. Finally remove any paint from the foreground (some will invariably get sprayed there, too) with a moist brush.

REPHOTOGRAPHING THE PRINT

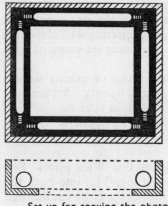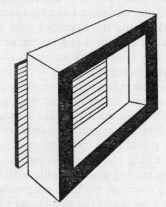

Set-up for copying the photomontage. *Left:* Lighting unit for even illumination. This consists of a frame with four tubular lamps mounted behind it, eliminating all shadows due to any raised edges of the pasted-up combination. *Right:* Arrangement of camera, lighting frame, and original. The frame should be as near as possible to the print to be copied, to avoid reflection of light into the lens.

We cannot present a completed cut-and-paste montage as a final print, since the handwork on it would be too obvious.

So we shall have to rephotograph the composite print. This provides a master negative from which we can make any number of prints without have to do cutting and pasting up afresh every time. It also makes it easier to remove minor imper-fections (obvious bits of cutting edge, etc.) by retouching.

While even illumination is essential for any copying job, we need special care in rephotographing a composite montage of this kind. We are concerned not only

142

with uniform brightness over a flat surface, but we must also avoid all shadows from any raised cutting edges.

Here the usual two lamps to the left and right of the camera may not be good enough. Even if they eliminate side shadows, they cannot do much about shadows at the top or bottom due to horizontal cutting edges.

The best way to really shadlowless lighting is a lighting frame.

Take a shallow wooden box at least 2 ft. square and cut out the bottom, leaving about 3 in. round all four sides. Inside the box behind each of these edges fit a long tubular lamp. Paint the inside of the box white.

For copying, place this frame in front of the picture. The latter will then be absolutely evenly lit from all sides by the four lamps without any shadows at all.

Set up the camera centrally opposite the frame, photographing the picture through it. The optical axis of the lens must be at exactly right angles to the picture plane. So square up the camera carefully to avoid any image distortion. The edges remaining of the bottom of the box will shield the lens from light from the lamps.

To prevent direct reflections from the picture surface into the lens, the light should come well from the side. So move the frame as near to the picture as possible. The lamps are too near only when the picture edges appear brighter than the centre.

Expose with a medium lens aperture, and adjust exposure and development times to obtain a normal negative. It should show good detail and a full tone range, so that after whatever retouching may be necessary it can easily be enlarged.

Retouching of the negative will probably be limited to touching up traces of the cutting edges. Here pencil retouching is particularly effective (p. 197).

THREE-DIMENSIONAL MONTAGE

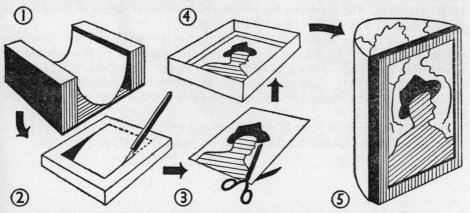

Mounting a three-dimensional montage. 1. Print the background negative on a bent sheet of bromide paper. 2. Cut out a frame from a box lid. 3. Cut out the foreground figure from a suitable print. 4. Stick the cut-out inside the front of the frame. 5. Fix the bent background print to the frame behind the foreground cut-out to complete the montage.

This is a special process which suggests a three-dimensional effect. We show objects in front of a curved background, so that they partly seem to blend into it,

143

and we cannot tell where the foreground finishes and the background begins.

As an example, let us show a figure in front of a suitable scene. Any background will do; we are not limited to that of the figure. The beauty of this method is that we can create entirely new settings.

First, make a whole-plate ($6\frac{1}{2} \times 8\frac{1}{2}$ in.), enlargement of the figure on thin paper. After processing and drying cut away all the background with scissors so that only the figure itself is left.

Next, make a 9×12 in. enlargement of a suitable background on matt paper. During enlarging curve the paper inwards between two boxes as described on p. 57, so that the boxes are about 7 in. apart.

With a sharp knife, cut out part of the centre of a whole-plate box of bromide paper, leaving just a frame. Thus cut a piece 6×8 in., so that the frame is $\frac{1}{4}$ in. all round. Then stick the cut-away foreground print behind the frame. If there is not enough foreground picture to stick to at least two sides of the frame, put the print between two glass plates $6\frac{1}{2} \times 8\frac{1}{2}$ in. and place just behind the cut-out frame.

Behind this fasten in the distorted 9×12 in. enlargement (trimmed to $8\frac{1}{2} \times 11\frac{1}{4}$ in.). Stick the two ends of it to the sides of the frame and curve the $11\frac{1}{2}$ in. of paper in between through an arc. The curvature should be the same as it was during enlarging.

Both the foreground and background prints can be hand coloured (p. 217) beforehand to give a still more effective result.

Looking straight at this set-up will produce an impression of a natural three-dimensional effect like a pair of stereo prints in a stereo viewer. The distortion on the curved background sheet is now, by viewing the similarly curved print, no longer apparent. The eye sees a flat image which, however, seems to stand out in space similar to a cyclorama on a theatre stage.

The shadow thrown on the background by the foreground picture can sometimes detract from the effect. We can therefore improve the result by illuminating the model from the inside. Thus a lid with a small electric bulb inside it may be put on top of the assembly. Alternatively, place the set-up on a pedestal consisting of a hollow small box without a lid and with the lamp inside it which shines onto the picture from below.

Often the foreground print is not translucent enough, and looks more like a silhouette. In that case varnish the back of the paper (No. **47**, p. 246).

LETTERING IN PHOTOGRAPHS

Nobody can stop us from painting or writing on our photographs with Indian ink or water colour. But the result will not be very pleasing because the writing will stick out of the photograph as something completely alien. To combine the writing and the photograph the former must be brought in as part of the photographic process, not afterwards.

There are various ways of incorporating lettering in a negative.

We can simply write it in with opaque ink or pigment (p. 186) to print white in the enlargement.

We can scratch it in with an engraving tool or write it in with *Farmer's* reducer, when it will print black.

All these methods have disadvantages.

The lettering must be written reversed left to right—which is not easy—and the results are usually anything but neat.

Most important of all, the negative is spoiled for good and can never be used again without the writing.

For that reason it is much better to go the longer way round, and introduce the lettering during printing.

BLACK LETTERING

Printing-in black lettering. **1.** Make a lettering negative by copying the word or words (drawn on a white card) in the camera. **2.** Print the picture negative in the normal way. **3.** Print in the lettering from the lettering negative (p. 140).

Draw black letters in any desired size on white paper in Indian ink. Faults can easily be touched up and corrected, either by painting over again with white, or by pasting pieces of paper over it and redrawing on top.

It is advisable to have the size of the lettering rather larger than will be needed later on. It is easier to work in a larger size, and subsequent copying on a reduced scale minimises the effect of any unevenness. The job can of course also be typeset by a printer.

Copy the drawing or printer's pull on a high contrast process or photo-mechanical film or plate. Develop in a contrast developer and finish in the normal way.

The resulting negative must show the lettering clear and transparent against a practically opaque background. If there is still any veil over the image of the letters, briefly treat the negative with *Farmer's* reducer. Block out any transparent spots and also the transparent plate edges with opaque medium.

Where the negative is to be used in the enlarger, the size and position of the lettering in the negative area is immaterial. For contact printing, however, the lettering must be copied so that it is in the right place and of the right size for the negative with which it is to be combined. The subject negative is therefore best held against the ground glass screen of the copying camera to check relative positioning.

The writing and picture are combined in two stages.

First focus the picture negative and make a pencil lay-out sketch (p. 107). Then expose the bromide paper behind this negative.

Put the pencil lay-out back in the paper holder, focus, and suitably position the lettering negative. Finally expose the bromide paper again to the lettering negative.

WHITE LETTERING

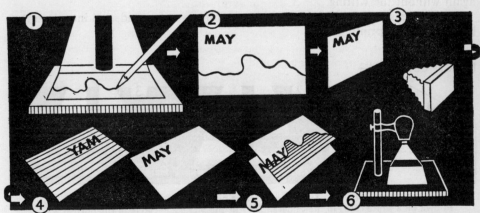

Introducing white lettering. 1. Prepare a lay-out sketch in the size of the finished print. 2. Draw or paint the lettering in the right place on the sketch. 3. Photograph in the camera so that the lay-out just fills the negative area. 4. Make a positive transparency from the lettering negative. 5. Bind up the picture negative and the transparency together. 6. Print as one negative (p. 140).

White lettering requires a little more preparation, but has the advantage that the negatives can later be printed together in one stage.

First place the picture negative in the enlarger and focus onto a large sheet of drawing paper so that the image just fills the paper. Roughly trace the picture shapes and masses in pencil, and decide on the most suitable position for the lettering.

Then draw and paint the lettering on this sheet in the right size to fit the lay-out. When this is finished and the pencil markings removed, copy the whole sheet on a reduced scale so that it again fills a negative of the same size as the picture negative. In other words the scale of reduction will have to be the reciprocal of the degree of enlargement used to make the lay-out.

Make the lettering negative on process material as before (p. 146) so that it shows the transparent writing on a dense black background.

Finally, contact print the lettering negative itself on to a high contrast film or plate to produce a positive transparency of the same size with dense black letters on transparent film. Since this transparency is now reversed left to right, it can be placed face to face with the original picture negative, and the two enlarged together. If the lettering on the transparency was dense enough, the letters will come out pure white.

SIGNATURES

Draw the signature on a large sheet of white paper in Indian ink, copy onto a plate or film of the same size as the usual negative size, and make a positive transparency.

In copying put the signature in the bottom right-hand corner of the negative area, so that it is in the required size for future use.

It is best to make two negatives and positives, one upright and one landscape shape, so that they can be used with either format. We shall thus have two negatives with the signatures transparent on black ground, and two positives with the signatures on black transparent ground.

For white lettering where the edges of the picture are dark, simply enlarge the positive in contact with the negative.

For black lettering on a light print, enlarge the picture negative first, and print in the signature afterwards.

OTHER KINDS OF LETTERING

Making various kinds of lettering. *Left:* Metal or cardboard letters on the printing paper. *Centre:* Plastic letters set up and photographed. *Right:* Textured letters by making a positive transparency from the lettering negative through a texture screen.

To make the lettering appear more pictorial, solid cut-out letters of various materials (cardboard, wood, plastic, etc.) can be set up and photographed against a black or white background.

147

For perspective effects photograph the letters obliquely. They can also be made to show shadows and texture.

Double print this lettering negative with a normal negative, directly or successively.

There are two ways of making patterned lettering.

For the first, simply cut the letters out of a texture screen and place them on the sensitive paper during printing or enlarging. This needs a certain amount of care to align the letters correctly.

Alternatively, a negative with transparent letters on black ground is used as before (p. 146). For printing in dark lettering place this negative in contact with a texture negative. The texture will then be reproduced in the letters.

Similarly for white letters with a pattern, make the positive transparency with a texture screen between negative and positive.

Transparent lettering where the image underneath shows through is equally simple.

If the lettering is to be dark, the procedure is the same as for printing in black letters (p. 145), except that the printing time for the lettering negative is reduced. The letters will then appear as overexposed image parts.

If the lettering is to be lighter with the picture image showing through faintly underneath, the method is much the same as it is with white letters (p. 146). But in this case the positive transparency should be very thin so that the letters are only light grey instead of black. They will therefore not hold back the image of the picture negative completely when printed together, but will allow it to print through more or less faintly.

Luminous white letters resembling neon signs are also made similarly to ordinary white letters (p. 146). But make the transparency from the transparent-on-black lettering negative by same size reproduction in the enlarger, and use a soft-focus attachment in front of the enlarger lens.

Finally for tinted lettering, print in white letters as before (p. 146), and paint them over in the finished print with suitable tinting dyes (p. 217). These dyes blend into the paper surface and do not show up even with glossy surfaced papers.

Section IV:

OFF THE BEATEN TRACK

PICTURES ON SILVER OR GOLD

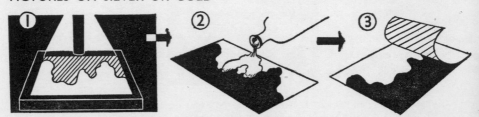

Silver or gold backgrounds. **1.** Make a thin transparency in the normal way. **2.** Coat the emulsion side with linseed oil or a suitable adhesive. **3.** Stick down a sheet of gold or silver paper or foil, and trim to shape.

We can achieve special effects in combination with gold leaf or silver paper. As the base will show a metallic surface instead of white paper, the image is enhanced in all its detail as if it were projected on a silver screen.

First make an enlarged transparency of suitable size (p. 120). Develop it to a low density; the shadows must on no account be heavy or black. The whole transparency should be much thinner than when used for projection.

After drying paint linseed oil, acid-free gum arabic, or Canada balsam diluted with a little xylene over gold or silver paper. Treat the emulsion side of the transparency in the same way, and press the two treated surfaces into contact, taking care to avoid air bubbles between them. Put this sandwich under pressure for a while.

Trim off the protruding paper edges, and put the picture into a frame. The glass of the transparency itself becomes the cover glass.

When we look at such pictures slightly from one side, all the details appear with enhanced highlight gradation.

While black images show up best against silver, a golden background goes well with brown toned transparencies. The sulphide toner (Nos. **41-42**, p. 245) is suitable for toning.

Toning also makes the image much more permanent, otherwise the intimate contact between the image layer and the binding medium may cause chemical changes which in time will discolour the picture. The risk is particularly great with linseed oil. So only use the latter with sulphide toned transparencies.

We can also increase the permanence of the image by sticking a piece of cellophane over the back of the picture to prevent access of air through the backing as far as possible.

150

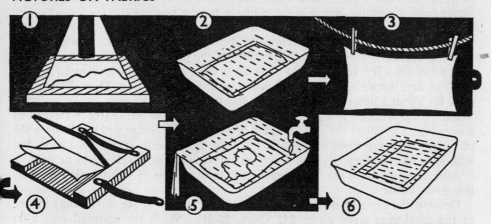

Daylight printing on fabrics. I. Make an enlarged paper negative in the size of the final print. Impregnate the base of this paper negative to make it more transparent. 2. Sensitise the fabric. 3. Hang up to dry in the dark. 4. Print out by daylight through the paper negative. 5. Wash the exposed fabric in the dark. 6. Fix in a plain hypo bath.

It is possible to sensitise materials like canvas, silk, or linen, and to produce prints or enlargements on them.

The materials can be sensitised either for daylight printing or for enlarging like bromide paper, though the latter is slightly more involved. On the other hand, daylight printing materials can only be printed by contact. So either the picture size is limited to that of the negative, or we must make an enlarged duplicate negative.

Prepare the duplicate negative via a transparency made by contact printing in the usual way. Enlarge the transparency on cut film, or on negative paper, which is a special bromide paper with a translucent, very even, and almost texture free base. To make the paper negative even more translucent, impregnate the back with a mixture of equal parts of castor oil and petrol or petroleum ether.

To prepare the material itself for printing, immerse it in a suitable sensitiser (Nos. 21-22, p. 242) for about 3 minutes. Push and prod it about well during that time with a glass rod. Then hang up to dry in the dark. Creases all over the sensitised fabric are simply ironed out with a moderately hot iron.

Print out the sensitised material by daylight in a printing frame behind a negative. When the image is about half as dense as intended (check by opening half the back of the printing frame from time to time) take the fabric out and wash for about 10 minutes in the dark in running water. Then put into a 5 per cent solution of plain hypo (*not* an acid fixing bath), wash well again, and dry.

Another method of sensitising fabrics produces pure dye images without any silver in them at all. It is based on the action of light on certain organic compounds which are capable of forming dyes. The action of light destroys the dye forming ability; in other words an image is formed where the material was not exposed

151

to light. As a result this process which is also known as diazotype gives a negative image from a negative, and a positive image from a positive.

Soak the fabric (preferably cotton) in a hot 1 per cent solution of primuline in water (not to be confused with primuline dyes) for 5–10 minutes. Work it about with a glass rod to ensure even distribution of the primuline. Then drain, rinse in cold water for a few seconds, and hang up to dry in a current of warm air.

When dry, immerse the prepared fabric in the sensitiser (No. 25, p. 242) in the dark for about a minute. Blot between sheets of blotting paper.

Expose immediately in a printing frame, with a positive transparency instead of a negative. The longer the exposure, the fainter the final image will be. Expose the material until a test piece exposed to the same light source at the same time, but without a transparency, gives just a slight colour with the developer to be used.

After exposure wash the transparency to remove traces of sensitiser left on it by the moist fabric.

Develop the exposed material by soaking (preferably in the darkroom) in one of the developers given on p. 242 (Nos. 26-31). Wash the material well after development.

The images are permanent unless exposed to strong sunlight for long periods.

To sensitise canvas for enlarging, use the following procedure. All operations, including preparation of the canvas, must be carried out in the dark, or by a deep red darkroom safelight. Otherwise the results may be fogged.

First soak the canvas in soap suds for 12 hours, wash well in running water, and dry in the dark. When dry, sprinkle with water and iron with not too hot iron.

Then soak for 20 minutes in the presensitising bath (No. 23, p. 242), dry in a warm dry place, and sensitise (No. 24, p. 242).

Lay the cloth in the bottom of a clean dish, and allow the sensitiser to flow over it. Break up any air bubbles with a glass rod. After 4 minutes pick it up by one corner, allow to drain (but do not squeeze out), and dry in the dark.

The canvas can then be used like bromide paper—exposing, developing, fixing, and washing it in much the same way.

LUMINOUS PICTURES

Producing luminous images. 1. Coat a sheet of plain paper with luminous paint. 2. Expose for a few minutes under a negative in the enlarger. 3. Switch off the enlarger light, and a glowing image will be visible in the dark.

Photographs which glow in the dark are made in the same way as pictures with metallic backgrounds (p. 150), except that paper coated with luminous paint takes the place of the silver paper or gold foil.

152

When such transparencies backed with luminous paint are exposed for a short time to a strong light, they begin to glow. They will go on glowing in the dark for several hours, until the effect fades and is regenerated by a fresh exposure to light.

Luminous paints can be bought, or made as described on p. 243 (Formulae Nos. 32-34).

The sulphur content of the paints would soon attack the transparency image unless this is already sulphide toned. It is therefore advisable to put a sheet of cellophane between the transparency and the painted paper.

Alternatively, a sheet of clear film can be cemented to the emulsion side of the transparency, and the paint applied directly to this film. In that case the powder is best mixed with a varnish medium instead of gum solution, so that it will stick to the film better.

Where a permanent picture is not important, the following short cut quickly leads to the same result.

Paint a card over with the luminous mixture, and lay it on the baseboard of the enlarger. Project an image on it from a positive transparency. As all this takes place in the darkroom, it is easy to see when the paper has started to glow sufficiently, by switching off the enlarger from time to time.

Naturally, the glowing image must be protected from any additional exposure to light, as otherwise it would be obliterated and the whole card would begin to glow uniformly.

NON-PHOTOGRAPHIC REPRODUCTION

Photography makes use of the action of light upon materials sensitive to it. We can however, at one stage of the process at any rate, dispense with the sensitive material and use the photographic image as a guide for making non-photographic pictures.

The image used may be either that projected by the enlarger onto the baseboard, or that of a finished print. In the former case we directly produce a positive in pencil or chalk, in the latter we draw a pen and ink image on top of the photographic one, and then remove the latter.

In discussing these photographic aids to non-photographic reproduction we do not intend to encroach on the field of free creative drawing, nor are we imitating it. Purists may not approve, but although our results may look like drawings, they are still photography in the sense that they are based on a real optical image. Only the method of reproduction is that of a drawing.

Finally, as with all processes which are not quite so rigidly tied to straight photographic reproduction, our possibilities of control are immensely widened.

DRAWING WITH THE ENLARGER

Focus the negative in the enlarger to the required size on a sheet of drawing paper pinned to the baseboard.

Now start to shade in the "positive" with a pencil or crayon to varying depths until the negative image is hardly visible and the paper presents a more or less even grey surface. This will be the case when the brightest image parts on the drawing paper are covered over most, while the light cannot get through the dense parts of the negative anyway. What in fact happens, is that we build up the density of the drawing in the same way in which the light from the negative builds up the densities of a print by its action on the sensitive paper.

We must of course work in the dark. But we may turn on the room light from time to time to check progress.

Finally, we can deal separately with details that need touching up.

PEN AND INK DRAWINGS ON PRINTS

For pen and ink drawings first make a light enlargement.

Then draw in the main details with a soft round pointed pen. Take care not to scratch the gelatine surface. For that reason also do not go over the same spot more than once at the same time; at the first stroke the gelatine swells and is then

154

easily injured. So allow each line to dry before putting another immediately next to it.

A matt paper surface makes quick drying easy, though very fine lines are best drawn on glossy paper. In the latter case take great care to avoid greasy finger marks, as the slightest trace of grease repels the ink.

The picture can be drawn in small thin strokes or in heavy outlines. But keep the style uniform throughout the drawing.

Once the picture is finished in its outlines and most important details, remove the silver image completely by *Farmer's* reducer (No. **35**, p. 243), so that only the pen work is left.

Then fill in large black areas with a brush and ink. Leave this to the last, because large areas of ink easily crack owing to the expansion and contraction of the gelatine during bleaching, washing, and drying.

Similarly, wait with any knifing until this stage (p. 205), to avoid damaging the gelatine layer too soon.

LITHOGRAPHS FROM PRINTS

This method, which must not be confused with photo-lithography, allows quick preparation of an original for immediate reproduction in any size and quantity. The materials needed are a litho stone, or litho transfer paper, and lithographic ink and crayons.

The methods of use are much the same as have been described on p. 154. Thus the image of the negative projected on the stone can be shaded in with litho crayon on the stone, or a pen and ink drawing made from the print in litho ink. This, however, is not made directly on the print, but on a sheet of transparent litho transfer paper placed on top of the print.

A block can be made straightaway from the original, ready for printing by the usual methods of lithography. The pulls will then be similar to the original in every respect.

EMANCIPATED TECHNIQUE

When photography leaves the world of reality rightly or wrongly allotted to it, anything may happen. It literally becomes photo-graphy—drawing with light— or at least simulates the effects of a pure Art of Light. In other words, it is tied less and less to its mechanical machinery, the camera, and can start off on fancy flights of its own. And therein lies the true scope for expression by the artist.

We can still start these excursions with a negative. It will of course not be a normal negative, for we shall shape it to our own requirement either by special processing or by aftertreatment. But we are still using a negative-positive process.

At the same time, the negative need not necessarily be one made in the camera. Any other image will do which is transparent, and lends itself to being combined with the printing paper for the short time needed to produce a print.

Finally, we can go further still, and dispense with the negative altogether. Then it is up to the printing paper itself, and the ever necessary light. It is up to our ingenuity in directing, obstructing, and moulding the various elements to our purpose.

But first let us see what we can do with a negative.

SOLARISATION

We can start adjusting the negative to our own wishes long before it is finished— while it is still in the developer.

The result of solarisation is a negative in name more than in fact. It is a negative in so far as it is the intermediate on the way to the final print. Strictly speaking it is both a negative and a positive, inseparably tied together, giving picture images of a peculiar character.

We need for this images with simple clear outlines. The background should be dark, or at least the subject should contain large areas of dark tone.

Develop an ordinary negative (on panchromatic film) until the whole image is clearly visible on the surface. The progress of development is best followed visually by a deep green darkroom safelight. Then expose the negative for a few seconds to a red darkroom light. This fogging exposure mainly affects the image parts so far undeveloped which have just begun to go black in the developer. These parts now develop fairly rapidly, as the emulsion is already thoroughly soaked in the solution, and soon catch up with the already developed portion.

Where metallic silver is deposited through decomposition of silver bromide during development, potassium or sodium bromide is also formed at the same time. This soluble bromide slows down development, and is in fact often added to developers for that reason; for restrained development means less fog.

156

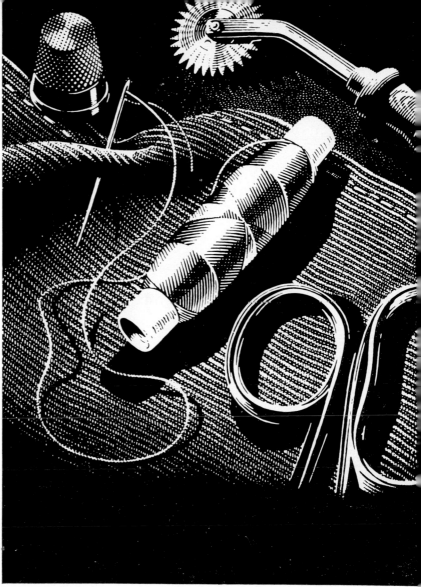

PEN AND INK DRAWINGS ON
PRINTS. *Left:* Original print. *Above:*
Pen and ink picture made by drawing
on the print with indian ink and then
bleaching out the silver image (p.154).

AP—N   157

DRAWING WITH THE ENLARGER.
Above: Print made from the negative in the normal way. *Right:* Pencil drawing produced by shading in the image projected onto a piece of plain paper on the enlarging easel (p. 154). The tone gradation and also the image can be changed at will to make the subject stand out.

158

LITHOGRAPHIC REPRODUCTION.
Left: Straight print. *Above:* Details traced onto litho transfer paper with litho ink, ready for making a lithographic plate (p. 155). Any unwanted part of the picture is simply omitted.

159

SOLARISATION. This is a process of partial reversal obtained during development of the negative (p. 156). *Left:* and *above right:* Prints from normal negatives. *Right:* Print from negative slightly solarised by exposure to a strong darkroom lamp near the end of development. *Above left:* Print of negative strongly solarised by exposure half way through development (p. 165).

PICTURE FROM A TUMBLER. *Left:* A normal photograph of a tumbler cannot show the whole of the image etched or painted on the glass. *Above:* Print obtained by wrapping sensitive paper round the tumbler and exposing with a lamp from the inside (p. 166).

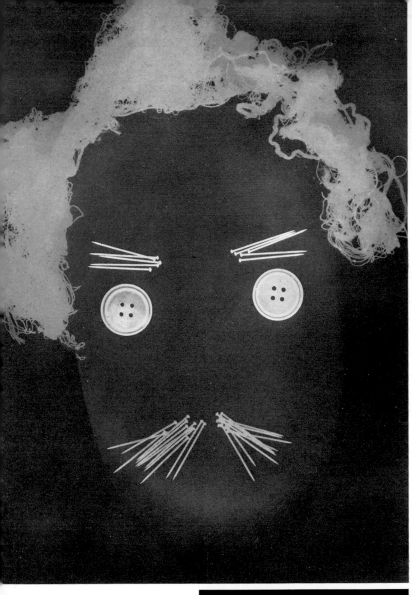

SIMPLE PHOTOGRAMS. *Above:* Outlines and shapes produced by placing buttons, pins, and mending wool on a sheet of bromide paper on the enlarging easel and exposing without a negative. *Left:* A practical use of a photogram like this is to provide a background for a tool box to keep all the tools in their proper places. *Right:* The parts of the fan in contact with the paper are sharp, the blades which were further away may hardly show at all (p. 167).

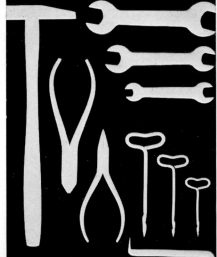

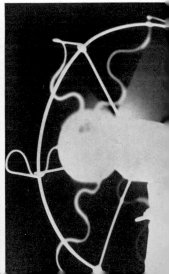

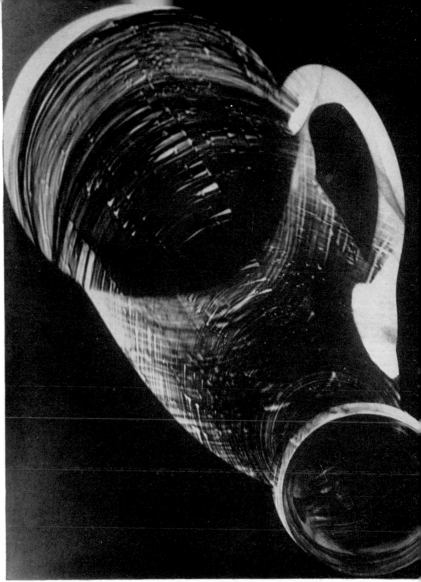

MORE ELABORATE PHOTOGRAMS.
Above: Photogram of a glass jug standing up and illuminated obliquely from the side (p. 168). *Left:* Photogram produced on a sheet of printing paper already exposed to a negative. The combination therefore includes both a photographic and a photogram image.

163

ARTIFICIAL LIGHTNING. *Above:* A spark between the discharge knobs of an influence machine or an induction coil will produce this pattern on a film or paper held in the spark gap (p. 169). *Right:* For a special effect the discharge can be made to go through a metal object like a cog-wheel, laid on the paper (p. 170).

164

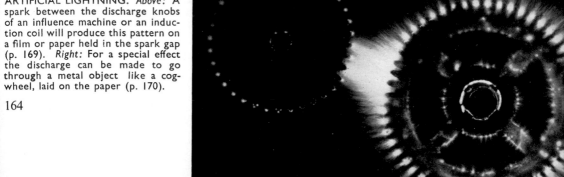

In this case the bromide concentration increases in the emulsion near the border line between already developed areas and those quickly developing after the fogging exposure. It forms there quicker than it can diffuse out of the emulsion, and by its mere presence almost stops development in those boundary areas.

After fixing, all the normally thin parts of the negative will be dense, in addition to the naturally dense highlights. Between these dense areas, however, a narrow transparent band—where the bromide had accumulated—remains. That band shows as a black outline in the subsequent print. This outline has a special graphic effect.

During exposure to the red light the thinner halftones are of course also affected and gain density while development continues. So it is important to hit on the right moment for the second exposure. Thus if the halftones in the finished negative are too dense, or altogether buried, the second exposure was too soon. For the next attempt, then, re-expose the negative later when the image is already further developed.

MELTING THE EMULSION

Distorted images by a molten emulsion layer. 1. Soak the plate in water for 10 minutes. 2. Leave to drain thoroughly. 3. Carefully heat over a spirit burner, tilting the plate to and fro to get the molten emulsion to run (p. 100).

We can produce distorted and grotesque effects by partially melting the gelatine layer of the negative.

In developing the negative for this process avoid tanning developers (such as hydroquinone or pyrocatechin), and also acid fixing baths.

First soak the negative well in water, and then hang up to dry for a short time until no actual drops of water are left on the surface. The gelatine should be evenly swollen, for every droplet would later cause uneven flow of the gelatine. The same applies to drops on the back of the negative because they have a cooling effect, and thus locally retard melting.

Plate and film negatives now require slightly different treatment.

Carefully warm plates in a horizontal position above a spirit burner or a gas flame.

For film negatives an electric hot plate must be used with some care, as celluloid easily catches fire.

As soon as the gelatine layer begins to melt (at this point the surface will become shiny), make it flow in the desired direction by turning or tilting the negative. It is advisable to stop the flow of the gelatine a little before the final effect is reached, as the layer still moves a little as it solidifies. Once the intended distortion is obtained, dry the film or plate horizontally.

We can produce wavy lines by partially warming individual portions of the negative. Allow the gelatine to flow alternately now in one direction, and then in another. But let it solidify completely between phases each time. A cool day is preferable to speed up this sort of work.

Through melting, parts of the negative also become thinner. This results in uneven density during enlarging, and the most distorted parts must be shaded during exposure (p. 59).

FLAT PICTURES FROM A CURVED SURFACE

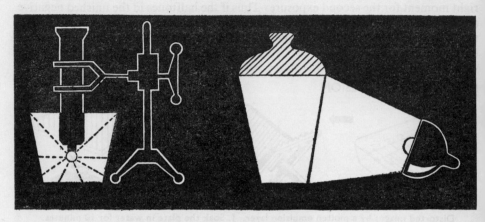

Pictures from vases and tumblers. *Left:* An image etched or painted onto a glass tumbler can be printed directly by wrapping the bromide paper round the glass. Exposure is by a small torch bulb in the centre of the tumbler (p. 161). *Right:* To reproduce images on opaque vases, the paper is wrapped round the vase and illuminated from the back.

Anyone who has tried to reproduce patterns from a curved surface will know that this is almost impossible in a single normal photograph. A number of exposures are required which are then combined to make the complete picture, similarly to panorams (p. 133).

There is, however, a way round this problem. We can often print patterns directly from the curved surface. For instance, we can wrap up a Greek vase tightly into sensitive paper (emulsion side inwards) and expose it to light. The rays coming through the paper which fall on white or light parts of the vase are reflected and act on the sensitive emulsion; while those which fall on the black parts are absorbed and do not produce any appreciable blackening of the paper. The result is a negative which can be reversed in processing or printed again to produce a positive.

This method, which is useful for opaque objects, is modified where transparent materials are concerned. We can print directly from tumblers or lampshades by wrapping sensitive paper around them, and exposing with a small light source in the centre.

166

The transparent object to be photographed is thus enveloped in a kind of sleeve which is pressed on by tying rubber bands round the outside. Cut off the protruding edge of the paper with a pair of scissors. Then introduce a pocket torch with a spotlight bulb in the centre. The filament of this type of bulb is almost a point. The smaller it is, the sharper will be the reproduction, as it is really a question of projecting the shadow of the pattern on the printing paper.

Place the light exactly in the centre so that the sides are evenly illuminated all round. Take care not to move it at all during exposure, or the shadows will be blurred. To make quite sure clamp the torch into a heavy retort stand or similar device.

To avoid moving the lamp when switching on the light, unscrew the base of the torch and turn on the switch. For the actual exposure carefully place the base in position, thus completing the electric circuit which lights the lamp. A separate outside switch is even safer. Usually an exposure of about 2–3 seconds will do the job.

The images obtained are of course reversed left to right. To get them the right way round, print them again. They will then at the same time become positive pictures.

SIMPLE PHOTOGRAMS

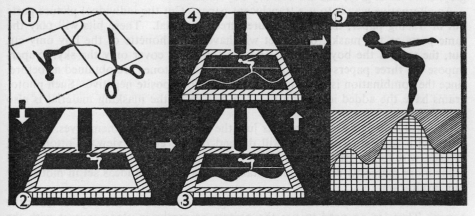

Photograms with masks. **1.** Cut three masks, one covering the background outline only, one the background and middle distance, and one for the foreground figure. **2.** Expose the printing paper with the first mask on it. **3.** Expose again with the second mask on top. **4.** Finally expose the same paper with the third mask on top of the other two, to get the finished print **5** on development.

Just as we can directly print from decorations on vases or glass tumblers, so we can reproduce the outlines of flat objects in a similar way, by-passing any negative.

For instance, we may place an etched flat glass dish on a suitably sized sheet of bromide paper and "print" it in the light beam of the enlarger without a negative. We need a point source of light which we easily get by completely stopping down

167

the enlarger lens. A really sharp projected beam is, however, only formed if the correct distances between lens, paper, and condenser are ensured by first setting the enlarger in the usual way, i.e. focusing a negative on the baseboard.

Further possibilities of printing objects directly on to sensitive paper lead to photograms. It is immaterial whether we use ready made objects or specially prepared masks.

A simple example will illustrate the technique. A picture is planned which shows a little black boy on a cliff in the sea, with the sky as background.

This composition needs three masks. One will cover only the sky. One will cover the sky and the sea. The third will cover sky, sea, and cliff, leaving out only the silhouette of the boy.

The print is made by three exposures in the clear beam of the enlarger light.

For the first, place the sky mask on the bromide paper so that all parts other than the sky receive a short exposure.

Then superimpose the mask for the cliff, which leaves only the cliff and boy uncovered for the second exposure.

Finally expose the paper under the cut-out for just the boy, and print the paper to give a really black tone.

After development the picture will show these tone steps: sky—white, sea—light grey, cliff—dark grey, and the solitary boy—black.

An alternative way is to use translucent paper. Cut the individual picture parts out of tracing paper, tissue, or texture screen material. These bits will play the same parts as the masks: one sheet will have the silhouette of the boy only cut out, the second the boy and cliff, and the third will cover only the sky. Superimpose the three papers and print as one. The same tones are obtained as before, since the combination is nothing more than one composite negative. Such photograms have the added attraction that the texture of the masking material is also recorded.

Obviously we can use real objects just the same, either by themselves, or combined with masks. The choice will depend on the end in view. Cotton wool, threads, wire loops, gramophone needles, wood shavings, lead shot, fish scales, and many more materials will provide suitable media to realise ideas set in motion by our inspiration.

There are further possibilities in altering the distance of the objects from the paper. There is no need to use the objects or masks in close contact with the paper surface. We can just as well interpose them in the light beam higher up. Unsharp diffuse images are formed if the objects are placed on a stage—a sheet of glass supported some way above the paper. The method is the same as for producing unsharp shadows in combination printing (p. 121).

PHOTOGRAMS OF SOLID OBJECTS

The third dimension is completely lost if we confine ourselves to the methods just described. The shape of anything standing up above the paper level can only record if the light beam is allowed to throw a shadow of the whole object on the sensitive paper. In other words, the light must not fall on the object vertically from above, but obliquely.

The solution is simple: either tilt the baseboard as for correcting distortion (p. 51), or incline the enlarger head; so that in either case the light beam falls on the objects a little from one side.

There is no real reason why we should not dispense with the enlarger altogether, and build up the objects on the paper on any convenient table, using one or more pocket torches as spotlights. Stronger light sources can also be used, but the exposures will be inconveniently short.

The outline of the base of the object will always be reproduced sharp. The cast shadow, on the other hand, becomes the more diffuse the higher up the part of the object is which throws it. This is the case particularly when we use the enlarger lens at full aperture, or employ any separate light source at random. We can therefore control the sharpness of the cast shadows by altering the lens aperture, or the focus of any spotlight used. The amount of adjustment needed will depend on the height of the object.

Moreover, instead of putting, say, a glass dish directly down on the paper, we can again support it some way above on the stage already mentioned (p. 123). This produces a cast shadow without a base shadow and thus has no solidity of outline at all.

Usually prints which show only cast shadows seem to be more intelligible, particularly as the shadows are reproduced white, and not black. Intelligibility, though, is not necessarily the keynote of photograms. They are after all, as a rule, highly abstract forms of pictorial expression.

LIGHTNING

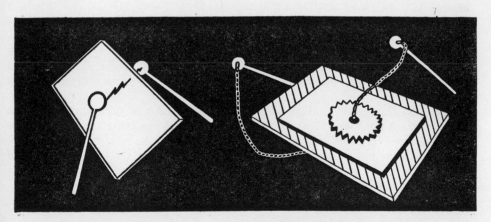

Producing artificial lightning. *Left:* A sheet of sensitised paper is held between the discharge knobs of an electric influence machine (p. 164). The flash forms its own image. *Right:* Another way of obtaining flash images is to place the paper on a metal sheet connected to one discharge knob, and place various metal objects on top, connecting them to the other knob by means of a thin chain.

A flash of lightning is about the only subject that can take a lifelike picture of itself—without a camera, merely by its own light action on the sensitive material. But as experiments with the real thing are apt to be chancy, we had better use weaker flashes which we can produce ourselves at will.

If an electric influence machine is available, simply hold a sensitive emulsion (film or paper) between the discharge knobs. During discharge the path of the flash is promptly recorded with all its branches.

The shape of the reproduced flash varies, depending on whether the emulsion side faces the positively or the negatively charged knob. In either case the figures formed diverge from the centre, and resemble the rivers and rivulets on a map.

Instead of turning to the discharge knobs, we can press into service any metal object, such as coins, cog wheels, and the like. They will then record their own image in the form of visible flashes along their outlines.

For this purpose lay a metal sheet on a glass plate, place the paper on it, and finally put a cog wheel, a bracelet, or something of the sort on top. Connect the bottom metal sheet to one discharge knob, and allow a fine wire or chain to hang down from the other so that it touches the metal objects lying on the paper.

As soon as the influence machine is set in motion, sparks begin to discharge from all projecting points between the poles, and thus indicate the shapes and outlines of the objects on the paper. In fact, they print themselves with innumerable tiny electrical discharges. A small turn of the wheels of the influence machine is quite enough for this purpose.

An electric "underexposure" is preferable, overdeveloping in a hard developer for contrast and density. Prolonged discharge on the sensitive material will produce too many superimposed flash images, giving an indistinct foggy result.

Section V:

AFTERTREATMENT, RETOUCHING AND FINISHING

AFTERTREATMENT OF NEGATIVES

Usually unsatisfactory negatives are best consigned to the waste paper basket, rather than wasting time messing about with them. They will only produce an inferior print in the end. Sometimes, however, an important exposure cannot be repeated and has to be enlarged at all costs, however bad the negative. Then we must try to get as much out of it as possible.

There are many things that can be wrong with a negative. It may be too dense or too thin, too contrasty or too soft, too grainy, or even scratched. And if the various methods of control by exposure and choice of paper grade (p. 28) are inadequate, we must treat the negative itself.

Strictly speaking, most of the methods to be described are, from the point of view of print making, not aftertreatment at all. If we intend to treat the negative, we must do so before making the prints.

In all cases chemical aftertreatment of the whole negative must precede any local aftertreatment and any retouching (p. 181).

TOO DENSE NEGATIVES

Beyond a certain degree dense negatives are not easy to print. The exposure times become inconveniently long, and often we shall find it difficult to obtain crisp enlargements with deep shadows and unveiled highlights.

Such a negative will therefore have to be reduced. The method depends on whether the gradation as well as the density of the negative needs modification.

If the negative is flat as well as dense, the contrast is increased during reduction by using *Farmer's* reducer (No. 35, p. 243). If the contrast is satisfactory and only the density needs reduction, we shall use a permanganate reducer (No. 36, p. 244).

With *Farmer's* reducer immerse the negatives to be reduced in the solution (preferably after a preliminary soaking in water) and keep them moving constantly. Observe the progress of the reduction by lifting the negative out from time to time. When they are sufficiently reduced, put them into clean water and wash for 30 minutes.

After treatment the negatives are thinner and at the same time somewhat harder in contrast, for *Farmer's* reducer attacks the shadow portions proportionally more than the highlights.

If the negatives are only too dense, bathe them in the permanganate reducer. The solution acts slowly, but move the negative about constantly until they are sufficiently reduced.

After a brief rinse place the negatives in a 5 per cent solution of potassium metabisulphite or sodium bisulphite which removes the brown stain. Finally, wash in running water and dry.

The permanganate reducer does not alter the gradation of the negatives.

TOO CONTRASTY NEGATIVES

If the negative is dense as well as hard, the permanganate reducer (No. 36, p. 244) helps a lot. Tone separation methods (p. 78) can also be tried.

The most useful methods of making the negatives softer are redevelopment after bleaching, or else toning the image blue.

For redevelopment, first bleach the thoroughly washed negatives. Leave them in the bleaching bath (No. 37, p. 244) until the image is milky white throughout. After a 15-minute wash redevelop by daylight in a soft-working (preferably fine-grain) developer (e.g. metol—No. 4, p. 238).

Stop development as soon as the negative has reached the required density. Viewed from the back of the film, the extreme highlights should still show some white silver chloride. This is subsequently dissolved away in a fixing bath (No. 16, p. 240).

If the resulting image is not yet soft enough, repeat the whole process from the beginning.

Where a fine grain developer is used for redevelopment, the grain of the negative image is reduced at the same time.

Blue toning for reduced contrast is based on quite a different principle. Just as yellowish light produces harder pictures, so blue light produces softer ones. We can utilise this by converting the black silver image into a blue one. The method also has the advantage that the negative densities let more light through when they are blue.

Immerse the thoroughly washed negatives in the blue toner (No. 38, p. 244) for 10 minutes. Then bathe for 5 minutes in a 3 per cent solution of sodium thiosulphate (hypo), wash well (not less than 30 minutes), and dry.

The blue toned negatives will give softer prints, while needing only short exposures.

TOO THIN AND SOFT NEGATIVES

These were usually underexposed and underdeveloped as well.

Nearly all methods of intensification increase the grain of the negative, since the additional metals or metallic compounds—chromium, mercury, copper, etc.—are deposited on the silver grains.

But where there is no silver image (or only very faint traces of one) nothing can be deposited. Where the shadow regions of the negative consist of clear film or glass, intensification cannot help much. It would only increase the contrast without doing anything about the shadow density. And whatever we achieve by a mere increase in overall density, we can just as well gain by reduced printing exposures.

Modification of too soft negative gradation is therefore of some use only when even ultra-hard bromide paper only gives flat and grey prints. If the negative is grey as well as soft, it may be worth while trying to enlarge it on ultra-hard contact paper which is harder still than the corresponding grade of bromide paper. The printing exposures will, however, be quite considerable.

If that does not get us anywhere, the methods available are: making a duplicate on a hard process film; intensification; or copying by reflected light (dark ground illumination).

MAKING A DUPLICATE

Print the negative either by contact or in the enlarger onto a high contrast film or plate (positive film, process plates, etc.). Develop in a contrast developer to produce a somewhat harder positive transparency. Repeat the process and print the transparency again onto a high contrast negative material to obtain a duplicate negative.

The result will show a considerably steeper gradation than the original. In desperate cases the whole process of making a duplicate via a transparency can be repeated with the new negative, to obtain a still harder result.

Obviously this somewhat involved procedure will also emphasise the grain of the original negative increasingly with each step. To avoid going from one extreme to the other, the process must only be carried far enough to give a reasonably usable negative which is not too grainy. Though we can subdue negative grain by various methods of diffusion (pp. 86-89), the image definition invariably suffers.

It is of course perfectly feasible to make soft duplicates from hard originals by printing onto a soft working material in the same way. There is, however, no real need for it, as we can achieve the same result more simply by reduction (p. 173).

INTENSIFICATION

One of the most reliable intensifiers is chromium (No. 39, p. 244). The increase in graininess is small, and the solutions are easy to use.

Immerse the well washed negative in the intensifier mixture until the image has gone completely orange buff. There must be no blackness left, not even when viewed from the back.

Rinse in water, and immerse in a 2 per cent potassium metabisulphite solution until the yellow stain has gone, and the image is pure buff in colour. Then transfer the negatives to a 1 per cent borax solution. Prolonged immersion in the metabisulphite solution is harmful.

Finally, redevelop in an ordinary negative developer (not a fine grain formula), or even a paper developer (Nos. 1-2, p. 237) until the image is completely black throughout. It is best to leave the negative in the developer for at least 10 minutes before taking it out for the final wash.

Another way of intensifying negatives is to sulphide tone them. In principle, the effect is the exact opposite of reduction by blue toning (p. 173). Here the sulphide image is brown-yellow. While its visual density is only slightly changed, the effective printing density and printing contrast are considerably increased.

The solutions and technique are the same as for sulphide toning for prints (Nos. 41-42, p. 245).

174

COPYING BY DARK-GROUND ILLUMINATION

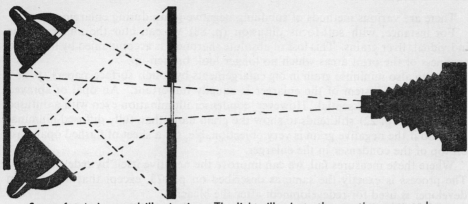

Set-up for dark-ground illumination. The lights illuminate the negative more or less from the side. In this way very thin images will show as a positive, and can be copied. The camera lens is shielded from direct light by a wide frame. The camera must be squarely opposite the centre of the negative to be copied.

A really hopeless case is a grossly underexposed negative.

The only way of doing anything about it is to copy the negative by reflected light in front of a black background. With such very thin negatives an image will show up when light falls on the surface at a certain angle, even though practically nothing may be visible when we look through the film.

We shall therefore illuminate the negative in such a way that we can rephotograph this image. As the image will appear as a positive, rephotographing directly produces a new negative. The required lighting set-up is known as dark ground illumination.

Put the negative in a broad frame with a small aperture in the centre just large enough for the negative. Place two ordinary household lamps so that the light strikes the negative evenly from behind this frame. Then put up a sheet of deep black paper some distance behind the negative (looking from the camera direction) with its centre in the optical axis of the camera lens. The paper must be shaded all round so that no light from the lamps falls on it.

Set up the camera opposite, facing the back of negative. The lens therefore looks through the negative at the absolutely black paper. The light from behind (which is itself shielded from the camera by the wide frame) shines on the negative and lights up those parts where there is a faint silver image. This illuminated image shows sufficient gradation for copying, and will produce quite a good negative on a contrasty process material. At the same time, the clear parts of the original negative without any silver image will still show up as black because of the black background behind.

The effect will be still stronger if we bleach the original negative beforehand in a bleacher (No. 37, p. 244). After drying, the image will be white, and thus even brighter when lit up.

This method only works if the original negative is absolutely free from fog. Any fog present would also catch the light and thus mask all traces of a weak image.

GRAINY NEGATIVES

There are various methods of subduing negative grain during enlarging.

For instance, with soft-focus diffusion (p. 88) we can blur the images of the individual silver grains. This loss of absolute sharpness is accompanied by increased evenness of the print areas which no longer look broken-up.

We can also minimise grain in big enlargements by rough surface papers (p. 28).

The lighting system of the enlarger is equally important. An opal or sprayed lamp is absolutely essential. However, condenser illumination even with a diffused light source (p. 22) still tends to show the grain more than fully diffused illumination. So if the negative grain is very objectionable, try a sheet of flashed opal glass on top of the condenser in the enlarger.

Where these measures fail, we can improve the negative itself by redevelopment. The process is exactly the same as described on p. 173, except that a fine grain developer is used for redevelopment after the bleach.

We must, however, keep one point in mind before deciding on redevelopment. Treatment with a fine grain developer usually makes the negative softer. That means it will subsequently require a harder paper grade. But the harder the paper, the more the negative grain is emphasised. Thus the final print may still be grainy, in spite of fine grain redevelopment.

The success of this method will therefore depend on the character of the negative concerned. The process should not give too soft a negative which would need a much harder paper.

We can also subdue grain with the help of a ground glass plate of the same size as the print. Place such a plate with the matt side up onto the bromide paper during part of the exposure time. The ground glass surface diffuses the rays falling on it, and thus blurs the sharp image of the grains. Naturally, overall sharpness is slightly reduced, too.

By adjusting the relative times of exposure with and without this diffusing plate, we can just make the grain disappear before unsharpness becomes too noticeable.

SCRATCHED NEGATIVES

Making scratches invisible. **I.** Pour a small pool of glycerine on a glass plate and carefully lower the negative onto it. **2.** Put another pool on top followed by a second glass plate. **3.** Squeeze out surplus liquid.

The ways of suppressing grain during enlarging are also useful for minimising the effect of scratches and other damage to the gelatine layer. In other words:

diffused enlarger lighting, soft-focus diffusion during exposure or part of it, and use of the ground glass plate just mentioned.

We can remove scratches in the gelatine layer, particularly if they are in the backing layer, and the image itself is not damaged.

To make a scratch invisible, we must restore the smoothness of the surface which has been broken by the injury. Every scratch in the gelatine is visible only because the light is refracted by its irregular edges. To cut out this refraction, we shall have to create a new continuous surface.

The best method is to embed the negative during enlarging in a medium of more or less the same refractive index as the gelatine. The procedure is the same as that of binding up specimens with Canada balsam to make microscope slides.

For our purpose the negative has to be mounted temporarily only during the exposure. So instead of Canada balsam we use glycerine or carbon tetrachloride.

First pour a few drops of the medium onto a clean glass plate the same size as the negative, lying on a sheet of blotting paper. Arch the film in the middle and carefully bring it into contact with the liquid from the middle outwards. The manipulation is similar to lowering a wet print onto the glazing plate (p. 45). The important point is that no airbells must remain between the glass plate and the film.

Now pour some more liquid over the film, and carefully lay a second similar glass over it. Again take care to avoid air bubbles. The excess liquid oozes out at the edges and is absorbed by the blotting paper.

As glass has nearly the same refractive index as glycerine or carbon tetrachloride, the film becomes a homogeneous mass between the two glasses. All scratches are filled up by the liquid, and become invisible.

After enlarging remove the film from this sandwich. If carbon tetrachloride was used, simply hang the film up to dry. With glycerine as the medium, the film must be washed first.

Another method which is particularly suitable for plate negatives consists of polishing the gelatine layer with jeweller's rouge. The idea again is to smooth down the jagged edges of the scratch.

Mix fine silver polishing powder or jeweller's rouge to a paste with turpentine. Smear a little of this on the negative, and polish until the surface is shiny. By this treatment the scratches which previously were something like microscopic precipices are reduced to gentle valleys, and are therefore hardly apparent.

Instead of smoothing the edges we may also fill in the scratches by a refractive medium. Simply paint in the scratch with a scratch-proofing lacquer by means of a fine brush.

Finally, various solutions can be used as employed in the motion picture industry for restoring used films. These are thin varnishes which on the one hand swell the gelatine layer, and on the other leave traces of varnish in the pores and scratches. The combined result is a new smooth surface to the film. To use such a varnish immerse the negatives in the solution, drain, and hang up to dry. These lacquer and varnish treatments must be applied after spotting (p. 185), but before pencil retouching (p. 197).

NEGATIVE RETOUCHING

Retouching in photography is a necessary evil. There should really be no need for it. Photographs could quite well hold their own unretouched, if only. . . .

Well, first of all, if only working procedure were perfect. But as things are, minor flaws keep cropping up here and there during the various stages of picture making. These are much more easily put right afterwards by touching up than by starting all over again.

Secondly, if only there were no human vanity. But our sitters nearly always want to look more impressive or beautiful than Nature has made them. They prefer a smooth face with noble features to one which could be called at all a "speaking likeness".

While the first case is a matter of rectifying small technical faults, the second means consciously changing the photographic picture.

Strictly speaking the two ways of subsequent picture correction are often distinguished as spotting, and retouching.

HOW TO AVOID IT

Spotting, as the name implies, covers the removal of all the various kinds of disturbing small spots and pinholes in the picture. The best cure is of course prevention by clean working. A few hints on how to cut out spotting afterwards will therefore not be out of place.

Above all, keep dust scrupulously away from the negatives. On enlarging, each speck of dust will form a large white dot or pinhole on the print.

Greasy finger marks and scratches are also avoidable by careful working, which will save subsequent laborious spotting.

The campaign against dust begins with drying the negatives after washing. Don't just take them out of the water and leave them to their own devices. There are always fine suspended particles present in the water, so before drying wash the negatives under the tap by hand. Otherwise these particles will dry into the gelatine.

Obviously the place where the negatives are dried should be free of dust, too. As, however, no room is ever absolutely dust-free, the main aim is to avoid stirring up the dust which is everywhere. Settled dust is harmless. So keep out draughts and don't walk about near drying negatives.

Even dry films may get dusty, though the dust can then be removed. They must therefore be cleaned just before enlarging or printing. But excessive vigour in cleaning may achieve exactly the opposite to the desired result. Vigorous rubbing induces an electric charge on the films and plates, and they then actually attract the dust suspended in the air. Therefore wipe the negatives clean slowly.

After drying, plates and 35 mm. films (which have no gelatine backing layer) may show traces of dried-up drops of water on the back, particularly if the washing water was hard. To remove these, put the negative face down on a clean sheet of paper. Breathe on the back, and polish with a soft piece of chamois leather or a piece of cotton wool. Repeat and continue until further breathing on the back shows no more traces of the deposit.

Negatives just cleaned should not be enlarged straightaway. The electric charge produced by rubbing must be given a chance to disappear, which will take a few minutes. Then put them in the enlarger after careful final dusting. That should be done with dry hands. However dry the hand is, traces of moisture will still cling to it, and these will help to take the dust with them. So wipe over the plates gently with the palm of the hand, or in the case of films pull them slowly through between the second and third fingers.

Even if the negative is now free of dust, the glass plates of the negative carrier—if the carrier has glass plates—are by no means clean yet. Here again, breathe on them and gently polish with a piece of wash leather before putting in the negative. It is always better to be too meticulous than not painstaking enough when dealing with dust.

Handle negatives carefully all the time to avoid injury. Make a habit of only holding them by the edges, and even there only with two fingers.

Finger-prints on the film are easily avoided by careful handling. Moist finger-prints are particularly dangerous. If we notice them immediately, no harm is done, but the negative must straightaway be soaked in water and dried again.

The same applies to water splashes on the gelatine. Once these have dried in, not much can be done. Sometimes, but only rarely, weak ammonia solution may help: soak the negatives for a few hours in water with a few drops of ammonia added, then dry without further washing.

Greasy finger-prints are fairly easily removed by polishing the negative with a piece of cotton wool soaked in carbon tetrachloride or trichloroethylene. Better still, wash the hands before handling negatives!

To preserve them in storage put them into thin translucent envelopes which will best protect them against scratches and other marks.

If they should by mischance nevertheless collect a scratch or two, these can, if not removed, at any rate be subdued (p. 176).

NEGATIVE OR POSITIVE?

After these preventive measures let us turn to the actual corrective methods available. We can divide them into two branches: negative retouching, and positive retouching (p. 203).

The decision as to whether to do the afterwork on the negative or on the print will depend on several considerations.

Firstly, it is easier to add density by retouching than to remove it. So if parts of the picture are to be lightened, we can do this best by darkening the corresponding portions of the negative. On the other hand, small areas to be darker in the final picture are treated directly on the print.

Secondly, certain types of print retouching—such as knifing—give themselves away by leaving marks on the paper surface. Here again it is best to treat the negative instead.

Finally, with something like a dozen prints from the same negative, print retouching is a dozen times more work. This factor by itself may turn the scales decidedly in favour of negative retouching.

EQUIPMENT

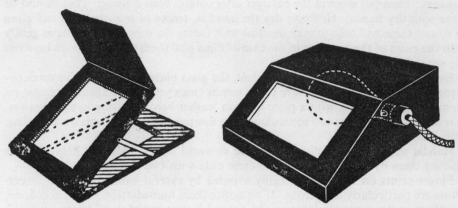

Types of retouching desks. *Left:* A simple retouching desk consists of a frame propped up above a white reflecting surface. Daylight reflected from the surface illuminates the negative in the frame. A screen above the frame keeps out stray light. *Right:* For artificial light an illuminated viewing box can be used with the light source behind a sheet of opal glass.

We have already dealt with some methods of aftertreatment on the negative, such as local reduction (p. 125) and subduing scratches (p. 176). These processes can be carried out without a retouching desk. We shall, however, need one for negative retouching proper.

The aim of the retouching desk is to provide a convenient base on which to work, and which shows the negative by transmitted light. It consists of an inclined frame with a ground glass screen in the centre. The light from the window or other suitable diffused source is reflected by a mirror onto the ground glass from behind and illuminates the negative placed on it. The frame is supported by a suitable stand or by leaning it against a ledge or some books, so that it cannot slide off.

Further materials and accessories are:

Red dye solution (neo-coccin or similar).

Retouching dye (grey).

Opaque medium.

Black water colour.

Sable brushes in various thicknesses.

180

Retouching pencils in at least four grades of hardness.
Retouching knife and stone for sharpening.
Retouching medium (matt varnish).
Stump.
Abrasive paste (turpentine and finely powdered pumice).

ORDER OF PROCEDURE

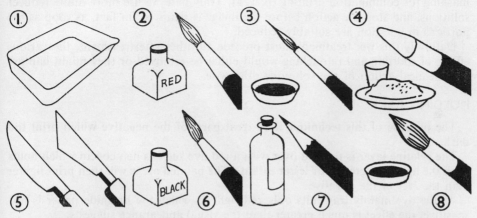

Stages in negative retouching. **I.** Chemical aftertreatment (p. 172), such as intensification and reduction. **2.** Holding back parts of the negative with red dye. **3.** Spotting with black water colour. **4.** Dry reduction with stump and abrasive paste. **5.** Scraping with the knife. **6.** Initial blacking out round the contours with black dye. **7.** Matt varnishing and pencil retouching. **8.** Final blocking out with opaque.

The summary of materials above gives already an indication of the diversity of the individual steps in retouching. These steps cannot, however, be carried out in just any order. So as not to make things unnecessarily difficult or even balk further work, retouching must proceed according to a definite plan.

The sequence of the single stages, whichever are needed, is as follows.

1. Chemical aftertreatment, such as general reduction and intensification, and local reduction (pp. 125 and 172).

2. Holding back parts of the negative with red or grey dye (p. 182). Any mistake here can be removed by washing the negative.

3. Spotting with black water colour or retouching dye (p. 185).

4. Local dry reduction with stump and abrasive paste (p. 187).

5. Knifing (p. 188).

6. Blocking out with dye (p. 183). This is the initial outline only. Final blocking out comes later.

7. Pencil retouching on the matt varnished negative (p. 197).

8. Blocking out with opaque (p. 184). This must come after pencil retouching, as it won't hold the matt varnish. Opaque itself, however, will take on top of the varnish layer.

The matt varnish does not allow any further knifing or spotting.
We shall now take these steps in their order.

CHEMICAL AFTERTREATMENT

The methods of chemical aftertreatment involving the whole negative have already been discussed (pp. 172–174).

Local wet reduction is much the same as mentioned in connection with chemical masking for combination printing (p. 125). Only here we use more dilute reducer solutions, and stop the action before the image is removed; in fact, as soon as the portions in question are suitably reduced.

Naturally this wet treatment must precede all other aftertreatment; the various effects of spotting and retouching would either be removed or they might hamper the chemical action of the solutions otherwise.

HOLDING BACK

The purpose of this technique is to treat parts of the negative which print too dark.

The gelatine layer is painted over with a red dye such as neo-coccin which holds back the light to a greater or lesser extent. The painted areas will then print lighter than the rest of the negative.

As the dye mainly transmits only red light to which the bromide paper is not sensitive, the effect is much greater than the visual appearance suggests.

The red dye can be applied anywhere where detail is still visible in the negative. Painting over empty detailless shadows will produce blind areas in the print.

We shall need two solutions; one dilute, and the other concentrated.

Often the dyes are supplied in the form of highly concentrated solutions. These are diluted to the required strengths.

The former should be just strong enough to leave a faint tint on white paper.

The stronger dye should already produce a definite colour, but nowhere near as strong as, say, red ink.

The art of holding back consists of producing a completely even area of colour on the negative portions concerned. The more dilute the solution, the less danger there is of forming blotches.

So first paint the dilute solution with a suitable sized brush over the gelatine side of the negative. The brush must not be too dry, as the gelatine immediately absorbs the water from it, and is then easily injured by the dry hairs of the brush. On the other hand, an excessively wet brush will leave droplets of dye on the negative surface, and thus produce uneven colour density. For that reason also keep the brush constantly on the move. Stopping on one spot for any time has the same effect as a dye droplet left on the surface; the gelatine underneath quickly absorbs excessive amounts of wet dye, again producing uneven results.

To blend the outlines invisibly into the rest of the negative, the brush should sometimes slightly go over the edges of the area in question, and sometimes stop just a trace short of them. Working on a wet (but blotted) negative will make the dye contours diffuse a little.

When the portion is evenly dyed with the dilute solution, start touching up details with the more concentrated dye.

As the covering power of the dye is apt to be deceptive, it is advisable to make a test print from time to time, letting the negative dry first. The ability to judge the effect by the appearance of the negative will come with some experience.

If the dye was applied too strongly, we can remove it again by soaking the negative in water.

Holding back is not quite so easy with most grey retouching dyes, as we usually cannot completely wash them out again. A trace always remains. Grey dye is fairly popular though, because the effect is more easily judged on the negative.

While the red dye is mainly used to hold back whole areas, the grey dye is more useful to strengthen individual detail.

The procedure with the grey dye is the same as it is with the red one. Start with highly dilute washes, and then go over to the stronger solution.

BLOCKING OUT: WHITE BACKGROUNDS

Blocking out a background. **1.** Paint a thin band with black dye round the outlines of the subject. **2.** Paint out of corners rather than into them (p. 184). **3.** Finally fill in all the area outside the band with opaque.

Sometimes we may have to modify the background of the picture; either because it is too distracting, or because we may want a special effect. The backgrounds which we can produce by hand are pure white, pure black, or neutral grey.

The simplest is a white background. It completely isolates the object in the print.

We produce it by blocking out the negative. All the image parts to be suppressed are painted over with an opaque medium or retouching dye.

The blocked out area does not show any transition in tone. Wherever we apply the blocking-out medium, it completely holds back the light. Wherever it stops, it does so with a sharp border. This may not always look very good. Such sharp borders often appear unphotographic, or are simply unsuitable for the subject. We only have to imagine hair or a fur collar bordering on such a background!

The first step therefore is to create a more or less diffused band around the outline to be preserved. The band should match the local boundaries between subject and background. For this purpose follow the contours on the emulsion side of the negative with a brush charged with black retouching dye. The dye, as opposed to water colour pigment, opaque, or other blocking out media, does not cover completely on the first application, but becomes denser the more often we paint over the same area. Previous applications of dye will not smudge, as the dye actually sinks into the gelatine, and does not form a layer on top of it. It is, however, difficult to wash out.

During painting over do not follow the contour very accurately. At one application of the dye the band may stop a little short of the outline, at the next it might slightly overlap. This helps to soften the transition.

Sharp corners cutting into the image must be painted from the pointed end outwards. Otherwise a small droplet of dye is left where the brush was lifted off the surface.

As we go on the band becomes denser and denser. Finally, when it is sufficiently opaque, wash out the inside edge with a large brush and plenty of water. The brush must always be moved from the edge into the painted area, not the other way round. Continue this washing out until the contours are sufficiently softened. If the dye has become too thin in places, paint more on.

When dry, completely block out the rest of the negative with opaque water colour pigment or opaque medium. Leave about $\frac{1}{8}$ in. of the original band uncovered so that the blocking out medium does not interfere with subsequent corrections.

If film negatives are used it is in any case advisable to paint the initial outline band on the back of the film (except with miniature films and certain sheet films which have no gelatine backing). Then finish complete blocking out on the emulsion side. This prevents any soiling or smudging during final corrections.

BLACK BACKGROUNDS

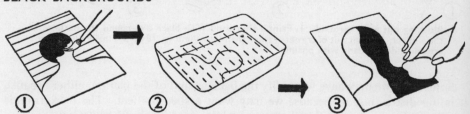

Bleaching out a background. **1.** Paint over the image parts which are to remain on the negative, with asphalt varnish (p. 191). **2.** Treat the negative in Farmer's reducer. **3.** Clean off the protective asphalt varnish layer with cotton wool soaked in petrol.

There are several ways of producing an empty black background.

One is local reduction (p. 125) where the unwanted negative parts are reduced with *Farmer's* reducer. We can do this either by painting directly on the negative (p. 126) with a fine brush, or by protecting the required image areas with asphalt varnish (p. 127) and bathing the negative in the reducer which removes the rest of the image. The latter method also gives very abrupt and sharp outlines.

Another way is again blocking out; this time, however, not on the negative, but on a positive transparency made from it. First paint the transparency round the outlines of the subject with retouching dye (p. 186), and then completely block out the unwanted image with blocking out medium. After drying simply contact print the transparency to make a new negative with a clear background which will print deep black in the final picture.

184

GREY BACKGROUNDS

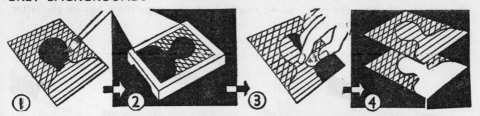

How to make a grey background. **I.** Block out all image parts required on the negative with opaque. **2.** Make a contact transparency. **3.** Remove the opaque from the negative. **4.** Bind the negative and transparency together in register and enlarge as one.

By clever combination of blocking out (p. 183) and negative-positive printing (p. 119) we can produce an even, neutral grey background.

On the negative block out the parts of the subject to be retained with ordinary opaque medium (*not* retouching dye).

When dry, make a positive transparency by contact printing. This transparency should be soft and fairly thin.

Then soak the negative in water until the opaque pigment is completely washed off. Wiping over the surface with the finger tips will help to remove the last traces of pigment.

Dry the negative again, and mount it face to face with the transparency. Shift the two to and fro until the images are in exact register. The positive detail in the background of the transparency then masks the detail of the negative image, producing a uniform grey. The subject itself, however, consists only of the negative image, since the corresponding area of the transparency is clear.

The hard contours produced by the opaque pigment are not too disturbing here. The outlines of the subject are never in such strong contrast to the background as when the latter is black or white. Instead, they are merely transitions between lighter and darker grey.

Water colour opaque and not retouching dye is used in this case because we have to remove the blocking out again afterwards. And the opaque medium washes off easily, while the dye does not (p. 186).

If, however, we want particularly soft outlines as obtained by dye painting (p. 184), preliminary tests must be made with the dye. Not every black or grey dye can be removed completely even after prolonged soaking (p. 185). Should the tests not be satisfactory, use strong neo-coccin in the same way as the black dye.

SPOTTING NEGATIVES

Despite most careful work, dust particles will settle on the film or plate in the camera. These produce tiny clear spots or pinholes. Small particles of gelatine emulsion which have chipped off and settled on the negative surface during development, will have the same effect. Finally, certain bacteria can get onto the negative during washing or drying, and literally eat away small spots of gelatine down to the film or glass base.

185

Whatever their cause, these pinholes must be removed. This is better done on the negative than on the print, as we would have to scrape them out on the latter, leaving a damaged print surface.

THE BRUSH

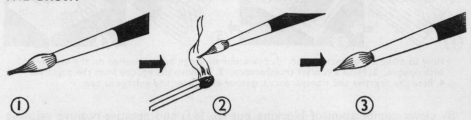

Preparing the spotting brush. I. Moisten the brush and draw the hairs to a point as far as possible. 2. Quickly pass the point through a flame, to burn off protruding hairs and leave a sharp point 3.

For spotting we shall need a sable brush. It should have a really fine point without any single hairs sticking out. These would bend over sideways when they come into contact with the negative surface, and so no longer produce round spots, but misshapen triangles.

Therefore burn off protruding hairs first. Moisten the brush with water and quickly draw it through the flame of a burning match. This leaves the bulk of the hairs untouched and only attacks single hairs sticking out which do not adhere closely to the rest.

DYE AND PIGMENT MEDIA

There are two kinds of spotting media—dye, and pigment.

The former is a solution which dyes the gelatine and is difficult to wash out (p. 185). When applied, the dye itself sinks into the gelatine, and leaves no trace on the surface. As it is transparent, it blends well with the image and does not become conspicuous even at high degrees of enlargement. But it can be used only where there is a gelatine layer it can dye. By itself the dye has practically no covering power.

Water colour pigment, opaque, and other pigment media are not solutions but suspensions of finely powdered pigment. They are body colours and form a layer of pigment on the surface. Combined with a suitable binding medium they can be applied anywhere, even on clear film or glass. At high degrees of enlargement they show the granular structure of the individual pigment grains. They have great covering power, and are therefore more suitable for complete blocking out. The surface film so formed is easily washed off.

There is a difference between spots caused by dust, where the gelatine underneath is intact, and spots which are actual holes in the gelatine layer.

The former can be removed by careful spotting with a negative dye; the latter need filling in with water colour or pigment spotting medium.

186

APPLYING THE COLOUR

For the actual job take up only very little dye with the brush. It must be as dry as possible, so that it will only just give off the solution when brought into contact with the surface. With too much dye, dark edges round the spot are unavoidable. These look like the edge of a crater, and make the fault worse instead of better.

As the grey retouching dye sinks into the gelatine, apply it by dabbing the pin-hole lightly with very dilute dye until the spot is dense enough.

With water colour pigment and similar media, however, we must fill in the spot by one application, as successive dabbing will smudge the pigment already there. Water colour pigment with a little gum mixed in is the only medium which can be used to fill in holes in the gelatine, as the glass or film underneath will not take the dye.

Where the spots to be filled in are large, cover them—in the case of water colour pigments—by putting many dots side by side until the required visual density is built up. With dye solution we can deal even with large spots by simply painting repeatedly over the whole spot.

In either case—and this applies particularly to the beginner with little experience—it is better to put on too much colour than too little. Even if the pin-holes are covered so strongly that they print white, we can quite easily spot them out on the print. But if they are too light on the negative, the print must be scraped (p. 205).

We have now reached the last of the wet and semi-wet retouching stages. They must all precede either dry reduction or pencil retouching. The negative may need soaking to remove mistakes in spotting or holding back, and it is best to get that over as soon as possible. Apart from the fact that such soaking may affect some of the dry work, retouching dyes do not take too well on either the roughened up surface after dry reducing and scraping, or on the varnished surface for pencil retouching.

Final blocking out of large areas with opaque can, however, be carried out even after pencil retouching on the varnish or on the back of the negative.

DRY REDUCTION

Tools for dry reduction with abrasive. *Left:* Various types of stumps may be used to apply the reducing paste. *Centre:* Large areas are treated with a thick stump. *Right:* For small areas (e.g. halation rings) a pointed stump is best.

Just as parts of the negative which print too dark can be held back with red dye, so too dense portions can be made lighter by local reduction. We have already dealt with the wet methods of chemical reduction (pp. 172, 173, 174). Dry or physical reduction is, however, preferable when only small negative areas need treatment.

Stir finely ground and sifted pumice powder or Kieselguhr into a mixture of equal parts of turpentine and petrol (or carbon tetrachloride) to produce a thin paste. Polish a little of this over the negative area to be reduced by means of a leather or paper stump. The process is really a very gentle grinding down of the surface. Only the abrasive is so fine that it leaves no visible scars.

Physical reduction needs patience. It takes several minutes before the negative area becomes visibly lighter. Continue polishing until the desired effect is obtained. But it is not advisable to speed up the process by extra pressure while polishing, as this easily leads to unevenness. Renew the abrasive paste frequently.

Finally, to clean the negative remove all surplus paste and rub the rest well into the whole negative with a fresh piece of cotton wool until no trace is visible.

To reduce areas with sharp outlines in this way, a mask is useful. Cut this out of old film so as to cover the image except for the parts to be reduced, and polish the negative as before.

KNIFING

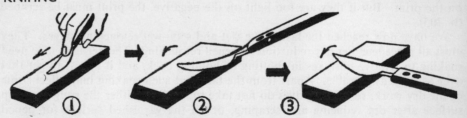

Sharpening a retouching knife. I. Move the knife to and fro on the stone, pressing the edge down with the finger. 2. At the same time swing the blade with a slight circular movement. 3. Repeat for stropping.

This technique of brightening up small image details is one of the most difficult methods of retouching. It requires practice as well as skill.

Any attempt to scrape a negative with a knife is doomed to failure if the knife is not good enough. It must be really sharp, and kept sharp all the time.

There are two kinds of stone for sharpening, whetstones and oilstones. The former resharpen the knife quicker, while the latter give the finest and smoothest edge and are used for the final polish. For sharpening on a whetstone we must have a few drops of water on the stone; on an oilstone a few drops of oil. We can speed up the work by using paraffin instead of oil.

To sharpen, lay the blade on the moistened stone and cover with the index finger almost up to the knife edge. While the finger presses the blade in close contact with the stone, sharpen the bottom side by moving it to and fro. Swing the hand slightly from the wrist to give the edge its necessary slight curvature. Without this wrist movement the cutting edge would be dead straight.

After treating one side of the knife turn it over and sharpen the other side in

HOLDING BACK. Disturbing or unnecessary parts in a picture can be subdued by painting over the corresponding areas in the negative with red dye (p. 182). *Left*: Straight print. *Above*: Subject made to stand out by holding back the background.

BLOCKING OUT. White back-
grounds are obtained by completely
painting out the background in the
negative (p. 183). *Left:* Print from
original negative. *Right:* Print from
partially blocked-out negative. *Above:*
Finished result.

190

BLACK BACKGROUNDS. One way of producing them is to paint a protective varnish over the subject, and then dissolve away the rest of the image in Farmer's reducer (p. 184). *Left:* Straight print. *Right:* Negative with important parts of image protected by varnish. *Above:* Print from reduced negative.

GREY BACKGROUNDS. Here the technique is a combination of the methods for black backgrounds and for blocking out (p. 185). *Left:* Original print. *Right:* Intermediate with shape of figure held back through blocking out. *Above:* Print from the negative pair with grey background.

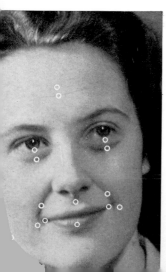

RETOUCHING NEGATIVES (p. 198).
Left: Print from original negative indicating the portions that need treatment. These are mainly wrinkles and disturbing shadows around the eye, nose, mouth, and neck. *Above:* Print from retouched negative.

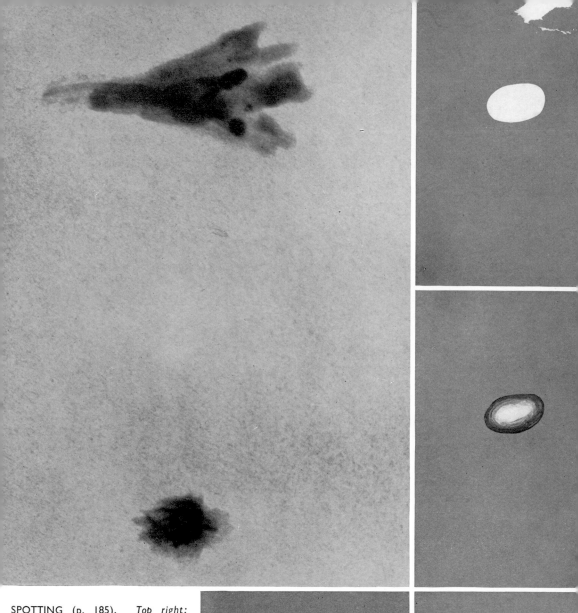

SPOTTING (p. 185).   *Top right:*
Magnified picture of a pinhole.
Centre right: Working on one spot
for too long swells the gelatine. The
spotting colour then settles in a rim
round the pinhole (p. 187).   *Bottom
right:* With some practice the pinhole
can be made quite invisible.   *Bottom
left:* It is better to apply too much
colour than too little.   If the pinhole
is completely filled in, it can still be
spotted in the print.   *Above left:* A
truly round spot is only possible with
a very pointed brush (*bottom*). A bad
point with stray hairs will produce an
irregular blotch (*top*).

194

PHYSICAL REDUCTION. *Left:* Print from original negative with diffused halo spots from the lamps. *Above:* Print from negative after reduction of halo areas by rubbing over them with a pumice paste or similar fine abrasive (p. 187).

195

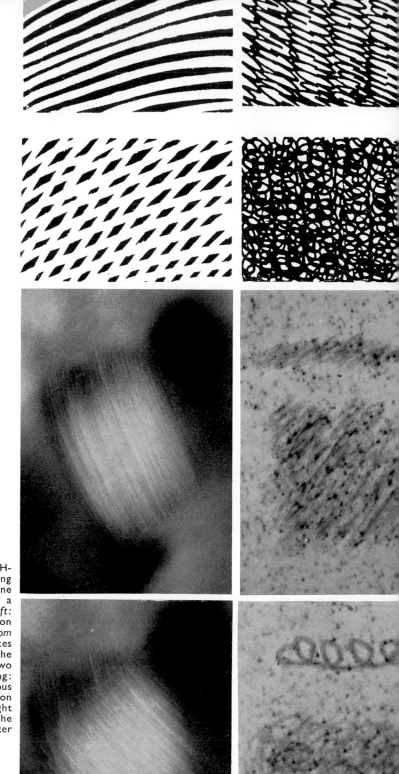

**KNIFING AND PENCIL RETOUCH-
ING** *Top left:* The strokes in knifing
are first made side by side in one
direction, and then overlaid by a
second set at an angle. *Centre left:*
First set of strokes on knifed section
of negative highly magnified. *Bottom
left:* When the second set of strokes
is superimposed, the texture of the
area is quite even. *Top right:* Two
types of pencil strokes for retouching:
short line shading, and continuous
scrolls. *Centre right:* Enlarged portion
of negative retouched with straight
pencil strokes. *Bottom right:* The
continuous scrolls blend much better
with the image grain (p. 199).

the same manner. The finger must always press on the blade only when moving forward against the stone (as if cutting it). Slacken the pressure going back.

Sharpening of both sides is followed by stropping. This is really a refined sharpening movement, done with less pressure, and the knife lying a little less flat on the stone. Otherwise the procedure is exactly the same.

The last stroke in stropping should always be on the side opposite to the direction of movement followed for scraping. As the fingers usually scrape from right to left, the side away from us (with the blade held ready for work) will be the one to receive the last stropping.

The more often we stroke the edge successively on this side, the keener it will become. The test for absolute sharpness is to place the edge on the nail of the finger sloping downwards. The knife must not slide off, but should feel as if it were sticking to the nail.

This test does not tell, though, whether the edge is also smooth. Only trying it out on an old negative will show. If the knife scrapes with uneven strokes, indicating a jagged edge, strop the blade again.

Finally smooth the edge on chamois leather or smooth cardboard, like a barber smoothes his razor.

Start knifing on the gelatine layer, by making parallel strokes, one after another, side by side. After working over the area change the direction of the strokes.

For the second lot make the strokes at an acute angle to the first ones. The third time round make them in a different direction again. This hides the direction of the strokes on the surface, and also helps them to blend together. The more sets of lines are superimposed, the better.

Just that is the difficult part. The heavy handed beginner usually removes so much of the gelatine layer the first time, that a second application is impossible.

One test of scraping skill consists of working over a larger area (say about $\frac{1}{2}$ in. square), so that no detail of the lines is visible. It is therefore worth while to practise on a useless negative to acquire the knack of it.

The knife must be placed vertically on the surface and should remove a very thin chip at a time without making a sound. A fine chirping noise already indicates that the blade is vibrating and not absolutely sharp.

PENCIL RETOUCHING

How to hold a retouching pencil. *Left:* Incorrect way; the hand is much too cramped. *Right:* Correct way; the hand is relaxed and can exercise the maximum control over placing and pressure of the pencil strokes.

What is commonly known as retouching proper is really almost exclusively pencil work on the negative.

Here we are mainly concerned with touching up portraits with a view to beautifying the sitters and make them look younger. Advancing age leaves its marks on every face. The youthfully smooth features become sharper; where the skin was evenly stretched before, wrinkles begin to appear. Nobody likes to notice wrinkles and sharpened features on his or her own face, until the photograph suddenly shows them to be there. Then the reaction is, "away with it!" So here pencil retouching comes in.

The many halftones and details on a negative of a human face are most easily mastered with the pencil because all the outlines and transitions can effectively be reproduced in terms of a pencil drawing.

Primarily it is the wrinkles which need attention. They show up in the negative as light lines under the eyes, along the sides of the nose down to the corners of the mouth, and on the neck. We can remove them quite well with a little skill by shading over them with the pencil.

As the gelatine surface will not take pencil work, we must first rub a retouching medium or matt varnish over it. This is usually a resin solution (No. **48**, p. 246). On drying it leaves a matt surface which will hold the pencil work.

Rub a drop or two of the varnish with a soft cotton rag over the gelatine surface of the negative, which absorbs it straightaway. Apply only very little; any excess not absorbed by the surface remains there as a tacky layer on the negative and soils it. Therefore polish this off thoroughly, and leave the negative to dry for about 15 minutes.

There are sheet films with the back specially matted for retouching. These will not need any varnish, we can work directly on the matted surface with the pencil.

For retouching we shall need pencils of several degrees of hardness. Soft pencils will give greater density, while light shading is produced with the harder ones. Usually a set of 4H, 2H, HB, and 2B pencils will be sufficient. The harder the pencil, the less visible will be the retouched area, as it consists of a larger number of fine lines superimposed on each other.

There is a definite limit to the density we can produce. While the density increases at first, it decreases again after going over the same spot for the sixth or seventh time. The pencil point begins to push the varnish layer aside until there is no more varnish underneath to take the pencil work. At the same time the spot is polished by the pencil until it will take no more. The thicker the varnish layer, the sooner this will happen.

Always start work with the hardest pencil. If the first stroke shows that the required density can be built up by about four or five applications, carry on. If not, try the next softer pencil.

The point of pencil retouching is always to match the tone of the treated portion exactly with the surrounding area, so as to blend in properly.

To make the detail of the pencil work disappear as far as possible, the pencil must be absolutely sharp, so resharpen it frequently on fine emery paper. Keep the strokes as small as possible.

Some retouchers work over the area with small straight, and almost parallel lines. The result will, however, be less visible by drawing tiny scrolls (p. 196).

198

They tend to imitate and blend into the negative grain, and negatives retouched in this way can be enlarged to a greater degree.

Failures in pencil retouching are due to excessively thick varnish coating, use of blunt pencils of the wrong hardness, coarse and too long strokes, and too heavy pressure on the pencil.

Unsuccessful pencil work can be removed with a piece of cotton wool soaked in petrol or carbon tetrachloride which washes off the varnish, pencil work, and all. Sometimes, however, such negatives cannot be retouched again because the portions to be treated were polished completely smooth by excessive pencil pressure the first time.

RETOUCHING MINIATURE NEGATIVES

Where small negatives are concerned it is even more important to prevent faults which will need touching up later on. This applies particularly to pinholes; the necessarily high degree of enlargement of the negative will make any such flaws very obvious. And however finely we spot them out, they will still be visible. With miniature negatives therefore spotting on the negative is almost out of the question.

Apart from that, however, we can apply most retouching methods described quite well to miniature negatives, provided that the work is of microscopic fineness. Skill is the first requirement.

Further, we shall need a suitable magnifying glass. To leave both hands free, this is best mounted in some way in front of the retouching desk. Special magnifiers fixed in an adjustable stand are particularly suitable. Still better is a watchmaker's magnifier used on the eye. This gives a greatly magnified view, but the eye must be brought right up to the negative.

Pencil retouching on a miniature portrait should not present any special difficulties. We can assume that the image of the head will be about $\frac{1}{2}$ in. high, and that is already large enough to work on individual features. Considering that the glass may magnify about two or three times, with a light touch the difference as compared with retouching a $2\frac{1}{4} \times 3\frac{1}{4}$ in. negative will not be too great.

Similarly holding back (p. 182) with red dye is quite practicable. The dye has no grain structure, and with a sufficiently fine brush even small negative areas can be treated without trouble.

One thing to avoid when working close to the negative, is breathing on it. This may make it moist and easily damaged. So keep the mouth shut!

To protect the emulsion layer against finger marks, stick a triangular card onto a piece of wash leather and use it as support for the hand, so that the wash leather is in contact with the negative.

199

An unsuccessful paper print need not be thrown away and repeated every time. In many cases, admittedly, attempts at aftertreatment waste more time than the print is worth. Quite frequently, however, even finished prints can be improved afterwards. Specially with large prints we shall think twice before discarding them. Sometimes a print may even be slightly overprinted on purpose, with a view to planned aftertreatment, to get the very best final result out of it.

CLEARING THE HIGHLIGHTS

Slight overexposure during enlarging, as well as diffusion of the rays forming the image, may lead to some veiling of the extreme highlights.

We can remove this greyness with *Farmer's* reducer. By this treatment the picture gains in luminosity and plasticity. In addition *Farmer's* reducer attacks the lighter portions of the image most, thus increasing the tone differentiation in the highlights.

To clear the prints immerse them after washing—or even after drying and re-soaking—in *Farmer's* reducer. The formula is the same as No. 35 on p. 243, but diluted 1 part with 5 parts of water to slow down the action. Clearing is still comparatively rapid, so stop the treatment a little too soon, as the reducer is still slightly active during subsequent washing.

If reduction goes on too long, the whole print becomes lighter. The image colour becomes unpleasant, for *Farmer's* reducer leaves a greenish black tinge on the black silver. This tinge does not appear while the action is still confined to the extreme highlights only.

To lighten the whole print (if it was overexposed and perhaps overdeveloped as well), reduce it in permanganate which does not affect the image colour. Here, too, use the formula (No. 36, p. 244) diluted, but a dilution of 1 part with 2 parts of water will be sufficient. The reducer works slowly anyway, and its action is easily controlled.

REMOVING YELLOW FOG

Warm developer or prolonged development times lead to very saturated black tones, but forced development often produces yellow stains or an overall yellow fog. This consists of finely divided colloidal silver which is deposited on the white paper base, often in irregular patches.

We may remove this yellow fog afterwards by treating the prints in a thiocarbro-mide clearing bath (No. 40, p. 244).

Immerse the prints in the solution for 5–8 minutes. As soon as the stain has gone, wash in the usual way for 30 minutes. Longer immersion reduces the overall density.

These yellow stains will usually also disappear during sulphide toning.

SULPHIDE TONING

Among the many processes for modifying the colour of the picture by after-treatment sulphide toning holds a special place. For apart from the almost universal black, brown is the most popular image colour.

Sulphide toning for brown tones also has the advantage that the results are really permanent, which is not the case with many other colour toning methods.

Prints for toning should have full black tones, and must have been fully developed (p. 39). Underdeveloped prints give unpleasant yellowish browns.

Immerse the prints in a suitable bleaching bath (No. **41**, p. 245) and move them about until all blackness has disappeared and the image itself is visible only as a yellow-brown trace. Then wash until the gelatine layer is completely free of the yellow-green colour of the bleaching bath. In this condition the pictures must be kept away from any trace of fixing solution, for this would dissolve away the whole image.

After the wash tone the prints in a thiocarbromide darkener (No. **42**, p. 245). The image gradually goes through yellow and reddish brown to a sepia brown tone. Then wash again and dry.

This process converts the silver image into one of silver sulphide, hence the name "sulphide toning". The older methods originally used sodium sulphide solutions for darkening, but those have a very unpleasant smell and make a well ventilated room necessary for working. Also, the hydrogen sulphide gas formed during toning with sodium sulphide is very harmful to all sensitive materials. Toning with sodium sulphide therefore had to be carried out well away from rooms where sensitive materials were stored.

Alternatively, we can use a selenium toner (No. 43, p. 245) which will give more reddish tones. The prints are not bleached, but simply immersed in the toner until the required image colour is reached. The longer the immersion, the warmer the tone.

GOLD TONING

Apart from the results of sulphide toning, only gold toned images are more permanent than the original.

Gold toning gives very fine blue-black or red images. It also has the advantage that it will greatly improve poor image colours due to exhausted developer or solutions containing too much potassium bromide.

Immerse the print in the toner until the desired tone is reached (No. **44**, p. 245), then rinse and leave for a few minutes in a 5 per cent hypo solution. Finally wash and dry as usual.

201

Ordinary black prints slowly turn deep steel blue in the toning bath. The longer the time of immersion, the bluer the result.

Warm tone prints on chlorobromide papers will give slightly warmer blue-blacks.

Greenish prints developed in an exhausted developer will lose their unpleasant olive-green tinge and turn greenish black.

On sulphide toned prints (p. 201) treatment in the gold bath will produce brownish red to chalk red colours.

OTHER TONING METHODS

Besides the toning processes already mentioned, our possibilities for producing coloured images are still very great.

At one time prints toned to all colours imaginable were highly popular. The glaring red, green, blue, and other colours produced by the better known metal toners are however not always pleasant, nor are the images very permanent. A further disadvantage is that the image is usually opaque. These toning methods are becoming more and more obsolete. An example is the blue toner (p. 244) which we have used to decrease the printing contrast of negatives (p. 173).

A more modern method is to produce coloured images by direct development (p. 84). We can easily apply this process to finished prints by bleaching them in a ferricyanide-bromide bleaching bath (No. **41**, p. 245) and redeveloping in the colour developer (No. **7**, p. 239). This produces brilliant and transparent dye images.

Similarly we may also use the methods of chemical colouring (p. 221). We can tone the whole picture by bleaching it in a mordanting bleach (No. **45**, p. 245) and then immersing it in a suitable dye bath (No. **46**, p. 245).

The methods for removing flaws or spots, and for afterwork to improve parts of the print will depend on the paper surface.

Glossy prints can only be treated with glossy water colour paints or with dye.

Semi-matt surfaces can be retouched with ordinary water colour pigment, or with retouching crayons (oil crayons) as well as by oil reinforcement.

Matt prints can in addition be treated with chalks. Knifing which is occasionally used to lighten print parts and to remove black spots, is really invisible only on matt prints.

The different methods of positive retouching, in their order of application, are:
1. Spotting with water colour (below).
2. Crayon work (p. 204).
3. Chalk treatment (p. 204).
4. Oil reinforcement (p. 205).
5. Knifing (p. 205).

SPOTTING

White pinholes due to dust are removed by carefully dabbing them with spotting colour. The colour used should have the same tone and the same gloss as the print.

For matt prints use black water colour pigment; mixing a suitable brown tone for sulphide toned prints. If the surface is semi-matt add a little gum to the water colour so that it dries with a slight sheen.

Glossy prints must be treated with high gloss paints, also with gum added. Alternatively they can be touched up with dye.

The working procedure with paint and brush looks very easy, but gives the beginner a lot of trouble. The secret lies in the right moistness of the brush. If this is too wet, dark edges are formed around a lighter central spot. If the brush is too dry, it yields colour only reluctantly and often produces too dark spots.

A good way of working is as follows.

Dip the brush in water and wipe it against the edge of the bowl so that it contains only as much water as its hairs can comfortably hold. Then with the whole brush take up some water colour from a palette, and brush onto a piece of paper; a spoiled print is ideal. Pull the brush over the surface away from the point, and at the same time rotate it slightly. In this way the brush gives off pigment, and at the same time forms a good point.

When the colour in the brush seems dilute enough, we can start spotting. Begin with pinholes in the densest parts. The colour should be slightly lighter than needed so that the right tone can be built up accurately by dabbing the spot several times. But do not dab too much, or the brush will smudge any colour already there.

During spotting the paint becomes more dilute and thus lighter. So proceed to the progressively lighter parts until the brush almost ceases to deliver any paint at all. Then take up fresh paint and start again in the denser areas.

Taking too little paint on the tip of the brush only wastes a lot of time, for we shall have to recharge the brush all the time. For the same reason avoid too small brushes, because they hold very little colour.

To treat larger spots, the brush must only just be moist. The gelatine swells if there is too much water present, and repels the colour which then settles in a rim around the spot.

Dyes are an exception; they remain irremovably where they are applied (p. 186). We can therefore use them to paint over whole areas to deepen grey shadows.

CRAYON WORK

If we use an ordinary pencil for positive retouching the treated areas become apparent by the shiny graphite layer. This does not happen with the special print retouching crayons. These are black oil crayons, and their sheen corresponds to that of semi-matt paper surfaces. Crayon work is easily smudged, though.

Use positive retouching crayons to make minor adjustments to the image itself. While spots are removed with spotting medium, uneven detail is more effectively toned down with the crayon.

Crayon work is most successful on fine grained or "Royal" type surfaces, because the surface grain diffuses and hides the individual crayon strokes.

As in the case of negative retouching with pencils (p. 197), it is a mistake to try to obtain too much density with too hard a crayon.

In any case retouching crayons should only be used for limited correction, as for instance strengthening an outline or toning down a catchlight.

CHALK WORK

The most suitable medium for working on large areas is artist's chalk.

Powder a little of these black or white chalks and rub into the print surface. White chalk uniformly lightens image areas, black chalk intensifies the blackness of individual portions.

If the areas to be treated are large, apply the chalk with a wash leather; for smaller parts a stump is more useful. It does not matter if parts within a larger area so treated are supposed to remain clear. The chalk is simply removed in those places with a plastic rubber (very soft artist's eraser as used for charcoal drawings).

The outlines of chalk work are always soft. To follow definite contours cut a mask out of tracing paper or cellophane and lay it over the parts to be protected. Then apply the chalk, starting on top of the mask, and rub or wipe into the print.

As the chalk is completely matt, it is only suitable for matt papers.

Prints to be treated with chalk must not have been knifed as yet. Any damaged spots in the gelatine surface hold the chalk particularly well, and become visible.

OIL REINFORCEMENT

As an alternative to chalk, areas can be strengthened by oil reinforcement.

This again must be done before knifing; partly because, like chalk, it shows up more in the knifed spots, and partly because if the gelatine layer is excessively damaged the oil may penetrate to the paper underneath and produce greasy spots.

Mix equal parts of Copaiba balsam, turpentine, and pure raw linseed oil, and add a little black oil paint. Rub the mixture over the print surface—particularly the shadow areas—with a soft flannel rag. Then, with a second clean rag remove the pigment from the lighter portions and highlights which must remain completely clear. Let the print dry for a few days in a dust-free atmosphere.

In case of difficulty in removing the excess colour from the print surface, moisten the clean rag with a few drops of turpentine.

KNIFING

Any attack on the print surface will be the more visible, the shinier the surface. If there are only small black dots to be removed, the slight surface injury is, however, preferable to the more obvious black dots. Knife work is only apparent when looking obliquely onto the surface, anyway.

Work with the retouching knife in the same way as when removing a spot of ink from our note paper. Carefully scrape off the surface without pressure until the density underneath is sufficiently reduced.

The beginner is usually much too impatient and scrapes the surface off in a few strokes right down to the paper base. This only makes things worse. The fault often lies with a blunt knife; keep it sharp all the time (p. 188).

Where we have gone too far with the scraping we can darken the spots again by very careful retouching with water colour.

The scraped portions are usually invisible on matt paper. On semi-matt or glossy surfaces the original gloss is restored as follows.

Put a drop of pale gum arabic solution on a glass plate. With a wet brush take off just so much that the gum still flows smoothly from the brush. Then paint over the scraped areas with the gum solution, carefully following the outlines of the knife work. If the surface is not glossy enough the first time, repeat when dry.

Where there are only minor scraped spots, waxing or varnishing the surface (see below) will also help a lot.

WAXING AND VARNISHING PRINTS

While wet prints may look satisfactory in both their tone range and depth of shadows, their quality is greatly reduced once they have dried. They may look dull and flat; the image has "sunk in". Only glossy papers are completely free from this effect, and dead matt ones suffer from it most.

If we subsequently give the surface a sheen, much of the original quality returns.

Shadows become deeper, detail more distinct, and the whole print brightens up and becomes crisper. The methods of achieving this are waxing and varnishing.

The former is analogous to polishing a floor, the latter to varnishing furniture.

For waxing the prints are rubbed over with a special paste containing a gloss resin (No. **49**, p. 246).

Take a little of the paste on a flannel rag and rub over the print until the surface has acquired a definite sheen. Irregularities in the surface, whether from water colour paint, or from knifing, usually disappear.

Prints to be waxed must not carry any crayon or chalk work on the surface; obviously this would be wiped off or at least smudged.

We shall obtain a higher gloss by varnishing the prints (No. **50**, p. 246).

There are various print lacquers and varnishes on the market; depending on their composition, they produce a more or less glossy coating. They can be poured over the print lying flat, or they can be painted on with a brush, or even sprayed on. The last method gives a more even covering (below).

Of the many commercially available print varnishes some have the unfortunate drawback that they contain linseed or other oil. If the print has been scraped, the oil may easily penetrate through to the paper base, and leave a dark greasy spot.

Pour the varnish over the print, and drain off the excess by one corner. Drying takes about 24 hours.

Diluted with an equal volume of petrol, most varnishes can also be painted on the print with a brush, though this may produce an uneven coating.

SPRAY VARNISH

The brilliance of a print can be restored to some extent even with ordinary Zapon varnish. The effect is not very apparent though, because Zapon varnish by itself gives only a semi-gloss. The varnish is diluted with at least an equal part of acetone, and can then be sprayed on the print with an ordinary spray as used to "fix" charcoal or chalk drawings.

Do the spraying in the open air, as the acetone vapour tends to irritate the throat. It is also inflammable.

Pin the print to a drawing board, and stand it up slanting against a wall or on an easel. If spraying requires too much effort, the varnish is still too thick.

Stop spraying immediately the print shows a uniform sheen. Excessive spraying would cause the drops to flow together and run down the print.

A second coat can be applied when the first one is dry (which takes a few minutes), and if necessary a third one later on.

By adding a glossy resin to the Zapon varnish we can considerably enhance the effect. Such artificial resins are used in the varnish industry to make cellulose lacquers more shiny. There are many kinds; for our purpose the palest (they are all more or less yellowish brown in colour) is best.

Dissolve 1 part of this resin in 10 parts of acetone with 10 to 20 per cent amyl acetate added if it does not dissolve easily. Then use this to dilute the varnish.

Instead of the spray an air brush worked by compressed carbon dioxide or by an air compressor can be used.

206

AIR BRUSHING

This technique goes beyond the limits of normal print improvement. At the same time it can only be carried out with special apparatus.

The purpose of air brushing is to obtain a perfect original for reproduction. By going over the print with an air brush, the photographic character of it will be preserved and yet the subject glamourised in appearance, conveying an impression of perfectness or precision often lacking in the straight photograph.

With industrial photographs which most frequently need air brushing the trouble above all is the background; we can rarely bring a heavy engine into the studio or even move it out of its often far too busy surroundings. If the print is to be air brushed, the setting does not matter in the least, we can produce any desired background on the print. And if the engine is to stand on a tiled floor, then we can add a tiled floor without making the afterwork obvious.

As the picture is considerably changed by air brush work, the print itself obviously no longer looks like a genuine straight photograph. It only regains its truly photographic character as a copy or reproduction. Air brush work is therefore almost out of question where we want to use the original print as the final picture. Nevertheless a certain amount of air brushing is possible even on the final print. For instance the sky of a landscape can be lightly sprayed over with dilute Indian ink to give it tone without the spraying becoming very visible.

APPARATUS

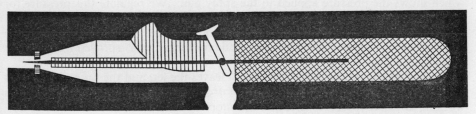

Construction of an air brush. The compressed air flows out through a small needle valve at the tip of the brush controlled by the finger lever. The air stream carries tiny droplets of paint from the reservoir with it.

For air brush work we need a spray gun, liquid carbon dioxide or other compressed gas in cylinders, or an air compressor, and paints.

The spray gun works on the same principle as a scent spray or atomiser. In the latter the scent is sprayed by pressure in fine droplets through a nozzle or jet. In the air brush the paint is similarly blown out by compressed air.

This is achieved by an accurately ground fine needle which at the same time is an air valve. We fill the reservoir of the apparatus with dilute paint solution, and connect it through a pipeline to a compressed air supply to blow out the paint. That happens when we open the valve by pressing a small lever. The needle which closes a fine jet is pulled back, and the compressed air can escape. On the way it carries some paint solution with it. As the mixture of air and paint streams out, the latter is dragged off the point of the needle in tiny droplets.

Obviously the finer the needle, the smaller the droplets will be. This also explains why an air brush is comparatively expensive: namely, because of the great precision and therefore high cost of the needle required. The air brush must accordingly be handled very carefully.

THE PRESSURE SUPPLY

The spray gun only works when we supply compressed air to it. Here the choice lies between cylinders of compressed liquid gases (air, carbon dioxide, nitrogen, etc.), or a means of producing pressure, such as a pump or electric air compressor.

Pressure pumps are very cheap in use. They involve pumping up a pressure reservoir by hand, much like pumping up a rubber tyre. Anybody who has ever done that will know that it takes quite an amount of physical effort; so much so that one's hands may tremble afterwards. But retouching needs a steady hand, and the preceding exertion is far from conducive to this. Pressure pumps are therefore not very useful unless we do the pumping up some time before use.

Electrically powered air compressors are much better because they are always at hand and ready. Their drawback is that they can only produce a limited amount of pressure. Owing to the piston movement the pressure in many compressors is not constant, either, but fluctuates periodically.

Compressed gas cylinders have none of these disadvantages. On the other hand they can be a nuisance if they suddenly give out during work.

Whichever method is used, the equipment should be fitted with a pressure gauge which shows the pressure applied to the spray gun. We regulate this pressure for the work in hand by means of a special reducing valve. The usual pressure should be round about 30 lbs. per sq. in. (about 2 atmospheres). A lower pressure will do for treating small areas from close-up, while for larger areas sprayed from farther away the pressure is increased.

The greater the pressure, the more paint leaves the jet, and the finer the droplets will be. The pressure should therefore not drop below a certain limit, even though working at lower pressures is easier and more controllable.

PAINTS

Not every paint can be used for air brushing.

In large spray guns used for spraying posters or for varnishing pictures, the choice of spraying medium is wide. These guns have a thick and blunt needle which produces comparatively large drops visible even with the naked eye.

For our purposes only highest quality water colours or special air brushing paints are suitable. These are particularly finely ground pigments so that the size of the particles cannot block the jet.

208

A block-up is the worst that can happen during spraying. A foam of colour immediately forms over the jet and spits large drops onto the print, spoiling the work.

The moral: mix the paints thoroughly and evenly so that no lumps are left.

Always keep the vessel containing the colour covered to protect it from dust.

Finally, use only best quality brushes to mix the paints; a single hair of the brush allowed to get into the mixture is fatal.

Once the paint is mixed it should not come into contact with the brush again. It is best introduced into the reservoir of the spray gun with a dropping tube. Some air brushes even have a special filling device similar to a fountain pen.

The paint—whether it is black, white, or a mixture of the two for any shade of grey—should be thin, but not watery. Too dilute colour slows down the work, while if it is too thick it does not leave the jet easily.

As air brush paints are body colours and cover everything underneath, we cannot simply darken a grey area by spraying black over it. Nor can we lighten it by just spraying with white. This would merely produce blind detailless portions. The required tint must always be mixed as a tint in a paint dish.

One point to note: almost any shade looks darker wet than when dry.

WORKING PROCEDURE

Before spraying on the print, test the depth of tone on a piece of plain paper. Also find the correct spraying distance to give the required amount of dispersion.

When the tone and distance are right, start spraying the print.

Go on spraying to the required light or dark tone. Usually this is obtained fairly soon, though it will take longer with dilute paint.

The print must not be sprayed for too long at a time, as the paper gets increasingly wet until it is unable to hold any more paint. As a result large drops will first collect on the surface and then start to run. So as soon as the paper begins to look shiny, stop spraying and give the paint a chance to dry before going on.

SPRAYING MASKS

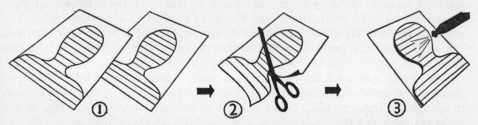

Spraying with a mask. 1. Make two identical bromide prints. 2. Cut out the parts to be masked from one of the prints. 3. Lay these bits on the other print, and spray over it.

With this free-hand method of spraying it is impossible to follow sharp outlines. It is easy to spray large areas in this way; smaller ones need more care, while fine lines and details require quite an amount of skill and practice.

In air brushing boundaries are inevitably gradual. Abrupt contours are only possible with the help of masks.

Masks can be made of all sorts of materials; each has its peculiarities. We can use gelatine or celluloid film, cellophane, waxed paper, tin-foil, or another print.

Tin foil has the advantage of being completely immune against water. But it can only be used where a transparent mask is not essential. It is, for instance, ideal for masking off straight lines.

In most other cases more or less transparent masks are better. As they always have to follow the exact outline of the portion to be air brushed, the only way to make the masks is to lay the material over the print and trace through. On gelatine or celluloid film this is easy with a needle: lay the film over the print, and engrave the outline with the needle point. If the film is thin enough, the two parts can usually be broken apart along the scratched contour. Alternatively, cut the mask along the scratch with a knife or scissors. It must fit accurately over the contour.

The masks become wet during spraying. Gelatine or cellophane begins to warp which is sometimes useful, but can also be a nuisance. Through this continuous warping the outline moves very slightly during spraying, and results in a softened boundary. Celluloid masks keep their shape and thus give a sharp contour even when they are wet. The same applies to waxed paper.

Instead of preparing the masks afterwards from the print, it is a good idea to make two enlargements on double weight paper straightaway. We can then use the better of the two as original for air brushing, and cut up the other to make the mask. This does away with all tracing.

Both sheets of bromide paper should come from the same packet, and the image printed in the same direction relative to the paper grain. Also, the prints must be dried under identical conditions. Otherwise they might shrink slightly differently during the various stages of processing and drying, and the images may fail to cover each other perfectly.

Put down the cut out mask—whatever kind—on the outline in exact register. As it will of course not stay there just like that—the air stream from the spray gun would blow it away at once—it must be weighed down. The heavier the weights, the better, as long as they are not too high. Flat pieces of lead or printers' reglets are most suitable. Arrange them side by side so that the mask is in close contact everywhere with the print. For when the spray is directed against the mask, the edges are liable to lift up, with the paint flowing underneath. When spraying from the mask onto the print, weights sticking up may throw "shadows" on the print.

When using masks it is easy to apply too much colour, as it is a little difficult to check the progress of spraying. Usually just a trace of additional density is enough to obtain the required effect. The snag is to estimate it while working, as the areas against which the result is to be compared are covered up.

The best way to keep everything under control is to spray sparingly, and look at the work once or twice in between by carefully lifting up the masks. However, this must only be done when the paint is completely dry.

Spraying needs planning. Spray large areas first with suitable large masks, followed by the smaller portions with successively smaller masks.

FINE DETAIL

There is a limit to the size of masks we can use. Too small masks can no longer be cut and weighed down efficiently.

We can still pin small masks onto the paper as a makeshift, but this, too, fails if the mask has to cover tiny detail. When, for example, a branch or twig is to be protected while the sky behind is sprayed, cutting a mask becomes very laborious.

In cases like this we paint a waterproof mask over the detail in question. Alternatively we can spray without any mask at all, and wash out the detail afterwards.

For painting a waterproof mask use an oily medium. Dilute boiled linseed oil with benzene or petrol until the solution is fairly thin, and then stir in finely powdered chalk.

Paint over the image detail with this white mixture. The benzene soon evaporates, and the linseed oil and chalk form a greasy mask which protects the image underneath during spraying.

As soon as the air brush work is dry, wipe the still tacky linseed oil off completely with a rag moistened with pure benzene. The sprayed areas are not harmed as the water colour is insoluble in benzene.

The other method of dealing with fine detail is to wash it out after spraying the whole area. Brush over the parts in question with a fairly large brush full of water, and blot off the dissolved pigment.

Don't try to do this all at once. First wash out the details only roughly, and then go over the required parts of the print surface again several times, always using fresh water in the brush, until all the colour is removed.

Do not use the brush itself to take off the colour, as that would unavoidably cause paint fringes. Always remove the dissolved paint with blotting paper.

This method is also suitable for correcting small faults in spraying.

As the sprayed surface is rough, it will readily take chalk or crayon work. Thus very fine lines to be preserved can be redrawn directly on the print, instead of washing out the colour.

SPRAYING CLOUDS

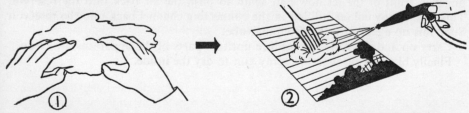

Clouds with the air brush. **1.** Pull about a piece of cotton wool of suitable size until it has the right shape for a cloud. **2.** Hold this down on the print with a fork and spray round with the air brush (p. 214).

We can introduce clouds directly by means of the air brush even when there is no sign of them in the picture.

Pull about a small ball of cotton wool until it has the shape of a cloud of the right size. Then lay this on the paper and hold it down by means of a fork held in the left hand. While spraying all round with the air brush, move the cotton wool about a little now and again. This more or less mechanically produces an image of cloud formations.

To make these more distinct, fray out a piece of blotting paper at random, put it near the edges of some of the clouds, and spray over once briefly with the spray gun.

EXERCISES

To get used to air brush technique, four exercises are recommended. These are graded free-hand spraying of an area, spraying a cube and a sphere with masks, and unaided spraying of a ring (p. 213).

With the first exercise the point is to produce a gradual even transition from black to white from one edge of the paper to the other.

The cube and sphere provide opportunity for practice with masks.

For the cube, lay the masks down on the paper, leaving each of the faces free in turn. Then spray these to different densities.

For the sphere cut a round hole in a suitable masking material (p. 210). Put this on the white paper, and build up the shading inside it to give an image of a sphere.

Free-hand spraying of a ring should offer practice in the steady manipulation of the air brush at short spraying distances and for small areas.

CLEANING THE AIR BRUSH

The air brush must always be cleaned immediately after use.

First empty the paint reservoir until no more paint leaves the jet. Introduce some clean water into the reservoir by means of a dropping tube, and rinse out several times by sucking up the water with the dropping tube and putting in fresh water. Continue until no trace of colour is left there.

Then fill up again with fresh water and spray this out through the jet. Put a finger in front of the jet now and again to push the air back into the reservoir. This washes any colour still left in the connecting channel back into the reservoir. Suck this up again with the dropping tube.

Carry on and repeat the procedure until all parts of the apparatus are clean.

Finally blow air through the spray gun to dry the inside.

AIRBRUSH EXERCISES. *Top left:*
Evenly grading a surface from black to
white. *Centre left:* Spraying a cube
with masks. *Bottom left:* Spraying
a sphere with a mask, and spraying a
tone to suggest roundness. *Bottom
right:* Freehand spraying of a circle
(p. 212). *Above right:* Air brushing
combined with photomontage. The
filament and candles were printed
together, and the shape of the lamp
sprayed in with the help of a mask.

AP—S   213

SPRAYING CLOUDS. *Right:* Original print. *Above:* Sky darkened and cloud shapes sprayed with cotton-wool as mask (p. 211).

PREPARING A PRINT for reproduction with the help of the air brush. *Left :* Original print. *Above :* The beams were brightened up by spraying with white paint, highlights put in, and bolts painted white. This sort of work needs accurate spraying masks.

215

BRIGHTENING UP a print with black dye. *Centre:* Original print from under-exposed negative. An octopus is never easy to photograph and under the conditions this flat and grey result was the best possible. *Top:* Painting the shadows black and touching up unsharp detail gives the print depth and life (p. 223).

THE CUT-OUT standing up desk pictures (*right*) are made by mounting a photograph on plywood and cutting out with a fretsaw. It then only needs a block of wood stuck to the back to support it (p. 230).

216

HAND COLOURING

It was to be expected that with the increasing use of colour photography hand coloured prints would be pushed into the background. But the opposite is the case. More colouring is done nowadays than ever before. The reason may be that coloured pictures as such are becoming more popular, and that colour photographs proper are sometimes disappointing. With poor technique they are no better than hand coloured pictures, in fact they are sometimes definitely inferior.

Photographs can be coloured with water soluble transparent dyes, with oil colours, or with coloured crayons. The first can be used on all surfaces, the latter two only on semi-matt or matt prints.

TRANSPARENT DYES

They are similar to the black and red retouching dyes used for negative retouching (p. 186).

They do not contain any pigment, but are truly transparent and allow all detail underneath to show through.

As before, the colours dye the gelatine and are not easily washed out.

Since they do not form a layer on top but sink into the gelatine, they need a special painting technique.

THE PRINT FOR COLOURING

Before going any further into the technique, let us have a look at the print to be coloured.

The lighter the image, the more brilliant and pure will be the colour effect. With dark prints the blackness of the picture shines through all the time, and may be so dominant in the heavier tones that the transparent dyes do not come into their own at all. Dark prints with saturated blacks usually look unpleasant and dirty when coloured.

So keep prints light with all detail clearly visible.

The black-and-white print can be coloured as it stands, or it can be sulphide toned first. The choice will depend on the print itself, and on the effects desired.

Where areas which have to remain black are few and far between, with portions to be coloured yellow, red, or brown in the majority, matters are considerably simplified by preliminary sulphide toning. In practice a portrait, for example, is better coloured on a brown print, as the face parts then already have a tone similar to the final one required. And if the sitter should have black hair, we can always paint that over again with blue-black dye.

On the other hand a picture of, say, a pianist with a dominating black area of the grand piano is better left black-and-white as it is before colouring.

One small point: It is easier to tint black-and-white prints than tones ones. The gelatine is slightly tanned during toning, and does not absorb the colours as easily and intensely.

WORKING PROCEDURE

Preparing the print for colouring. 1. Put a wet handkerchief over a sheet of glass a little larger than the print. 2. Lay the print on top. 3. Squeegee down evenly. 4. Remove any surplus surface moisture with a second handkerchief.

For colouring the print must be wet.

Soak an old handkerchief in water, spread it over a sheet of glass of suitable size, and lay the print on top. Go over it with a roller squeegee to get it really flat, and blot the surface with a second dry fluffless cloth. The purpose of the wet cloth underneath is to keep the print moist longer.

Keep little glass bowls handy on the working table to dilute the colours. The dilution has to be fairly considerable; only one or two drops of the dye are needed.

As in retouching, start work with dilute colour, going over later to a more concentrated solution. Again it is better to paint over the same area several times with dilute washes rather than once with concentrated dye. This gives more even colour in large areas such as the sky.

The next job is to apply the colour to the print without leaving brush marks. This can only be done successfully by working boldly with as large a brush as possible. There is no need to worry over accurate outlines. Provided the colour is dilute enough, not much harm is done by going beyond the boundaries now and again.

As an example let us take the task of colouring a landscape print.

The largest area—in this case probably the sky—is painted first.

Apply the brush, well filled with dye solution, to the print and straightaway set it going in all directions to distribute the colour everywhere over the sky as quickly as possible. Keep brush continually on the move without interruption, and immediately disperse every droplet formed.

After a short time the brush is empty, while the colour has been absorbed by the print surface. Recharge the brush and apply more dye in the same way. Slowly but surely the sky goes bluer and bluer. Less dye is now also being absorbed. When the tint is right, take the dry cloth and wipe off the surplus solution from the face of the print.

When painting the sky, outlines do not matter much. The top and the sides are, after all, the picture edges, and the landscape itself probably borders onto the sky with some mountains or fields.

Owing to haze, mountains are bluish anyway, so they can have some blue over them.

The green colour of fields or woods is made up by mixing blue and yellow (below). So these too can be painted over with a thin wash of blue, and then a second time with yellow to produce the green.

Finally, paint in details within fields or trees more slowly with a small brush which also makes it easier to keep to the outlines. Uneven colour is hardly noticeable here as it disappears among the detail in these image parts.

MIXING COLOURS

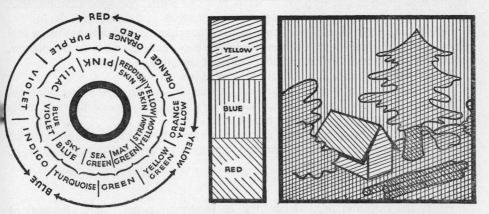

The colour circle. *Left:* A large range of the colours in nature can be reproduced by using just red, yellow, and blue. The colour circle shows how mixing the three basic colours produces all the intermediate tints. *Right:* As an example, we can apply this principle to a simplified landscape. Thus blue and yellow produce the varying shades of green, brown contains some of each colour, and so on.

Some preliminary thought on the colour mixtures possible will save much laborious manipulation later on.

In principle it is possible to work with no more than three colours: yellow, blue, and red. We can produce any shade by mixing two or all of these three.

In this case the dyes are mixed not before painting, but during the actual work, namely by applying the colours alternately. The tints obtainable can be seen from the colour chart (above). Any two of these basic colours give a new one, which in turn can lead to further tints.

The chart applies to pure colours only. It therefore does not include for instance brown which is a degraded colour.

We produce brown by mixing red and green (which then contains all three dyes). The colour will be cooler the more green is present, and warmer the higher the proportion of red.

Black, which strictly speaking is not a colour at all, can also be obtained by mixing all three basic colours. But as these mixtures invariably have some colour tinge, black is best produced with a separate dye as used for spotting (p. 186).

COLOURING DETAIL

When the large areas have been coloured, the progressively smaller ones are painted in.

After the ground colouring of a portrait, for instance, tint the cheeks next. The wet surface here makes diffused outlines easy.

Red for the lips or the colour of the eyes can be applied at the end when the print is already more or less dry.

Thus we gradually build up the picture until we have to make up our minds to regard it as finished and stop. It is better to do so a little too soon than too late, for beyond a certain point we are apt to lose ourselves in unimportant detail.

Before finishing it is, however, important to consider the delicate halftones and tints. These are present everywhere, and only they really give life to the picture, apart from the fact that without them the print merely looks cheap.

Thus every white area has delicate blue shadows.

Every face has a fine greenish tinge near the temples, and faint violet eye shadows.

Blonde hair shines through the individual strands slightly greenish, while really black hair is never pure black, but blue-black.

Much can be learned about these intermediate tones by looking at a good genuine colour transparency. And these tints are important for good colouring technique.

CRAYONS

Where the coloured print is on matt or semi-matt paper, some afterwork is possible with coloured crayons.

With a few lines we may add detail to large areas, while in places we can tone down the depth of black shining through, for the dry coloured crayons act as body colours.

Some crayons can also be worked wet, which means a different and independent colouring technique altogether. There are water soluble crayons, and fat soluble oil crayons. Whilst the water soluble ones are not suitable for colouring itself, but only for afterwork, we can completely colour a print from beginning to end with oil crayons.

WATER CRAYONS

The water soluble crayons are used where the larger print areas are already painted in. The prints must, however, be dry.

Shade over the individual small areas in the colour required, and distribute the colour by painting with the wet brush.

Minute details can be drawn directly on the wet surface and will then be specially accentuated in colour.

220

OIL CRAYONS

Oil crayons can be used to colour large or small areas. The print should be on semi-matt or matt paper, but not dead matt.

Rub over the print surface first with a soft rag moistened with a mixture of equal parts of pure linseed oil and turpentine, so as to leave a slightly oily surface film.

To use the example of the sky again, shade the area at random with a few strokes of the blue crayon. Then rub the pigment over the area with a stump or a wad of cotton wool. As the crayon dissolves in the oily film, the colour easily spreads quite evenly. Where it has overstepped a contour remove it again with a fresh piece of cotton wool.

Small areas are of course worked over with correspondingly small stumps which must be fresh each time, and not carry any other colour. For this purpose cut triangles out of blotting paper and roll them up into small sticks. According to the size of the triangles this gives larger or smaller pointed stumps.

A print coloured in this way will, however, take about a week to dry. During that time it must not be touched at all.

OIL COLOURING

Anybody who is familiar with the technique of oil painting and its special points can obtain good results even with oil colours.

We shall have to use a substitute for linseed oil as medium, as this slowly attacks the black silver image and turns it brown.

One merit of oil colouring is that the paint dries slowly. While it is still wet, we can produce any colour blending by painting over in different colours. On the other hand once the paint is dry we can paint over again and make corrections without interfering with what is already there. The print surface must, however, be oil proof.

Most glossy and semi-matt papers are suitable provided the print surface is undamaged and has no knife work on it. The oil of the paints will ooze through the smallest injury in the gelatine layer spread into the paper base, producing a dark grease spot. Papers with natural rough surfaces are best coated with a collodion layer first.

We have to distinguish between opaque oil paints and transparent varnishes.

Only the latter are of any use for our purpose, as the body pigments are not transparent enough to allow the print image to show through.

To dilute the paints and increase their transparency, use Canada balsam diluted with Oil of Lavender. Alternatively, to speed up drying use a mixture of Copaiba balsam and oil of turpentine for diluting the colours.

When the varnish is dry paint in highlights with white paint. For this purpose any white opaque oil pigment will do.

CHEMICAL COLOURING

The methods of colouring mentioned so far involve painting over the existing print. The image remains unchanged, with just the various colours added. Whatever parts are black, remain black, and a really black background deprives any dye or paint on top of its colour.

With chemical colouring the black silver image is removed, and the blackness replaced by pure colours which can be suitably chosen for every part of the picture. Such pictures look considerably more colourful, and with some skill in the choice of colours and manipulation they may be practically indistinguishable from proper colour prints on paper.

Chemical colouring is lengthy and requires practice. It is lengthy because of the long soaking times which can, however, be filled in with other work. We shall easily acquire the knack of the method once we have become reasonably familiar with the process.

Glossy surfaced papers are best. But they should not be dried by hot glazing afterwards, as that may change the colours.

The prints themselves must be brilliant, showing full detail; they must have been thoroughly fixed and washed. Dense blacks in the shadows are, if anything, desirable; particularly as the black image is removed anyway, and cannot interfere with the colours.

After washing, bleach the prints in a special mordanting bleacher (No. **45**, p. 245).

When the black image has completely disappeared, wash for at least 10 minutes. The prints can then be coloured straightaway.

Work in the same way as with dyes on the wet print. Only here special dyes (so-called mordant dyes) are used. Suitable ones are thioflavin T or auramine (yellow), safranine A (red), and methylene blue (blue). These three should be sufficient, particularly when working as described on p. 219. Additional colours can, however, be used: chrysoidine 3R (orange), methyl violet (purple to violet), and methylene green (green).

All these powdered dyes are dissolved in slightly acid distilled water (No. **46**, p. 245).

When using the basic three dyes apply them in the order blue—red—yellow.

First paint over all image parts to be blue with the blue dye solution. There is no need to follow the outlines in this process.

Cover green parts either with blue or green.

Then paint over the red portions with safranine, and the orange ones with either safranine or chrysoidine.

Finally apply the yellow dye over the parts to be yellow, and also on top of the blue over parts to be green (if no separate green was used), and on top of the red over parts to be orange (if no separate orange was used).

The colour chart (p. 219) will again indicate possible halftones and tints.

Paint over the print until the picture areas have absorbed enough colour. Not only the image portions will be coloured, but also the rest of the gelatine. For the dyes "develop" the almost invisible bleached image, and at the same time also tint the areas which should remain white. While this does not matter for the final result, as we shall subsequently wash out the unwanted tint, it complicates judging the effect during working. There experience will help.

As soon as the colours seem to be right, soak the print for 2–3 hours in water. This may with advantage be changed a few times during that period. During this

222

time the dyes are washed out of the gelatine and only remain in the parts of the original image itself. There they correspond exactly to the original densities. Washing out may be speeded up by adding a little acetic acid to the water.

With too long soaking the mordanted image areas may lose some dye, too, for the colours are not absolutely fast even there. Soaking for 24 hours would remove all the dye, and leave the print colourless again.

A sort of race takes place during soaking. Blue has the greatest tendency to leave the image, yellow the least. This explains the importance of the order of application. If the blue is applied first, it has the most opportunity to cling to the mordanted image grains. The red is not so well off, as many "places" are already "occupied", while the yellow gets the worst deal of all. But as it adheres best, the dye remains effective even with the comparatively fewer grains left for it to adhere to. Though the more mobile blue partly leaves the image, it can afford to do so; enough remains behind to be still effective.

USING BLACK DYE

Even black and white prints can be improved by means of the colouring technique used with transparent dyes. Only here we use just one dye; black.

While this method has nothing to do with creating a coloured picture, we shall deal with it here because it follows from the technique of colouring and is identical in every respect.

We can improve beyond all expectation really hopeless pictures which we may not be able to repeat. We only have to paint them over with dilute transparent black dye. This specially applies to prints which at their best are flat and grey and just look useless (p. 216).

Paint the wet print over with the dye by means of a brush in the same way as described on p. 218, in order to intensify the grey and dark grey tones. In this way we can create blacks which were not there in the print at all, and give increased strength to the picture.

As before, start with very dilute washes of dye, gradually going over to more concentrated solutions for the darker tones, right up to the pure blacks.

TINTING THE PAPER BASE

While tinted papers (ivory, cream) are easily obtainable, we may occasionally have only white paper of the required grade or surface at hand just when we want to make a tinted print.

We can easily remedy this by tinting the finished print afterwards.

Almost any dilute dye solution is suitable. Bathe the print in it, and hang up to dry after a quick rinse. But do not lay the print to dry on muslin or blotting paper (p. 43).

Even weak tea or coffee will do in an emergency. For a specially warm tone add a few drops of red ink to the liquid.

This tinting must of course be done before applying water colour pigments, crayons, or oil colours to the print.

PRINT FINISHING

After drying the finished prints often have uneven edges, and they are sometimes cockled and wavy instead of being flat. Particularly in the larger sizes they are also too thin to be handled. There is always great risk of creating or injuring them.

Small prints are usually mounted in albums, but we shall pass this over, for there is really nothing to it.

The larger proper sized enlargements, which are the main subject of this book, are not usually stuck into albums, if only because of their size. But in their present state they still look somewhat rough and unfinished, except if they are pictures for press reproduction when we can leave them as they are, provided we have glazed them (p. 44).

TRIMMING

Prints are best trimmed with a guillotine or similar trimmer. Where the output of prints is high such a trimmer will save much time. Working with it is so simple that it needs no lengthy description.

Trimming by hand, particularly of large prints, is a little more involved.

With large prints first flatten them after drying to take out the curl (p. 44). That, however, does not by any means make them really flat. Therefore wipe over the back with a sponge soaked in water and wrung out as far as possible. The prints must not become wet, only slightly moist. After treating several prints in this way, lay them face to face and back to back on top of each other, and leave overnight, weighed down with a large sheet of glass or a flat board. The next morning they will be completely flat and ready for trimming.

Another way is to lay the moistened prints face up on a sheet of intensely dried blotting paper or newspaper. Either of the latter is first held in front of the fire or an electric radiator until it is so dry that it nearly, but not quite, begins to scorch. Finally put a clean sheet of paper over the print, and a sheet of glass or a board on top to weigh it down. The paper then quickly draws the moisture out of the prints.

For trimming lay the prints face up on a hard paste-board or wooden board, and cut along the edge of a steel ruler (or the edge of a sheet of plate glass ground absolutely straight).

Use a razor blade or sharp knife for cutting. With a wooden board as support (which is best avoided if possible) the cut must go diagonally across the grain of the wood. Cutting straight across will produce a jagged edge, while along the grain the cut will not be even, as the knife tends to follow the grain. And this is never straight.

PASTE MOUNTING

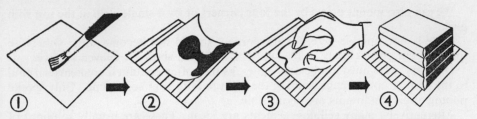

Mounting a print with paste. **1.** Rub the paste well into the back of the wet print. **2.** Carefully lower the print onto the mount. **3.** Wipe over to press down. **4.** Put under pressure for a few hours.

We can now mount the print on stiff board or mounts, or put it behind a cut-out frame.

For ordinary mounting the whole back of the picture is stuck down on heavy cardboard sheets, or on plywood.

There is a difference between simple glueing down and proper wet mounting. For the former we always use a glue, for the other a paste (e.g. No. **51**, p. 246).

Glues contain little water and have great adhesive power. Pastes, on the other hand, contain a lot of water and have comparatively small adhesive power.

The water content of the paste is important in mounting, for the back of the print must be wet and softened so that it stretches. Only when the paper is wet through can we mount it without folds or wrinkles. When the water evaporates the paper contracts again and adheres closely to the support. For that reason only completely smooth mounts will do for wet mounting, as any texture would be ingrained on the print surface.

The support must also be fairly thick and solid, otherwise the tension of the paper as it dries will bend it inwards. A thin sheet of paper is therefore often stuck to the back of the mount at the same time so as to counteract the warping produced by the print.

To mount the print, place it face down on a large sheet of newspaper, and evenly brush the paste over the back of the print with a large brush. Rub the paste well into the paper until the print is soft and limp. Do not try to speed this up by using too much paste. Always apply it thinly.

Then take the paper and carefully lower it onto the mount. Press down with a clean cloth, working from the centre outwards to push out all air bells. Finally leave to dry under pressure.

When the paper has become taut, raised spots may occasionally appear underneath the print. These are either particles of dried up paste broken off the edge of the paste pot, or hairs which have come out of the brush. Therefore carefully examine the back for any foreign matter and remove any hairs with tweezers before placing the print on the mount.

Take special care over mounting glossy prints. No trace of paste must get onto the surface, either by handling with sticky fingers or by smudging of any paste oozing out at the edges. Once the high glaze is spoilt, it cannot be restored again.

225

MOUNTING WITH GLUE OR CEMENT

We can also mount prints by the four corners or by a single strip at the top with glue.

Paste is not suitable here, for the corners should not become soft. Otherwise they will cling too closely to the support, and thus show an uneven surface.

Ordinary glues must not be used either, as they often contain ingredients harmful to the photographic image, causing the print to fade after some time. Only special photographic mountants are permissible.

Alternatively, many cellulose cements are ideal. These are usually solutions of cellulose in amyl acetate or acetone. Rubber solution (p. 132) will also do very well.

For mounting smear a little of the mountant or cement with the fingers on the corners of the print from the inside outwards. Place the print on the mount, and leave to dry under light pressure.

Alternatively a strip of mountant can be smeared along the top edge of the print.

DRY MOUNTING

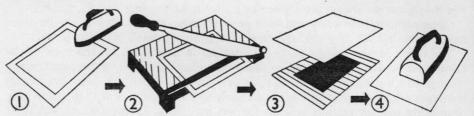

Mounting with tissue. 1. Tack down a sheet of tissue (slightly larger than the print) to the back of the print with a hot iron. 2. Trim tissue and print. 3. Place on mount and cover with clean paper. 4. Apply hot iron.

This method of mounting does not involve either paste or glue. Instead the medium is a resinous tissue which melts during mounting and binds the print and mount firmly together.

The procedure is simple:

Cut a sheet of dry mounting tissue a little larger all round than the print, and lay it on the back of the latter. Touch it in several places with the tip of a hot domestic iron. This melts the resin in those places which immediately stick to the print. Now trim print and tissue together and lay them on the mount in the right place. Put a clean sheet of thin card on top, and go over the whole with the hot iron.

As the resin melts underneath, the print is firmly mounted onto the support. Press the iron evenly all over the print surface to avoid pressure marks and uneven mounting.

The temperature of the iron is important. If the iron is too hot, the tissue will stick to the mount, but not to the print. If it is too cold, the tissue will stick to the print, but not to the mount.

The best temperature will have to be found by experience. It depends on the tissue itself, the weight of the paper base of the print to be mounted, and on the thickness of the covering card.

There are also special dry mounting presses which allow the whole print to be put under pressure simultaneously. This is particularly useful with large prints.

The method of dry mounting has the advantage that no tension is produced between print and support. Thus the mount cannot cockle. Dry mounting is also eminently suitable for glossy prints; there is nothing to spoil the glaze, as the process takes place under the exclusion of water.

PLATE MARKS

Embossing a plate mark. I. Place the mount over a sheet of stiff cardboard of the right size. 2. Press along the edges of the card from the back of the mount. 3. The shape of the card is now imprinted on the front.

Before mounting the prints we can give the mount itself a plate mark. This is a sunk area impressed on the mount, with the print inside it. When printing copper plate engravings or etchings such a plate mark is formed by the edges of the printing plate, so applying it to photographic mounts is strictly speaking not "in style".

First we need a large smooth sheet of heavy cardboard support. The plate mark itself is impressed on the mount with a thin card cut to the required size.

This should always be a little larger than the print. Thus for a whole plate ($6\frac{1}{2} \times 8\frac{1}{2}$ in.) enlargement, cut the card 7×9 in., leaving $\frac{1}{4}$ in. all round. If we wish to put our signature under the print we can make one of the sides longer. So for an upright $6\frac{1}{2} \times 8\frac{1}{2}$ in. print the card will be $7 \times 9\frac{1}{4}$ in., leaving $\frac{1}{4}$ in. space at the top and the sides, and $\frac{1}{2}$ in. underneath for the signature and title. A horizontal print under these conditions would require a space of $7\frac{1}{4} \times 9$ in.

Place the card to make the plate mark on the mount in the right position in the middle. If the mount has a different front and back, place the card on the front where the print will eventually go. Then lift up the two with one hand underneath the mount and one hand on top of the card, pressing them together with the spread out fingers. Without shifting them, turn them over face down onto the cardboard working support, and carefully withdraw the hand from underneath. The other hand must press down all the time on the back of the mount. This should be the left hand; change over if necessary.

This particular step is somewhat simplified as far as manipulation is concerned if the impression card is lightly stuck on the mount with a couple of dabs of rubber solution. This is easily removed later.

Then make the plate mark by pressing the mount onto the edges of this card with the cap of a fountain pen or some similar smooth round object. Take this in the right hand and place the rounded end on the back of the mount somewhere near the middle. Pull it towards the edge with slight pressure until the edge of the card underneath is felt. At this point the pen slides off slightly, as if it had slipped into a hidden cavity.

Now go along this edge, pressing down well all the time. This impresses the first side of the plate mark. Its ends can also be felt without any trouble.

Then get hold of the whole working support with the right hand (the left is still pressing down on the mount all the time) and revolve it through a quarter turn. This brings the second edge round for pressing down.

Repeat until all four edges are impressed in this way.

Finally lift off the mount and the impression will be clearly visible. The print is mounted into this sunk area by its four corners, or along a single strip at the top (p. 226).

FRAME MOUNTING

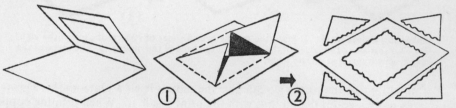

Types of frame mounts. *Left:* Usual folding frame mount with cut-out. *Right:* Making a frame with rough edges. **I.** Cut through the diagonals of the frame area. **2.** Fold back the four triangles formed, and tear off.

We can also improve the appearance of the mounted print in another way. Thus we may cover the mount with a wide frame with a cut out window which just comes to lie over the print.

The opening should be slightly smaller than the picture area. Thus for a print 6×8 in. the inside size of the opening would be $5\frac{5}{8} \times 7\frac{5}{8}$ in., covering at least $\frac{3}{16}$ in all round the print.

For cutting the window first place the print in the right position on the back of the mount to be cut. Indicate each corner of the print with a pencil mark, and join up the corners with the help of a ruler. Make the cut itself just a little inside these lines.

There is no need to draw a second set of lines, though. Just place the ruler about $\frac{1}{8}$ to $\frac{1}{4}$ in. inside each line and parallel to it, then cut along the ruler with a sharp knife. Stop just short of the corners, and cut these through separately from the corner outwards. This avoids half cutting into or through them.

The inside edges of the window can also be torn out. This gives them a slightly frayed appearance, not unlike old-fashioned hand-made paper. The procedure is as follows.

After marking the back of the mount in pencil as before, again place a ruler just inside the lines, and scratch along the ruler with the knife, without, however, cutting through the paper. This should be as uniform as possible along all four edges. Then place the ruler diagonally across from corner to corner, and really cut through the mount. Repeat with the other diagonal.

The inside area now consists of four triangles. Raise each one up from the centre, and bend outwards along the scratched edge. Crease down sharply, and tear off the triangles along their base, producing a straight torn edge. This edge will be more obviously frayed if it is moistened with a brush and a little water before tearing off. It will then tear like blotting paper.

The print can be stuck against the back of the window aperture with adhesive tape.

Alternatively, it may be mounted on a second mount of the same size as the outside of the frame, and the latter placed on top over the print. The two can be joined together by glueing or cementing the outside edges or by binding them with passe-partout tape.

As a final alternative, the mount may be cut double size, and folded in half in the middle. The aperture is cut in the top half, while the bottom half carries the print.

BOX MOUNTING

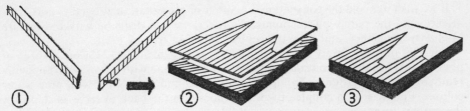

Making a box mount. 1. Cut four strips of wood for the sides of the box, and join together. 2. Mount the print on stiff card of the same size as the box. 3. Fix to the box and smooth down edges.

This procedure and also the one on p. 230 are rather out-of-the-way methods for mounting prints. One thing about them is that they give the photographs an emphatic impression of "presence".

First mount the enlargement with paste (p. 225) onto thick tough cardboard of the same size, and mount another sheet of paper on the back to prevent warping (p. 225).

Then make a frame out of 1 in. thick wooden battens. Cut these into single lengths with a fine saw. However, do not make the saw cuts straight, but at an angle of 45 degrees. Four lengths are needed; two of them, measured from tip to tip, are the same length as the long side of the print, and the other two correspond exactly to the short side. Glue them together to form a rectangular frame, and in addition fasten with thin nails. The heads of the nails should be nipped off just before they are completely knocked in, so that the nails disappear in the wood.

When the frame is dry, glue the mounted print on top so that the outside edges coincide exactly with the frame. The whole should now look like a box which is hollow underneath and carries the print on top.

When dry, smooth down with sandpaper small irregularities where the cardboard mount and the frame join and then paint the sides. Whether this is done with varnish, water colour, or other paint, as well as the colour used, is largely a matter of taste and depends on the result intended.

When they are hung up on the wall, such prints have an appeal undiminished by the outside intrusion of any frame or the like.

CUT-OUTS

How to mount a cut-out. **1.** Mount the print on plywood and cut out the subject with a fretsaw. **2.** Fix a wooden block to the back of the cut-out so that **3** it can stand upright (p. 216).

If we wish to avoid the conventional manner of presentation altogether and draw attention to the purely photographic character, we can dispense with the picture boundary altogether, and have the subject standing free by itself.

For this purpose firmly mount the whole enlargement (p. 225) on a sheet of plywood. When dry cut out the subject along its outline with a fretsaw, completely removing the background. Sandpaper the edges and paint over with grey water colour. Finally stick a couple of wooden blocks on the back to serve as stand for the cut-out print.

These pictures not only have a commercial use (e.g. shop window advertising, exhibitions, etc.) but also provide mantlepiece or desk decorations in the home. The subject is depicted without any of the trimmings that usually go with it; it will attract attention wholly by its own merits.

Section VI

APPENDIX

THE RESULTS

In following the printing process step by step from the negative to the finished print, we have assumed that all the steps were successful and that the print will only need minor touching up (p. 175).

However, if the print is not all it should be, we must find out where the fault lies, and what we have to do when we make a fresh print.

TONE AND CONTRAST

The print is grey and flat. It has no properly black shadows nor really bright highlights.

(*a*) CAUSE: The paper was too soft.
PREVENTION: Use a more contrasty grade (p. 30).

(*b*) CAUSE: Development time was cut short to compensate for overexposure.
PREVENTION: Reduce exposure so that the print can be fully developed for at least 2 minutes (p. 39).

(*c*) CAUSE: The developer was too warm or completely exhausted.
PREVENTION: Use fresh developer and watch the temperature (p. 19).

The print is too contrasty, with heavy shadows, detailless highlights, and hardly any half-tones.

(*a*) CAUSE: The paper was too hard.
PREVENTION: Choose a softer grade (p. 30).

(*b*) CAUSE: The developer was too cold.
PREVENTION: Warm it up to 65–68° F. (18–20° C.).

(*c*) CAUSE: The developer contains too much potassium bromide, usually because a negative developer was chosen.
PREVENTION: Use the right formula for the right paper (p. 237).

(*d*) CAUSE: The print was underexposed and overdeveloped.
PREVENTION: Increase the exposure so that the print is fully developed in 2 minutes (p. 39).

The print is too light.

(*a*) CAUSE: It was underexposed.
PREVENTION: Give a longer exposure time (p. 32).

(*b*) CAUSE: It was underdeveloped.
PREVENTION: Develop for the full time (p. 39).

(*c*) CAUSE: The developer was exhausted or too cold.
PREVENTION: Do not overwork the solutions (p. 241) and keep them at the right temperature (p. 19).

The print is too dark.

(*a*) CAUSE: It was overexposed.
PREVENTION: Reduce the exposure (p. 32).

232

(*b*) CAUSE: It was overdeveloped.
PREVENTION: Keep to the 2–2½ minutes development time (p. 39).

(*c*) CAUSE: The developer was too warm.
PREVENTION: Watch the development temperature (p. 19).

The image is greenish or brownish in colour. There is no proper black.

(*a*) CAUSE: Development time was too short.
PREVENTION: Develop for the full 2–2½ minutes (p. 39).

(*b*) CAUSE: The developer is exhausted.
PREVENTION: Use fresh solutions (p. 241).

(*c*) CAUSE: The developer contains too much potassium bromide.
PREVENTION: Use the correct formula (p. 237).

The prints appear "dead" after drying.

CAUSE: The image has "sunk" into the paper. This often happens with matt surfaced papers.

PREVENTION: Allow for this in print making by using a harder paper. Wet prints always appear more brilliant than dry ones. This brilliance can usually be brought back by varnishing or waxing the print.

FOG AND STAINS

The print shows an even or uneven overall grey fog.

(*a*) CAUSE: The darkroom lamp was too bright or of the wrong colour.
PREVENTION: Test the safelight (p. 16) and adjust accordingly.

(*b*) CAUSE: The paper was too old or badly stored.
PREVENTION: Use fresh paper and keep it in a cool dry place. With old paper add potassium bromide or a developer improver to the developer to reduce fog.

(*c*) CAUSE: Developer was too warm.
PREVENTION: Watch the temperature (p. 19).

(*d*) CAUSE: Developer contains too little potassium bromide (for instance, contact developer used for bromide paper).
PREVENTION: Use correct formula (p. 237).

(*e*) CAUSE: Stray light in the darkroom, or unexposed paper not properly wrapped up when white light was switched on.
PREVENTION: See that the enlarger or printer is light-tight and that no white light escapes into the darkroom during working. Pack away all sensitive paper before turning on white light.

The print shows yellow stains all over (can sometimes be removed, p. 244).

(*a*) CAUSE: The developer was contaminated with fixer.
PREVENTION: Take care not to splash solutions about. Never dip the fingers in the developer or fixer (p. 18). Keep the fixing forceps out of the developer (p. 18). Don't immerse the developer forceps in the acid rinse or fixer (p. 18).

(*b*) CAUSE: Intermediate rinse was insufficient or used for too long.
PREVENTION: Change rinsing water regularly. Still better, use an acid rinse (p. 240). Move the prints about in it for at least 10 seconds (p. 39).

(*c*) CAUSE: The print was underexposed and forced in development.
PREVENTION: Increase exposure and develop for not longer than 2–2½ minutes (p. 39).

The prints have black, yellow-brown, or violet stains, because development has continued in the fixing bath.

(*a*) CAUSE: Prints were allowed to stick together.
PREVENTION: Move the prints about when they are first immersed in the fixing solution.

AP—U

(*b*) CAUSE: The prints were not fully immersed in the fixer.
PREVENTION: Keep the prints under the surface with the print paddle (p. 40).

(*c*) CAUSE: The rinse was insufficient or used too long.
PREVENTION: Renew the rinse water frequently, and use an acid rinse (p. 240).

(*d*) CAUSE: The fixing bath was exhausted.
PREVENTION: Do not overwork the solutions (p. 241).

The print fades or turns yellow or brown on keeping.

(*a*) CAUSE: The print was fixed for too short a time or in an exhausted fixing bath.
PREVENTION: Fix for at least 10 minutes (p. 40). Do not overwork the fixing bath (p. 241).

(*b*) CAUSE: The print was insufficiently washed.
PREVENTION: Wash for at least 30 minutes in running water (p. 42). Use an alkaline rinse to remove as much acid as possible from the paper base (p. 241).

UNEVEN DENSITY

Print has mottled or patchy appearance.

(*a*) CAUSE: The print was greatly overexposed and underdeveloped.
PREVENTION: Reduce the exposure and develop fully (p. 39).

(*b*) CAUSE: The print was not moved about during development, or the developer was exhausted.
PREVENTION: Rock the dish constantly while developing (p. 39). Use fresh developer (p. 241).

(*c*) CAUSE: Old or stale paper.
PREVENTION: Add a developer improver to the developer.

(*d*) CAUSE: Very rarely: uneven coating of the paper (faulty manufacture).

The print shows areas of uneven density with sharp irregular boundaries.

CAUSE: The developer did not act simultaneously on the whole print surface.
PREVENTION: Immerse the print in the developer in one movement (p. 38). Large prints may have to be soaked in clean water for about a minute before development to ensure even wetting by the developer.

The print shows areas of uneven density with sharp straight boundaries.

CAUSE: The prints were allowed to stick to each other in a fresh or too strong fixing bath. The covered parts of the print were protected from the action of the strong fixing solution which slightly reduced the rest of the print.
PREVENTION: Use a fixing bath of the right strength, and move the prints about in it, particularly at first (p. 40).

The print shows light and dark markings in the shape of round or oval concentric rings.

CAUSE: These are Newton's rings which are formed through uneven contact between the back of the film negative and the glass of the printer or enlarger negative carrier.
PREVENTION: Reduce the pressure on the film. Place a cut-out mask or a blank film or a piece of cellophane between negative and glass. Breathe on the back of the negative. If possible use a glassless negative carrier.
With miniature films the best method is to roll them up for a few days with the emulsion side outwards. It should not give any trouble then.

234

PHYSICAL FAULTS

The print shows blisters with the gelatine leaving the paper base in places.

(*a*) CAUSE: Developer, rinse, and fixer were at different temperatures.
PREVENTION: Keep the temperature of all solutions more or less the same (p. 19).

(*b*) CAUSE: Stop bath or fixing bath contains too much acid.
PREVENTION: Use correctly made up formula (p. 240).

The prints curl very strongly during drying, are hard, and develop deep cracks when flattened out.

CAUSE: Too rapid, too intense, and too long drying, particularly after hardening in a formalin bath (p. 241).
PREVENTION: Dry the prints slowly at normal temperatures or with only moderate heat (p. 43), and flatten out before they are bone dry (p. 44). If prints are brittle and horny, they are best resoaked and dried again.

The print surface is rough and has a white scum on it.

CAUSE: Hard water, particularly during washing.
PREVENTION: Soak prints for a few minutes in 1 per cent acetic acid solution immediately before drying.

MISCELLANEOUS TROUBLES

The print is not sharp.

(*a*) CAUSE: The negative was not sharp.

(*b*) CAUSE: The enlarger was not properly focused.
PREVENTION: Focus accurately, using a focusing negative if necessary (p. 31).

(*c*) CAUSE: The negative was not quite flat in the enlarger.
PREVENTION: Check the negative carrier. If the films are buckling because of the heat from the enlarger lamp, let the apparatus cool down before continuing work.

(*d*) CAUSE: Enlarger vibration.
PREVENTION: Do not move, or knock against, the enlarger during exposure. Do not move about unnecessarily while exposing (p. 38).

(*e*) CAUSE: Dirty enlarging lens.
PREVENTION: Carefully clean the lens.

(*f*) CAUSE: Negative and printing paper not in proper contact in printer or printing frame.
PREVENTION: Check the pressure plates and pressure springs.

(*g*) CAUSE: Negative placed in printer with the emulsion side *away* from the paper.
PREVENTION: Print negative the right way round.

The print shows small white spots which were not present on the negative.

(*a*) CAUSE: Dust settled on the negative or the paper during exposure.
PREVENTION: Carefully brush off all foreign matter before exposing the paper (p. 178). Clean negative and negative carrier. Keep away cigarette ash, etc.

(*b*) CAUSE: Airbells settled on the paper during development.
PREVENTION: Remove airbells with the foreceps as soon as they are noticed in the developer.

The print shows small black spots which were not present in the negative.

CAUSE: Developer not completely dissolved. Small particles settle on the paper during development and blacken it there.
PREVENTION: Filter developer during use. Generally these spots can be removed (p. 205).

Black marks similar to pencil lines on the print.

CAUSE: The emulsion surface was rubbed before development or during development (e.g. with the print foreceps).

PREVENTION: Handle the paper carefully.

GLAZING FAULTS

Glazed prints stick to the glazing plate or show patterned surface markings.

(*a*) CAUSE: Glazing plate dirty.

PREVENTION: Clean carefully (p. 46).

(*b*) CAUSE: Glazing plate damaged or matt in places.

PREVENTION: Get a new glazing plate.

(*c*) CAUSE: Gelatine surface of print too soft and swollen through long soaking.

PREVENTION: Harden the prints in 2 per cent formalin solution before glazing.

The glazed prints show oyster shell type markings.

(*a*) CAUSE: Glazing press was opened before the prints were properly dry, or the pressure was uneven.

PREVENTION: Keep the prints under even pressure all the time during glazing until they are completely dry (p. 46).

(*b*) CAUSE: Glazing press was too hot or unevenly heated.

PREVENTION: Watch the temperature. Follow the working instructions supplied with each glazing machine. Possibly a newspaper laid over the prints may make drying more even.

The glazed surface is pitted and shows matt spots.

(*a*) CAUSE: Air bubbles or dust were present between the print and the glazing plate.

PREVENTION: Put prints down with sufficient water and squeegee thoroughly (p. 45).

(*b*) CAUSE: The glazing surface was dirty or damaged.

PREVENTION: Examine the surface with a magnifying glass to see if the chromium plating is beginning to come off.

(*c*) CAUSE: The print surface has been excessively hardened and does not make perfect contact with the glazing surface.

PREVENTION: Do not harden the prints too much before glazing. After resoaking in water with a few drops of ammonia added, try to reglaze the print.

The originally clean prints come off the glazing machine with brown stains.

(*a*) CAUSE: The prints were not washed sufficiently. The action of heat and fixing salt left in the print surface has locally toned the image brown.

PREVENTION: Wash prints for glazing particularly well.

(*b*) CAUSE: The apron was dirty or contaminated.

PREVENTION: Keep it clean.

FORMULAE

The simplest way of obtaining the developer, fixer, and other solutions required, is to buy them ready made.

Packets or tablets are dissolved according to the instructions enclosed, while liquid developers are simply diluted.

Alternatively, the formulae can be made up at home from the individual chemicals. This makes slightly more work, but is cheaper in the long run.

In any case use use only reputable branded chemicals.

The final volumes of solution for the British and metric versions of the formulae below are not the same, but they are the most convenient ones for each system. The British and metric amounts of each chemical are therefore not interchangeable. The composition of the developer is, however, the same in each case.

NORMAL PRINT DEVELOPERS

1. BROMIDE AND CHLOROBROMIDE DEVELOPER FOR BLACK TONES

Metol			60	grains	3.5 grains
Sodium sulphite, anhydrous	1 ounce	175	grains	35	grams
or crystals	2 ounces	350	grains	70	grams
Hydroquinone			150	grains	8.6 grams
Sodium carbonate, anhydrous			2½	ounces	63	grams
or crystals	6 ounces	350	grains	170	grams
Potassium bromide			33	grains	1.9 grams
Latitol U			1½	ounces	37	c.cm.
Wettol			190	minims	10	c.cm.
Water to make			40	ounces	1000	c.cm.

For use dilute 1 part with 2 parts water.

Instead of the Latitol U a similar amount of other developer improvers (Ilford IBT, Johnson 142, etc.) can be used. In the same way, the Wettol may be replaced by any other commercially available photographic wetting agent, such as Johnson 326, Kodak Wetting Agent, etc.

Development takes about 2–3 minutes at 65° F. (18.5° C.).

The above is the M.C.M. "New Winchester" formula. It gives rich black tones on bromide papers, or warm black tones on chlorobromide papers.

For blue-black tones on contact papers the following formula of the Ilford ID36 or Kodak D158 type is recommended.

2. CONTACT PAPER DEVELOPER

Metol			53	grains	3	grams
Sodium sulphite, anhydrous			2	ounces	50	grams
or crystals			4	ounces	100	grams
Hydroquinone			½	ounce	12.5 grams
Sodium carbonate, anhydrous	2 ounces	350	grains	70	grams
or crystals			7½	ounces	188	grams
Potassium bromide			16	grains	0.9 grams
Water to make			40	ounces	1000	c.cm.

For use dilute 1 part with 1 parts water.

Development of contact papers takes about ½–1 minute at 65° F. (18.5° C.).

VARIABLE CONTRAST DEVELOPERS

The contrast of the print can be influenced to some extent by the choice of developer (p. 64).

In addition to the normal metol-hydroquinone bromide paper developer the following are needed:

3. HYDROQUINONE CONTRAST DEVELOPER

Sodium sulphite, anhydrous	4	ounces	100	grams
or crystals	8	ounces	200	grams
Hydroquinone	2	ounces	50	grams
Sodium hydroxide	2	ounces	50	grams
Potassium bromide	I	ounce	25	grams
Water to make	40	ounces	1000	c.cm.

For use dilute 1 part with 6 parts water.

For better keeping qualities the sodium hydroxide can be made up separately as a 10 per cent solution, and added in the proportion of 1 part to every 14 parts of working solution.

4. METOL SOFT DEVELOPER

Metol	60	grains	3.5	grams
Sodium sulphite, anhydrous	I	ounce	25	grams
or crystals	2	ounces	50	grams
Sodium carbonate, anhydrous	¾	ounce	19	grams
or crystals	2	ounces	50	grams
Potassium bromide	18	grains	I	gram
Water to make	40	ounces	1000	c.cm.

For use, dilute 1 part with 1 part of water.

Finer control of intermediate contrast is possible by mixing the normal bromide paper developer (p. 237) with the hydroquinone or the metol formula in varying proportions.

Alternatively, we can develop in one developer until the shadows and medium tones are just visible, and after a quick rinse in clean water transfer it to the other solution for complete development.

TONE SEPARATION DEVELOPER

For redevelopment during the chemical tone separation process (p. 82) the following developer is necessary:

5. PYROCATECHIN SURFACE DEVELOPER

A. Potassium metabisulphite	175	grains	10	grams
Sodium sulphite, anhydrous	4	ounces	100	grams
or crystals	8	ounces	200	grams
Pyrocatechin	1½	ounces	38	grams
Water to make	40	ounces	1000	c.cm.
B. Sodium hydroxide	1½	ounces	38	grams
Potassium bromide	35	grains	2	grams
Water to make	40	ounces	1000	c.cm.

For use take equal parts of A and B, and add 13 parts of water.

WARM TONE DEVELOPER

We can develop warm black to brown tones on chlorobromide papers by using the following formula:

238

6. WARM TONE DEVELOPER

Sodium sulphite, anhydrous	2½ ounces	63 grams
or crystals	5 ounces	125 grams
Hydroquinone	120 grains	7 grams
Sodium carbonate, anhydrous	3 ounces	75 grams
or crystals	8 ounces	200 grams
Glycin	120 grains	7 grams
Potassium bromide	14 grains	0.8 gram
Water to make	40 ounces	1000 c.cm.

The tones obtainable are usually best found by trial and error. The following table will give some guidance on which experiments can be based.

WARM TONES ON CHLOROBROMIDE PAPERS

Image Colour	Exposure	Dilution of Developer	Development Time	Extra 10% Potassium Bromide per 100 Part Working Sol.
Warm black	Normal	Full strength	2 mins.	None
Brown black	2 × normal	1 : 5	4–6 mins.	8 parts
Brown	3 × normal	1 : 10	8–12 mins.	12 parts
Red brown	4 × normal	1 : 15	12–15 mins.	12 parts

DIRECT COLOUR DEVELOPERS

To produce dye images by direct development (p. 84), the following formulae are needed.

7. COUPLING DEVELOPER

Dimethyl paraphenylene diamine	18 grains	1 gram
Sodium sulphite, anhydrous	88 grains	5 grams
or crystals	175 grains	10 grams
Potassium carbonate	350 grains	20 grams
Water to make	40 ounces	1000 c.cm.

Instead of the dimethyl paraphenylene diamine a similar quantity of a proprietary colour developing agent such as *Genochrome* may be used. In that case use only half the amount of sodium sulphite.

To make up the working developer, take 10 parts of the above solution, and add to it 1 part of any of the following couplers or mixture of couplers. The working solution does not keep, so discard it after use and make up a fresh lot each time.

8. PURPLE COUPLER

Paranitrophenyl acetonitrile	14 grains	0.8 gram
Alcohol	4 ounces	100 c.cm.

9. YELLOW-BROWN COUPLER

Cyanacetanilide	7 grains	0.4 grams
Alcohol	2 ounces	50 c.cm.
Acetone	2 ounces	50 c.cm.

10. YELLOW COUPLER

Ortho-chloroacetoacetanilide	18 grains	I gram
Alcohol	4 ounces	100 c.cm.

11. YELLOW-GREEN COUPLER

Dichloro-ortho-cresol	16 grains	0.9 gram
Alcohol	4 ounces	100 c.cm.

12. BLUE-GREEN COUPLER

Dichloro-alpha-naphthol	18 grains	I gram
Alcohol	4 ounces	100 c.cm.

13. BLUE COUPLER

Alpha-naphthol	12 grains	0.7 gram
Alcohol	4 ounces	100 c.cm.

The alcohol in each case should preferably be methyl alcohol, but rectified spirit or industrial methylated spirit (colourless) will also do.

RINSES

For rinsing the prints after development plain water is quite suitable. An acid rinse, however, is better because it immediately arrests the action of the developer carried over with the print. It thus prevents stains, prolongs the life of the acid fixing bath, and ensures that the lightest highlights of the print remain particularly clear and unveiled.

14. ACETIC ACID RINSE

Glacial acetic acid	40 minims	2 c.cm.
Water	40 ounces	1000 c.cm.

15. BISULPHITE ACID RINSE

Potassium metabisulphite		
(or sodium bisulphite)	2 ounces	50 grams
Water	40 ounces	1000 c.cm.

FIXING AND HARDENING BATHS

There are two types of fixing baths: acid fixers, and acid hardening fixers.

The former are suitable for general use. The latter harden the gelatine emulsion during fixing, and are therefore particularly useful in hot weather (or in tropic climates), as well as for glossy prints which are to be glazed by heat (p. 45).

16. ACID FIXING BATH

Sodium thiosulphate (hypo) crystals	8 ounces	200 grams
Potassium metabisulphite		
(or sodium bisulphite)	I ounce	25 grams
Water to make	40 ounces	1000 c.cm.

17. ACID HARDENING FIXING BATH

Sodium thiosulphate (hypo) crystals	10 ounces	250 grams
Sodium sulphite, anhydrous	$\frac{1}{2}$ ounce	12.5 grams
or crystals	I ounce	25 grams
Glacial acetic acid	290 minims	15 c.cm.
Boric acid	130 grains	7.5 grams
Potash alum	265 grains	15 grams
Water to make	40 ounces	1000 c.cm.

Dissolve the chemicals in the above order, except for the potash alum which must be dissolved separately in about one-quarter of the final amount of water. This is then added to the main solution when cold.

An acid hardening fixer can also be made up with chrome alum. This is easier to prepare, and the fresh solution has stronger hardening properties. However, it does not keep well, and loses its hardening properties within a day or two, whether it is used or not. This deterioration can be seen by the change of colour from violet to greenish.

If therefore there is no special reason for using a hardening fixer, the simple acid fixing bath is perfectly satisfactory.

18. CHROME ALUM ACID HARDENING FIXER

Sodium thiosulphate (hypo) crystals	8 ounces	200 grams
Potassium metabisulphite (or sodium bisulphite)	I ounce	25 grams
Chrome alum	88 grains	5 grams
Water to make	40 ounces	1000 c.cm.

Fixing takes not more than 10–12 minutes.
In hot weather an after-hardening bath may also be used.

19. FORMALIN HARDENER

Formalin solution (40%)	2 ounces	50 c.cm.
Water to make	40 ounces	1000 c.cm.

The prints are immersed in this solution for 10 minutes before washing.
Where prints have been kept in the acid fixing bath for a long time, the paper base takes up a lot of acid which washed out only very slowly. Such prints are best immersed in a neutralising solution for a few minutes before washing.

20. NEUTRALISING BATH

Sodium carbonate, anhydrous	175 grains	10 grams
or crystals	I ounce	25 grams
Water	40 ounces	1000 c.cm.

EXHAUSTION

Neither the developer nor the other solutions must be overworked.
Exhausted developers give prints of poor quality and greenish black colour.
An exhausted fixer does not fix properly.
An overworked acid rinse leads to contamination of the fixer and stains on the print.
In the case of the developer formulae Nos. 1 and 2 given on page 237, 35–40 ounces (1000 c.cm.) of working strength solution will develop about 100–120 quarter-plate ($3\frac{1}{4} \times 4\frac{1}{4}$ in.) or 9×12 cm. prints, or the equivalent in other sizes. After that the useful life of the developer is more or less over, and its action no longer under control.

The acid rinse should be renewed more frequently. The same quantity will do for about 60 prints of the same size. If plain water is used for the rinse, it should be replaced twice as often.

Of the fixing baths, Nos. 16–18 35–40 ounces (1000 c.cm.) will fix about 250 quarter-plate ($3\frac{1}{4} \times 4\frac{1}{4}$ in.) or 9×12 cm. prints, or the equivalent. While at this point the fixing bath is not yet completely exhausted, it must not be used any longer, or the prints may fade later on.

241

SENSITISERS

For printing on fabrics one of the following sensitisers may be used. They will both sensitise the fabric for daylight printing (p. 151).

21. SENSITISER FOR BROWN-BLACK TONES

Ferric oxalate	$\frac{3}{4}$	ounce	19	grams
Oxalic acid	40	grains	2.2	grams
Silver nitrate	130	grains	7.5	grams
Distilled water to make	4	ounces	100	c.cm.

Dissolve in the above order.

22. SENSITISER FOR BLUE-GREY TONES

A. Ferric ammonium citrate	1	ounce	25	grams
Citric acid	175	grains	10	grams
Distilled water to make	4	ounces	100	c.cm.
B. Silver nitrate	178	grains	10	grams
Distilled water to make	4	ounces	100	c.cm.

For use take equal parts of A and B.
For enlarging on canvas or similar materials use this formula (p. 151).

23. PRESENSITISER FOR ENLARGING CANVAS

Potassium iodide	70	grains	4	grams
Potassium bromide	$\frac{1}{2}$	ounce	12.5	grams
Cadmium bromide	70	grains	4	grams
Distilled water	40	ounces	1000	c.cm.

Dry in a warm dry place, then sensitise.

24. SENSITISER FOR ENLARGING CANVAS

Silver nitrate	175	grains	10	grams
Citric acid	44	grains	2.5	grams
Distilled water	14	ounces	350	c.cm.

DIAZOTYPE

This process (p. 151) produces coloured images by daylight printing.

25. DIAZOTYPE SENSITISER

Sodium nitrite	70	grains	4	grams
Oxalic acid	105	grains	6	grams
Water	40	ounces	1000	c.cm.

The solution must be made up cold, and used straightaway.

26. DIAZOTYPE YELLOW DEVELOPER

Carbolic acid	175	grains	10	grams
Water	40	ounces	1000	c.cm.

27. DIAZOTYPE ORANGE DEVELOPER

Resorcinol	$\frac{1}{4}$	ounce	6	grams
Sodium hydroxide	160	grains	9	grams
Distilled water	40	ounces	1000	c.cm.

28. DIAZOTYPE BROWN DEVELOPER

Pyrogallic acid	$\frac{1}{2}$	ounce	12.5	grams
Water	40	ounces	1000	c.cm.

242

29. DIAZOTYPE RED DEVELOPER

Beta-naphthol	$\frac{1}{4}$	ounce	6	grams
Sodium hydroxide	140	grains	8	grams
Distilled water	40	ounces	1000	c.cm.

30. DIAZOTYPE BLUE DEVELOPER

Eikonogen	$\frac{1}{2}$	ounce	12.5 grams	
Water	40	ounces	1000	c.cm.

31. DIAZOTYPE PURPLE DEVELOPER

Alpha-naphthylamine	$\frac{1}{2}$	ounce	12.5 grams	
Oxalic acid	22	grains	1.2 grams	
Water	40	ounces	1000	c.cm.

After this developer rinse the fabric in a 5 per cent solution of tartaric acid and dry without further washing. The naphthylamine should be pure, as impurities in the commercial grade chemical may cause cancer if handled carelessly. For that reason it is also advisable to wear rubber gloves when working with naphthylamine. The smell can be removed from the hands and dishes by rinsing in the sensitiser solution.

LUMINOUS PAINT

32. RED LUMINOUS PAINT

Barium carbonate	2	ounces	50	grams
Sulphur (powdered)	130	grains	7.5	grams
Lithium carbonate	22	grains	1.2	grams
Sodium carbonate, anhydrous	$\frac{1}{2}$	grain	0.03	gram
Rubidium carbonate	1	grain	0.05	gram

33. YELLOW LUMINOUS PAINT

Strontium carbonate	2	ounces	50	grams
Sulphur (powdered)	130	grains	7.5	grams
Lithium carbonate	22	grains	1.2	grams

34. BLUE LUMINOUS PAINT

Strontium carbonate	2	ounces	50	grams
Sulphur (powdered)	70	grains	4	grams
Lithium carbonate	22	grains	1.2	grams
Calcium hydroxide	$\frac{1}{2}$	ounce	12.5	grams
Potassium sulphate	11	grains	0.6	gram
Bismuth nitrate	$\frac{1}{2}$	grain	0.03	gram

In each case fuse the mixtures together for about 45 minutes (careful—sulphur fumes!), and grind up finely after cooling. Then mix the powder to a paste with thin gum arabic solution, and paint over paper with a brush (p. 153).

REDUCERS

For reducing density and increasing contrast of negatives we can use the *Farmer's* ferricyanide reducer and the permanganate reducer (p. 244).

35. FARMER'S REDUCER

Potassium ferricyanide, 10% solution	1 part
Sodium thiosulphate (hypo), 10% solution	5 parts
Water	6 parts

The solutions must be mixed immediately before use. The yellow mixture decomposes within about 15 minutes, and loses its activity as the colour fades.

36. PERMANGANATE REDUCER

Potassium permanganate, 1% solution	1 part
Sulphuric acid, 10% solution	1 part
Water	18 parts

To reduce contrast, a good way is to bleach the negative and redevelop in a soft developer (p. 173).

37. BLEACHING BATH FOR REDEVELOPMENT

Copper sulphate (blue vitriol)	4	ounces	100	grams
Sodium chloride	4	ounces	100	grams
Water to make	40	ounces	1000	c.cm.
Sulphuric acid, concentrated	1	ounce	25	c.cm.

The sulphuric acid must be added to the solution slowly with constant stirring.
An alternative method is to tone the negative blue (p. 173).

38. BLUE TONER FOR NEGATIVES

A. Potassium ferricyanide	175	grains	10	grams
Potassium bichromate, 1% solution	25	minims	1.3	c.cm.
Water to make	40	ounces	1000	c.cm.
B. Ferric ammonium alum	370	grains	21	grams
Water to make	40	ounces	1000	c.cm.
C. Oxalic acid crystals	2	ounces	50	grams
Water to make	40	ounces	1000	c.cm.

Just before use, pour together equal parts of A, B, and C. The mixed solution is slightly sensitive to light, and should therefore be used by *subdued* daylight only.

INTENSIFIER

The chromium intensifier is useful to increase both contrast and density of negatives (p. 174).

39. CHROMIUM INTENSIFIER

A. Potassium bichromate	1	ounce	25	grams
Water to make	20	ounces	500	c.cm.
B. Hydrochloric acid, concentrated	1	ounce	25	c.cm.
Water to make	20	ounces	500	c.cm.

Just before use, the two solutions are mixed as follows:
For medium intensification take 1 part A and 1 part B.
For greater intensification take 2 parts A, 1 part B, 1 part water.
For still greater intensification take 3 parts A, 1 part B, and 1 part water. This solution acts rather slowly.

CLEARING BATH FOR PRINTS

The thiocarbamide bath will help to remove yellow stains due to forced development of prints (p. 200).

40. THIOCARBAMIDE CLEARING BATH (PRINTS)

Thiocarbamide	350	grains	20	grams
Citric acid crystals	175	grains	10	grams
Water	40	ounces	1000	c.cm.

This solution keeps well.

TONERS

41 BLEACHING BATH FOR SULPHIDE TONING

Potassium ferricyanide	6	ounces	150	grams
Potassium bromide	4	ounces	100	grams
Water to make	40	ounces	1000	c.cm.

For use dilute 1 part with 4 parts of water.

42. THIOCARBAMIDE DARKENER FOR SULPHIDE TONING

Thiocarbamide	44	grains	2.5	grams
Sodium hydroxide, 10% solution	1	ounce	25	c.cm.
Potassium bromide	1	ounce	25	grams
Water to make	40	ounces	1000	c.cm.

This can also be made up at five times the above strength and diluted for use.

43. SELENIUM TONER

Sodium sulphite, anhydrous	6	ounces	150	grams
or crystals	12	ounces	300	grams
Selenium powder	105	grains	6	grams
Ammonium chloride	7½	ounces	188	grams
Water to make	40	ounces	1000	c.cm.

Dissolve the sodium sulphite first in hot water, and add the selenium to the boiling solution. When it is all dissolved, cool and add the ammonium chloride.
For use dilute 1 part with 9 parts water.

44. GOLD TONER

A. Ammonium thiocyanate	175	grains	10	grams
Sodium chloride (cooking salt)	175	grains	10	grams
Hydrochloric acid (conc. pure)	77	minims	4	c.cm.
Distilled water to make	40	ounces	1000	c.cm.
B. Gold chloride	18	grains	1	gram
Distilled water to make	4	ounces	100	c.cm.

The solutions will keep well in brown bottles.
For use pour 1 part B into 10 parts A.
The mixed toner can be used repeatedly until exhausted.

CHEMICAL COLOURING

45. MORDANTING BLEACH FOR CHEMICAL COLOURING

Copper sulphate, 10% solution	4	ounces	100	c.cm.
Potassium citrate, 10% solution	6	ounces	150	c.cm.
Glacial acetic acid	135	minims	7	c.cm.
Ammonium thiocyanate, 10% solution	2	ounces	50	c.cm.

Add the ammonium thiocyanate solution last, when the others are already well mixed. The mixture must be clear, otherwise it is useless. Mix just before use, and throw away afterwards (p. 222).

46. DYE SOLUTION FOR CHEMICAL COLOURING

Dye	18	grains	1	gram
Glacial acetic acid	½	ounce	12	c.cm.
Distilled water	40	ounces	1000	c.cm.

Use at this strength. For dyes, see p. 222.

245

VARNISHES

47. TRANSPARENT VARNISH

Tricresyl phosphate	2	ounces	50 c.cm.
Petrol	2	ounces	50 c.cm.
Acetone	20	minims	1 c.cm.

Use this varnish to increase the transparency of prints mounted in front of an illuminated background (p. 143).

48. MATT VARNISH FOR RETOUCHING

Gum dammar	$\frac{1}{2}$	ounce	12 grams
Oil of turpentine	3	ounces	75 c.cm.
Petrol	3	ounces	75 c.cm.
Oil of lavender	40	minims	2 c.cm.

Place this mixture inside a vessel in a dish of warm or hot water until completely dissolved. *It is inflammable.*

49. WAXING PASTE FOR PRINTS

White wax	4	ounces	100 grams
Oil of turpentine	4	ounces	100 grams
Dammar varnish	70	grains	4 grams

Warm the wax and oil of turpentine together until melted, then stir in the dammar varnish When cold, this solidifies to a paste.

50. GLOSSY VARNISH FOR PRINTS

Gum dammar	175	grains	10 grams
Sulphuric ether	3	ounces	75 c.cm.
Petrol (pure)	3	ounces	75 c.cm.

The resin must be dissolved in the cold, as the mixture is *very inflammable*. Owing to the great risk of fire this varnish is not suitable for spraying.

MOUNTANT

51. STARCH MOUNTING PASTE

Dissolve about 3 ounces (75 grams) of wheat or rice starch in 40 ounces (1000 c.cm.) of water, smoothing out any lumps. Then, with constant stirring, warm up the turbid mixture on a water bath. As soon as the liquid has become more or less transparent, allow to cool. Leave to stand for 24 hours before use. To prevent growth of moulds, about 40 grains (2 grams) of salicylic or benzoic acid can be dissolved in the water before adding the starch. Otherwise the paste will not keep for more than a couple of days.

Use as described on p. 225.

INDEX

247

250

ALL ENQUIRIES
relating to this book or to any photographic problem are
answered by the Focal Press without charge if a
stamped addressed envelope is enclosed for reply.

if you are interested

not only in how to enlarge

but also in what are the

technical reasons

for what you are advised to do

turn to this book

it admirably complements the one

you have just read

ENLARGING

The Technique of the Positive

By C. I. Jacobson, Ph.D.

Enlarging is more than a mechanical process. It is capable of improving the photograph and varying its effect. Individual enlarging work is based on the ability of the photographer to judge his negatives and to choose his apparatus, his paper, his chemicals. Modern materials are products of scientific research and need to be handled in accordance with its findings. Turning these into terms of practical experience, this manual offers reliable help both to professional and amateur. It is comprehensive and outspoken, averse to any darkroom casualness and chemical gossip.

58 photographs, 78 diagrams, 304 pages, 75 formulae, 33 tables

$7\frac{1}{2} \times 5$ inches, cloth bound, price 17/6 (postage 9d.)
(U.S.A. price $4.50)

Seventeenth Edition

FOCAL ENLARGING CHART
By W. D. Emanuel
Measures exposure, ensures sharp focus, converts stop and speed; includes a precision-test negative and a Focal focusing negative.

Price 9/6

HOW PHOTOGRAPHY WORKS
By H. J. Walls
Unfolds the scientific background of photographic processes in a panorama of facts and reasoning—covering optics, chemistry, visual perception, in relation to black-and-white and colour images.
352 pp., 167 illus.

Price 42/-
(U.S.A. price $8.50)

DEVELOPING
By C. I. Jacobson
Practical advice on negative technique, choosing the right chemicals and getting the right negative, passed on in straightforward language.
328 pp., 140 illus., 14th ed.

Price 19/6
(U.S.A. price $4.95)

PHOTOGRAPHIC OPTICS
By Arthur Cox
Every photographer should be able to discriminate between lenses just as he knows how to choose films or filters. It pays to know how they work and how to work with them.
376 pp., 352 illus., 11th ed.

Price 17/6
(U.S.A. price $5.75)

COLOUR FILMS
By C. Leslie Thomson
Covers negative as well as reversal materials, and includes exposure, processing, manipulation, as well as full recommendations on how to get the best results from any colour films.
296 pp., 150 illus.

Price 42/-
(U.S.A. price $7.95)

THE COLOUR BOOK OF PHOTOGRAPHY
By Lucien Lorelle
A full account of colour photography on a practical level—in terms of pictures rather than of processes—abounding in useful facts and hints.

212 pp., 132 illus., 4th ed.

Price 15/6
(U.S.A. price $3.95)

AMATEUR CARBRO COLOUR PRINTS
By Viscount Hanworth
Shows how to do a first-rate job with amateur means. The author gives detailed, step by step explanations.
188 pp., 33 illus., 3rd ed.

Price 12/6
(U.S.A. price $3.00)

SUCCESSFUL COLOUR PHOTOGRAPHY
By C. Leslie Thomson
Helps you to create imaginative colour pictures of any subject, anywhere, at any time, with any light.

144 pp., 112 illus.

Price 9/6

LIGHTING FOR PHOTOGRAPHY
By W. Nurnberg
The technical roots of artificial lighting, the advantages and limitations of different light sources, the principles of their practical use.

176 pp., 286 illus., 13th ed.

Price 21/-
(U.S.A. price $4.50)

MAKING AN ENLARGER
By Hugo van Wadenoyen and John Holtam
Efficient designs for eight enlargers with numerous adaptations and refinements, based on materials available and suitable for easy construction.

82 pp., 75 illus., 19th ed.

Price 4/6

PHOTO TECHNIQUE
By H. J. Walls
Surveys the theoretical principles of all aspects of photography, from light to lenses and from films to apparatus, and shows how they are applied in practical picture making.
384 pp., 305 illus.

Price 25/-
(U.S.A. price $4.50)

EXPOSURE
By W. F. Berg
Helps to pick the right tools and materials, to suit filters to film and subject, to determine the correct exposure.

448 pp., 200 illus., 2nd ed.

Price 21/-
(U.S.A. price $5.00)

RETOUCHING
By O. R. Croy
This book points out the ways, picks the tools, explains the best methods and shows correct examples.

200 pp., 304 illus., 2nd ed.

Price 17/6
(U.S.A. price $4.50)

COLOUR PRINTS
By Jack H. Coote
Goes into the many and various methods of making colour prints, covering in detail negative-positive processes.

328 pp., 44 illus.

Price 25/-
(U.S.A. price $4.95)

COLOUR SEPARATION NEGATIVES
By Philip Jenkins
Explains the practical and theoretical aspects, covering equipment, techniques, methods for separation negatives from the subject and from transparencies, masking and materials.
272 pp., 115 illus.

Price 42/-
(U.S.A. price $8.50)

AMATEUR DYE TRANSFER COLOUR PRINTS
By Viscount Hanworth
The procedure of dye transfer printing described in detail from the theoretical as well as the practical angle.

176 pp., 85 illus.

Price 15/-

SUCCESSFUL FLASH PHOTOGRAPHY
By L. A. Mannheim
How any flash works and how to work it; describes all flash equipment and the way to make some of your own.

160 pp., 139 illus.

Price 9/6

LIGHTING FOR PORTRAITURE
By W. Nurnberg
With extreme clarity and profuse illustrations, the author of Lighting for Photography here describes the manifold possibilities of lighting the human face.
192 pp., 509 illus.

Price 21/-
(U.S.A. price $5.00)

THE LEICA WAY
By Andrew Matheson
Covers the whole technique and art of Leica photography, both with the latest equipment and older models and accessories.
432 pp., 352 illus.   **Price 25/-**
    (U.S.A. price $4.95)

THE CONTAX WAY
By H. Freytag
Up-to-date facts and authoritative advice on all Contax equipment applied to every conceivable Contax subject.

288 pp., 286 illus., 6th ed.   **Price 21/-**
    (U.S.A. price $4.50)

THE CONTAFLEX WAY
By H. Freytag
Comprehensive, methodical and authoritative, this book describes in non-technical terms all the models and explains the use of their accessories.

312 pp., 274 illus.   **Price 25/-**
    (U.S.A. price $4.95)

PICTURE-MAKING WITH THE REFLEX
By H. S. Newcombe
A guide to the materials and methods for the most effective use of the modern roll film reflex camera.

256 pp., 90 illus.   **Price 21/-**
    (U.S.A. price $4.95)

HOW TO TAKE PHOTOGRAPHS THAT EDITORS WILL BUY
By Ronald Spillman
A specialist in the field of feature photography shares his success secrets and shows the way to profit from pictures.
224 pp., 97 illus.   **Price 19/6**
    (U.S.A. price $4.50)

POSING PATTERNS
By L. E. Broome
A pictorial guide to posing for photographers, students and models; the text analyses the poses illustrated.
208 pp., 1226 illus.   **Price 35/-**
    (U.S.A. price $10.00)

THE TECHNIQUE OF BIRD PHOTOGRAPHY
By John Warham
Including a guide to identification, this book can be followed by the amateur with little knowledge of photography or of birds.
200 pp., 208 illus.   **Price 25/-**
    (U.S.A. price $4.95)

CLOSE RANGE PHOTOGRAPHY
By C. H. Adams
Explains how the amateur can achieve large-scale photographs of small subjects with home-made and inexpensive equipment.
192 pp., 64 illus.   **Price 21/-**
    (U.S.A. price $4.50)

SIMPLE ART OF MAKING FILMS
By Tony Rose
The simple technical facts that every owner of a cine camera needs to know, and the refinements that make the difference between good and bad amateur films.

256 pp., 100 illus.   **Price 25/-**

THE ROLLEI WAY
By L. A. Mannheim
A composite work, built from the experience and advice of leading photographers, dealing with essential points of Rolleiflex or Rolleicord practice.
304 pp., 358 illus., 6th ed.   **Price 25/-**
    (U.S.A. price $4.95)

THE RETINA WAY
By O. R. Croy
Will put the whole Retina technique safely in your hands and bring all the subjects of Retina photography within your easy reach.
336 pp., 236 illus., 9th ed.   **Price 21/-**
    (U.S.A. price $4.95)

MY WAY WITH THE MINIATURE
By Lancelot Vining
A veteran of London's Fleet Street, Lancelot Vining is here as open-minded and progressive as he is generous in his advice.

260 pp., 109 illus., 13th ed.   **Price 19/6**
    (U.S.A. price $4.50)

35 mm. PHOTO TECHNIQUE
By H. S. Newcombe
Technical factors of film, exposure and development producing the perfect negative are put into the language of common sense for the practical man.
328 pp., 148 illus., 13th ed.   **Price 19/6**
    (U.S.A. price $4.50)

PHOTOGRAPHS AND THE PRINTER
By Frank H. Smith
This book tells how and why and what sort of photographs will give the best results when printed by the printer.

176 pp., 116 illus.   **Price 12/6**
    (U.S.A. price $3.00)

GLAMOUR IN YOUR LENS
By James Macgregor
Shows what anyone can do anywhere with a camera and a pretty girl.
160 pp., 80 illus.   **Price 12/6**
    (U.S.A. price $1.95)

ALL THE PHOTO TRICKS
By Edwin Smith
Shows how startling pictorial effects, fantastic variations of reality and amusing deceptions of the eye are worked.

280 pp., 157 illus., 6th ed.   **Price 17/6**
    (U.S.A. price $3.95)

AMATEUR PHOTOMICROGRAPHY
By Alan Jackson
The methods and equipment used in photomicrography, an interesting hobby as much as a scientific technique.
184 pp., 70 illus., 7th ed.   **Price 15/6**
    (U.S.A price $3.00)

COMPLETE TECHNIQUE OF MAKING FILMS
By P. Monier
A comprehensive introduction to sub-standard cinematography for amateurs and semi-professionals—from the single shot to the story-telling sequence.
304 pp., 176 illus.   **Price 30/-**
    (U.S.A. price $6.00)

THE FOCAL
ENCYCLOPEDIA
OF
PHOTOGRAPHY

2,000 articles: 1¼ million words
1,468 pages, 385 photographs, 1,500 diagrams
Bound burgundy buckram, stamped silver
Price £5 5s.
(U.S.A. price $20.00)

THE FOCAL ENCYCLOPEDIA will do the job of a whole library. This single volume holds the right answers to any question on photography—ready for prompt reference. It contains more information than many books put together. Much of it could not easily be found elsewhere. A great deal of it has never been published before.

THE FOCAL ENCYCLOPEDIA covers completely the vast technology of photography and follows up all its uses for picture making. It defines terms, identifies personalities and quotes rules. It recalls past developments and records the present state of progress all over the world. It sums up scientific theory and instructs in up-to-date practice. It presents all the facts that matter, explains "why" and shows "how". It hands out advice based on first hand knowledge, expert skill and reliable authority.

THE FOCAL ENCYCLOPEDIA is specially written in plain, readable and commonsense English. It was carefully planned and set out in alphabetical order for easy reference. You will be able to find, instantly master and put to good use, all the information you need from whatever angle you look for it.

THE FOCAL ENCYCLOPEDIA is the only work of its kind in the world. A unique, up-to-date and universal source of photographic knowledge and an unfailing tool of practical help to any photographer, student of photography, professional and amateur, advanced and beginner alike.

THE FOCAL ENCYCLOPEDIA can take the place of a photographic library; and no library is complete without it.

See it at your bookseller or photographic dealer or write for full prospectus to Focal Press

PERSPECTIVE

A Quarterly Review of Progress in Photography, Cinematography, Sound and Image Recording

PERSPECTIVE is the only journal of its kind in the world.

Authoritative, accurate and concise—it presents the sum total of all the important, informative and interesting news on the economics, technology and research published by the leading periodicals throughout the world.

It reports on new products, their uses and their markets. It inquires into novel problems and applications in science, industry, medicine, commerce, education and administration. It offers intelligence from expert contributors and correspondents in research and industrial centres in every country.

Unique as a journal and reference book in one—it watches trends, publishes up-to-date surveys, analyses statistics, lines up digest summaries, abstracts new patents, signposts vital news. It translates messages of significance into words of common sense.

Published four times a year: March, June, September, and December. Fully illustrated by graphs, diagrams and photographs. 400 pages per volume. Size crown quarto (10 × 7½ in.). The annual subscription is £2 12s. 6d. ($7.50, DM 30,00, S.fr. 32,00) post free.

PERSPECTIVE is obtainable only through direct subscription exclusively, from the publishers Focal Press Ltd., 31 Fitzroy Square, London, W.1.

256